ENDORSEMENTS FOR
LEADERSHIP BY THE GOOD BOOK

"Through a collection of stories, David Steward captures the essential elements of what it takes to successfully lead people. Serve, love, risk, invest, trust, and so much more beautifully form a leadership template that you'll immediately want to replicate. But not so fast—let this book minister to you as God, through David, not only refines your leadership style but reconnects you with Him, the ultimate business adviser. *Leadership by the Good Book* has changed my life." **—Cynt Marshall**
CEO, Dallas Mavericks

"David Steward is an incredible leader who has helped to shape the future for so many people not just in the technology sector but across life. His vision for WWT and, more importantly, his passion of helping others have been an inspiration for me personally. We are all so fortunate to have such an incredible human being who has done so well in life now working even harder to help others achieve a level of personal and professional success." **—John W. Thompson**
Venture Partner, Lightspeed Venture, and
chair of the board, Microsoft Corporation

"In *Leadership by the Good Book*, David Steward has written a profound, timely, and timeless book. The wisdom within its pages demonstrates the power of God and David's willingness to be used by God. The knowledge shared will accelerate you toward greater integrity, improve your excellence at work and home, and fortify your faith. This book is a must-read for anyone looking to go to the next level as a leader, professionally and personally. **—DeVon Franklin**
Hollywood producer and
New York Times bestselling author

"All you have to do is see the table of contents, which presents you with a reality many do not think is possible: How you can lead a life of meaning and service to others, and be as successful as David Steward? The secret he reveals is so powerful—meaning and service to others is success…and it produces results. Thanks for this gift, David."   **—Dr. Henry Cloud**
psychologist, author, and leadership consultant

"As a lifelong educator, I have found that the higher education mission is balanced by morals and ethics of individuals. *Leadership by the Good Book* is an extraordinary read, authored by an extraordinary man. David Steward is truly God's servant, whose life exemplifies one of humility. This book serves as a spirit-led guide to finding one's potential and purpose. Through faith and by following godly principles you, too, will be inspired to become a servant leader."   **—Dr. Henry Givens Jr.**
president emeritus, Harris-Stowe State University

LEADERSHIP
—— BY THE ——
GOOD
BOOK

Timeless Principles for Making an Eternal Impact

DAVID L. STEWARD

WITH BRANDON K. MANN

Foreword by T. D. Jakes

FaithWords

New York • Nashville

Copyright © 2020 by Biblical Business Training, Inc.

Cover design by Brand Navigation
Cover copyright © 2020 by Hachette Book Group, Inc.

FaithWords
Hachette Book Group
1290 Avenue of the Americas, New York, NY 10104
faithwords.com
twitter.com/faithwords

First Edition: May 2020

FaithWords is a division of Hachette Book Group, Inc. The FaithWords name and logo are trademarks of Hachette Book Group, Inc.

The publisher is not responsible for websites (or their content) that are not owned by the publisher.

The Hachette Speakers Bureau provides a wide range of authors for speaking events. To find out more, go to www.hachettespeakersbureau.com or call (866) 376-6591.

Unless otherwise noted, Scripture quotations are taken from the Holy Bible, New International Version®, NIV®. Copyright ©1973, 1978, 1984, 2011 by Biblica, Inc.™ Used by permission of Zondervan. All rights reserved worldwide. www.zondervan.com. The "NIV" and "New International Version" are trademarks registered in the United States Patent and Trademark Office by Biblica, Inc.™ | Scripture quotations marked ESV are taken from the ESV® Bible (The Holy Bible, English Standard Version®), copyright © 2001 by Crossway, a publishing ministry of Good News Publishers. Used by permission. All rights reserved. | Scripture quotations marked KJV are taken from the King James Version of the Bible. Public domain. | Scripture quotations marked NKJV are taken from the New King James Version®. Copyright © 1982 by Thomas Nelson. Used by permission. All rights reserved. | Scripture quotations marked RSV are taken from the Revised Standard Version of the Bible, copyright © 1946, 1952, and 1971 National Council of the Churches of Christ in the United States of America. Used by permission. All rights reserved.

Library of Congress Cataloging-in-Publication Data
Names: Steward, David, 1951- author. | Mann, Brandon K., author.
Title: Leadership by the good book : timeless principles for making an eternal impact / David L. Steward, with Brandon K. Mann.
Description: First edition. | New York : FaithWords, 2020.
Identifiers: LCCN 2019049252 | ISBN 9781546013273 (hardcover) | ISBN 9781546013266 (ebook)
Subjects: LCSH: Leadership in the Bible. | Leadership—Biblical teaching. | Leadership—Religious aspects—Christianity. | Christian leadership.
Classification: LCC BS680.L4 S74 2020 | DDC 253—dc23
LC record available at https://lccn.loc.gov/2019049252

ISBNs: 978-1-5460-1327-3 (hardcover); 978-1-5460-1326-6 (ebook)

Printed in the United States of America

LSC-C

10 9 8 7 6 5 4 3 2

To my Lord and Savior Jesus Christ, thank you.
*"For God so loved the world, that He gave His
only begotten son, that whosoever believes in Him,
should not perish but have everlasting life."*
John 3:16 NKJV

To the love of my life, Thelma, God's precious gift
to me and our family.
*"Many women do noble things, but you surpass
them all." Proverbs 31:29*

To David II, Kimberly, and Mary, we are blessed
to call you our amazing children, as you are
beautifully and "wonderfully made." You are a
manifestation of God's great love.
*"Children are a heritage from the LORD, offspring
a reward from him." Psalm 127:3*

To David III and Julian, God's greatest
miracles to us all.
*"Grandchildren are the crown of the aged, and the
glory of children is their fathers."*
Proverbs 17:6 ESV

CONTENTS

Section 4: INVEST

Section 5: RISK

Section 6: TRUST

Section 7: SHARE

Section 8: FOLLOW

FOREWORD
by T. D. Jakes

Being a servant leader requires deep faith. While some degree of risk is required in every area of our lives, leaps of faith are vital when creating something new and sustaining its growth. Whether it be a nonprofit, a ministry, a start-up, a side hustle, or an expansion of an existing business, you must step out in faith to reach new heights. Based on my experience and observations, I'm convinced risk-taking faith is *the* hallmark of successful entrepreneurs and gifted leaders.

No one knows this better than my friend David Steward and his coauthor Brandon Mann. I can't think of better teachers to illustrate the relevance of Biblical principles in business and leadership. They understand that leadership by the Good Book is not only a matter of following the example set by Jesus and obeying the imperative instructions of the sacred Scriptures—they know these principles also show us how to become servant-leaders fueled by passion, purpose, and divine power.

This principle of daring to venture forward when the security and safety of the status quo offers satisfaction permeates the pages of the Bible. The Good Book is filled with heroes of faith—Noah, Moses, Abraham and Sarah, David, Ruth, Rahab, and Gideon, to name a few—who trusted God despite all odds and what their human senses were telling them. In Hebrews we find a list of many of these saints, a Faith Hall of Fame as it's often called, spotlighting these men and women who dared to trust

God for more than they could imagine, those who were willing to walk by faith and not by sight. Their emergent qualities—courage, patience, purpose, hope, discipline, service—inspire us not only in church but in our homes, cubicles, boardrooms, and online offices as well.

Anyone who has dared to imagine new possibilities and taken the necessary action to ignite change knows that faith fuels you forward. Human history is filled with these dynamic dare-takers and their spirit of overcoming adversity with faith in what could only be imagined. If we were to list a few members of an Entrepreneurial Hall of Fame, we might find the perseverance of Thomas Edison and the tenacity of the Wright Brothers, the inspired genius of George Washington Carver, and the dedication of Marie Curie. From recent decades, we would not be surprised to see entrepreneurial leaders such as Cathy Hughes and Bill Gates, Oprah and Tyler Perry.

Although many entrepreneurs and leaders excel in a variety of fields—many of them in more than one—they know that the beliefs in our hearts affect the thoughts in our minds, the words on our lips, and the actions we take. When leaders live from the belief that others, including employees at every level along with customers and community members, deserve to be treated like they themselves want to be treated, they embody the essence of faith required to inspire others to pursue their own God-given potential.

Servant leadership based on the Bible is rarely taught in business schools and MBA programs, but the wisdom David and Brandon share in this book is indispensable for leaders who want to maximize their potential without compromising their character. Throughout these pages, they emphasize a vital truth that often gets eclipsed by competitive convenience and egocentric climbers in today's tech marketplace and social media ubiquity: Leaders who succeed at the expense of their integrity have conquered nothing but momentary milestones, no matter how lucrative or lustrous their temporary trophies may be. As the Good Book reminds us, "What good is it for someone to gain the whole world, yet forfeit their soul?" (Mark 8:36).

The kind of servant leadership distilled in these pages reminds us that every relationship counts, from the website to the warehouse, and from the mind-set to the marketplace. Servant-leaders have aligned their faith in practical ways that contribute excellence to those around them. They value each and every person from the top of the organization to the customer making the smallest purchase, from the entry-level employee who just graduated to the emeritus board member who continues to serve long after retirement.

David Steward's brand of leadership is about serving the person and not just the account, the spiritual need and not just the product order. His bottom line carries eternal significance, not just fiscal profitability. Through his amazing, anointed, and admirable journey with World Wide Technology, David has been forced to proceed by faith every step of the way. He has married his work ethic to the ethics of his work! He has relied on God to lead, guide, and direct and has obediently made serving the Lord the only priority. David embodies the essence of the exhortation we find in the New Testament: "Whatever you do, work at it with all your heart, as working for the Lord, not for human masters, since you know that you will receive an inheritance from the Lord as a reward. It is the Lord Christ you are serving" (Col. 3:23–24).

I aspire to do the same, working as unto the Lord in all that I do. In fact, I'm often asked by up-and-coming leaders how I manage to juggle my many entrepreneurial and creative endeavors with leading my ministry and pastoring my flock at The Potter's House. My answer is simple: I make sure that everything I do exercises the gifts and opportunities God has given me to serve Him by serving others. Business is never just business and ministry emerges from the pulpit as well as the prospectus. Instead of segregating my interests, gifts, and ministries, I'm inspired by leaders like David Steward to serve in all capacities as the Lord leads.

Without a doubt, I know your ability to lead by serving will be ignited by the passionate wisdom in these pages. Whether you're just starting your career, making a switch into a different field, launching a new venture, or transitioning into a higher level of leadership, this book is your field guide to blazing a trail of triumph over trials and discovering the joy and fulfillment that comes from following God and leading by the Good Book. Whether you want to invest in an eternal legacy of vocational Christian ministry, to serve those in need through a nonprofit, or to succeed in business by making the Golden Rule your measuring stick, this book is for you!

—T. D. Jakes

A NOTE TO READERS

Thank you for reading our book. Undoubtedly, David Steward's message will bless and encourage you. As you turn these pages, you will hear David's voice, experience his passion, and be inspired by his perseverance. I have the privilege of enjoying his friendship and learning from him on a daily basis, and it is a gift for which I am eternally grateful!

Candidly, however, David would prefer that this book not be written from a first-person perspective in his voice. David does not want anything, including his own voice or perspective, to come between you and the Good Book, the Holy Bible.

Therefore, please keep in mind that while these stories are told from David's perspective, he wants you to know that they are really God's stories. This book is not about what David has done but about what God has done in and through David's life. "And we know that in all things God works for the good of those who love him, who have been called according to his purpose" (Rom. 8:28).

David and I encourage you to open your Bible alongside this book and to focus on hearing God's voice as you read the following pages.

To God be the glory,
Brandon K. Mann

INTRODUCTION
by Brandon K. Mann

W hy another leadership book?" you might ask. David Steward and I asked the same question before beginning this endeavor. Here is our answer: God has shown us how Biblical leadership principles can dynamically transform the way people lead and work.

Envision your business, industry, department, practice, school, organization large or small being led by men and women of integrity who seek excellence and understand the power of love and forgiveness. Imagine what it might feel like to work there...Can you see people flourishing at all levels? New hires, middle management, and executives working together. It's not perfect (or fake in that way that comes from pretending it is), but there is teamwork and collaboration. Everyone seeks to communicate effectively. All share core values that ensure each person has an opportunity to contribute their unique skills and perspectives to the organization's success.

Can this vision be realized, or is it simply a fantasy?

World Wide Technology (WWT) has realized this vision, and your organization can, too. With annual revenues exceeding $12 billion, WWT is the largest African American–owned business in the world. Founded by David Steward in 1990, WWT provides technology solutions to the world's largest companies and gets ranked year after year as one of the best places to work by *Fortune*, Glassdoor, and many others. Beginning as a small start-up of five people in four thousand square feet in suburban St. Louis, WWT has grown into a global powerhouse with thousands of employees and millions of square feet, managing billions of dollars in technology systems and solutions.

When David started WWT, however, his ambition was not to build a multi-billion-dollar company. He had a very different goal in mind. "I wanted my company to be my ministry," he explains. "It was an opportunity for me to live out the lessons of the Bible and for me to be God's ambassador in the business world. As 2 Corinthians 5:20 says, 'We are therefore Christ's ambassadors, as though God were making his appeal through us. We implore you on Christ's behalf: Be reconciled to God.'"

David and I share this passion for encouraging and equipping Christians to be ambassadors in the business world. So much so, that following God's call, I formed a Bible study group at my office in 2008. My coworkers and I met Thursday mornings before work and discussed how we could apply God's Word to work topics like teamwork, leadership, and customer service. We used David's first book, *Doing Business by the Good Book*, as our curriculum. In the beginning, all of the attendees worked at Cassidy Turley (now Cushman & Wakefield), a commercial real estate firm where I was an executive.

These first study groups where the genesis of what has become Biblical Business Training (BBT), a global nonprofit ministry that God called me to form in 2009. In 2010, I resigned from corporate America to serve as BBT's first executive director, and David was a founding board member. BBT's mission is to help people apply Biblical principles at work. Through BBT, God continues to show us how Biblical leadership principles can transform the ways people lead and work.

I can't think of anyone more qualified to fulfill this mission than David Steward, who models Jesus' leadership like no other leader I've ever met. God brought us together in 2002 while David and I were both mentoring the same small-business owner. Shortly after meeting David, I asked him to be one of my mentors, and since that time, he has poured into my life and set an example that inspires me every day. So, it is only fitting that our book focuses on Biblical leadership examples.

For within the pages of Scripture, you can discover some of the greatest Biblical leaders, from Moses and David to Solomon and, of course, Jesus Himself. The leadership principles demonstrated by these iconic figures stand the test of time. Whether warring with hostile neighbors or telling parables set in their agrarian society, these Biblical leaders share shockingly relevant wisdom for us today in our tumultuous world of advanced technology.

So again...why another leadership book, especially one from David? David's first book, *Doing Business by the Good Book*, provided a broad review of how Biblical principles can be applied to all aspects of work, from being an entrepreneur to branding and networking. This book is focused sharply on helping men and women apply Biblically based leadership principles.

To that end, following each chapter you will find a "Your Leadership Flywheel: Learn, Live, Lead, Legacy" section. Each of these sections includes several self-reflection questions regarding the application of the Biblical leadership principles included in the chapter, as well as a prayer. These sections are named for BBT's leadership development model, the *Leadership Flywheel*™. You can learn more about the Leadership Flywheel at the end of the book. David and I encourage you to explore all of BBT's resources at www.B-B-T.org. **All proceeds from the sale of this book go directly to BBT, helping to sustain and support the ministry. Thank you for your support!**

God has shown David and me, through WWT and BBT, how Biblical leadership principles can transform the way people lead and work. And I believe He is also igniting a similar vision in you.

Remember when I asked you to envision your business, industry, department, practice, school, organization large or small being led by men and women of integrity who seek excellence and understand the power of love and forgiveness? And to imagine what it might feel like to work there? I'm convinced this vision gives you a glimpse of how Biblical leadership principles can transform the way you lead and work.

You don't need another book on leadership to collect dust on your desk or sit idly on a shelf. My hope is that this book will be a field guide, one that you will return to again and again as God continues to fulfill all the incredible potential that He has placed within you as you seek to serve those entrusted to your care. So wherever you are—in your life, in your relationships, in your career—I pray that you will be inspired, empowered, and equipped by the Biblical principles contained in these pages to lead your families, your teams, your ministries, and your businesses by the Good Book!

SECTION 1
Serve

CHAPTER 1

SERVE A HIGHER PURPOSE

*Whoever wants to become great among you must be your ser-
vant, and whoever wants to be first must be slave of all. For
even the Son of Man did not come to be served, but to serve,
and to give his life as a ransom for many.*

Mark 10:43–45

I did not set out to create a multi-billion-dollar company.

When World Wide Technology (WWT) was launched in
1990, I wanted to build a world-class company that would help
transform the world through technology. Little did I realize in
those early days, but God certainly knew, that our journey as a
company would not only transform the world through technology but also serve a higher purpose and become a true ministry.

In the six years that preceded the founding of WWT, God
had taught me many lessons about the blessings and burdens of
entrepreneurship. I acquired and started several companies during the mid-to-late 1980s, after transitioning from a blessed and
successful career in corporate America. However, the darkest
time of my entrepreneurial journey was yet to come.

Within three short years of starting WWT, I was at an all-time
low. I vividly recall sitting in my small office in the dark. The
darkness was both external and internal. Externally, the power
was out, literally, because of a powerful thunderstorm. However, that storm and the darkness it caused paled in comparison

to the emotional and psychological darkness that I was experiencing. WWT was in dire straits from a business development standpoint, and cash was in short supply because of, let's say, a creative allocation of significant cash that one of my associates chose to make.

So there, in the darkness, I sat as the thunder echoed in my mind from the storms outside and inside. Then the phone rang. Expecting more bad news, I tentatively picked up the handset. The voice on the other end wasn't the gruff one of a banker, supplier, or customer, which I was anticipating. Instead, it was the sweet voice of my mother-in-law. Thelma's mother, also named Dorothy like my own mother, has always been more than a mother-in-law to me—she is truly my mother-in-love!

Like her daughter, my precious wife, Dorothy always knew what Scripture would help me experience God's peace. "David," she said, "God told me to call you and tell you to read Psalm Ninety-One. I don't know why God wanted me to do this right now, but He does and I'm sure you do, too. I love you and God does, too!"

After thanking her and saying goodbye, I quickly opened my Bible to Psalm 91. As I read, I knew why God told her to share this Scripture with me. Reading these powerful words of God's protection and provision inspired me. They renewed my strength and became my scriptural backstop whenever I felt the darkness closing in again. I encourage you to read Psalm 91 now. Its sixteen verses will bless you; I know firsthand.

While our bleak situation at WWT did not change overnight, my dependence on God's Word for leadership guidance deepened dramatically. As the prophet Isaiah writes, God's Word does not return void! Receiving and resting in God's Word enabled me to see Him as the source, not WWT, our employees, bankers, or customers. Even while I was buying groceries for my family at 7-Eleven, on a credit card that I couldn't afford to pay off at the time, I heard from God that it was going to be OK.

From that point on, my leadership approach was informed

and influenced by the teachings of the Holy Bible. I promised God that if He allowed WWT to survive, I would ensure that WWT was a ministry. Well, almost three decades later, God has enabled WWT to not only survive but thrive!

And true to my promise to God, I have endeavored to shape WWT's culture and core values based on the teachings of the Bible. WWT is a platform where we could exercise the leadership principles seen in Scripture. I wanted to serve as God's ambassador in a company focused on serving others. This company would be a ministry that spreads the Word of the Lord. We were not going to preach per se; I simply wanted WWT to draw people closer to God.

I'm a living testament, flawed though I still am, that Biblical leadership principles rooted in God's Word are indeed applicable today. With the incredible success of WWT, it's easy to draw a line of cause and effect to prove my point. But you must understand this line is not short, nor is it straight! Through the many ups and downs along the way, WWT's success reflects God's goodness and the power of the principles of leadership within the Good Book, that divinely inspired collection of history, poetry, prophecy, and letters known as the Holy Bible.

I believe I would be just as strong in my faith and just as content if God had not blessed WWT with such audacious global success. I believe this because I know the way I've led my life, my family, and my business endeavors would not be any different regardless of their success. Anything I know about leadership begins and ends with my relationship with God. I sincerely believe that putting Him first in all I do makes a tremendous difference in my personal purpose as well as my mission, motivation, and management in business. Having this higher purpose gives me a different perspective than most business leaders. Focused on God and His principles for leadership, I'm more concerned with the eternal than the urgent, the person than the product, the relationship, not the ROI.

And my relationship with Him—as well as with others and with what I do with the life I've been given—all comes down to service.

FIRM FOUNDATION

Like most people, my attitudes about God and faith, about leadership and how to treat people were influenced by my upbringing. Fortunately, I was blessed with a firm foundation for the leader God created me to be. I was born in Chicago, but I grew up in Clinton, Missouri, a small town of five thousand during the 1950s. Like most places in our country at that time, Clinton was segregated, a reality I encountered every day—on the bus to school, in the classroom, at the drinking fountain, on the playground, or anywhere else I happened to venture. I vividly remember having to sit in the balcony at the movie theater, not being able to swim at the public swimming pool, and not being allowed to eat at Wiley's Restaurant because it was whites only—the list of indignities was a long one.

Despite this challenging cultural environment, I was blessed to grow up in a loving home with two devoted Christian parents. My father was the first entrepreneur that I saw. He was an auto mechanic who supplemented our family's income by providing "shade tree" auto repair, as well as janitorial and trashing-hauling services. When there weren't jobs available, he created them. I have always admired that about him. My mother ran our very small home, no small feat with eight of us kids in the family and no indoor bathroom! She also volunteered at church and helped other families in our neighborhood. We were so poor that I like to joke we didn't live on the other side of the tracks—we lived *on* the tracks! Nonetheless, we had a small six-acre plot of land that allowed us to own a couple of cows, keep a few hogs, and raise chickens. We also had a vegetable garden, which my mother tended—and taught us kids to cultivate—almost every day except in the winter. Speaking of winter, Mom was also a canner, who enjoyed hosting "canning parties" to make sure our family and many others had canned the fall harvest, so we all had enough vegetables to last us through the winter. Miraculously, our little farm provided enough food so that our family of ten never went hungry.

I tell you this not for sympathy or to underline just how far God has brought me in achieving success. I share my humble beginnings with you so you can understand just how crazy it was for me to quit my job, risk my life savings, and blaze my own trail! When you follow God in how you live, learn, and lead, it won't always seem logical on paper or make sense to others. Most people I knew, including members of my family and close friends, questioned my sanity at the time.

This restlessness within my soul emerged when my career seemed to be at its peak, but it had started long before while I was still a boy back in Clinton, sitting in Sunday school and learning about Biblical heroes like Moses and Daniel. I wanted to emulate them and, in my own unique way, serve others by being their leader. The greatest inheritance that I received from my parents is the love of Christ. Therefore, at an early age I knew that God loved me—that He loved all people, black or white, rich or poor—and that He had a special purpose in life for me. I understood that God loved us so much that He sent His Son to live on Earth as a baby born in a smelly stable and to die as an innocent man nailed to a cross. Jesus' life on Earth was about overcoming the odds, overturning the corrupt establishment, and relying on His Father's love and power in all that He did. Jesus loved everyone—fishermen and tax collectors, sick people and prostitutes.

From a young age, I felt called to lead and to love people the same way. Don't get me wrong: I never thought about parting the Red Sea or spending a night in the lions' den, let alone walking on water. But I liked the idea of being a good shepherd leading his flock of other people who also wanted to serve other people. After seeing the ways prejudice and racism poisoned people's hearts in our segregated community, I wanted to make a difference and unite a group of diverse people around a common, worthwhile cause, a higher purpose. I dreamed of building a company that would focus on treating all people—employees, customers, even competitors—the way I wanted to be treated.

When I felt compelled to take a huge leap of faith and start WWT, I had already been blessed with so much in my life. By almost everyone's account, I was successful. Married to my beautiful wife, Thelma, a registered nurse, and father to our two children, I had worked my way up to the position of senior account executive with Federal Express. In fact, in 1981 I was named our company's salesman of the year. Fred Smith, the company's great founder and CEO, personally presented to me the trophy, a silver ice bucket engraved with my name, at the company's hall of fame dinner. While I felt incredibly honored to receive the award, I also felt this odd discomfort. I can remember peering inside that silver bucket and feeling as empty as it looked. I didn't want to spend the rest of my life meeting sales quotas and then wake up in my seventies one day, wondering why I didn't do more with my life.

Not long after being named salesman of the year, I resigned and bought a consulting firm that audited and reviewed freight charges for shippers. The company's owner, Leo Moore, operated two companies, one in Kansas City and the other in St. Joseph, Missouri. At age sixty-five, Leo was getting tired of the daily 110-mile round-trip drive between the two cities and wanted to slow down. I offered to buy Leo's company in St. Joseph for $100,000, and he agreed that I could pay him over time out of cash flow, since Thelma and I were basically living paycheck to paycheck.

My friends and family members still tried to talk me out of it.

LEAP OF FAITH

"David, you're a FedEx sales rep," one of my siblings said to me. "Why would you walk away from a high-paying job to start your own company? You don't know anything about building a company and leading others!"

Someone else warned, "David, you're a salesman, and you're only responsible for yourself. You've never had people report to you. What makes you think you can build an organization when you don't have any leadership experience? If you leave FedEx, you'll be making a huge mistake that will ruin your life, your wife's life, and your children's lives."

Keep in mind these were my relatives and close friends! And I knew they loved me and were giving me what they believed was good advice. I could have played it safe and remained in corporate America, worked my way up the ladder, and stuck around until my retirement account kicked in. Had I followed that career path, people would have said, "David did well for himself and his family." It would have been a good life, one that many people would have enjoyed with contentment.

But the God I knew and loved was compelling me to look beyond what was logical or safe and instead to step out in faith. During that season when God began accelerating my passion to lead, I returned to a couple of my favorite Bible verses. One defined the importance of following my dream, and the other reminded me of the faith required to see it realized. "Where there is no vision, the people perish" (Prov. 29:18 KJV) had always encouraged me to remember the importance of seeking God's vision for my future, a dream to pursue. Combined with a verse from the New Testament, "Now faith is the substance of things hoped for, the evidence of things not seen" (Heb. 11:1 KJV), I knew it was time to have faith in the vision God had given me.

These verses echoed in my heart, reminding me to see beyond circumstances and to try to see what God has for us through His eyes. I believed that where God wanted to lead me was so extraordinary it reminded me of Ephesians 3:20, because it went beyond anything I could think, dream, or ask for on my own. With strong faith combined with hard work and tenacity, I refused to let cynics discourage me and define my future.

Throughout all the obstacles I faced, I never stopped believing that God's power deep inside me would guide me to overcome all the challenges I faced. Why would God do this? Because He loves me and wants me to fulfill the potential that He placed inside me, and inside you, too! Remembering God's love fueled my hope—and as the reality of what I had done set in, I was going to need every ounce of God's love I could receive.

A BIGGER LEAP

Being on my own meant that no supervisor would ever be looking over my shoulder to approve or disapprove a decision I made—or to help or advise me. My corporate lifeline was cut, and I was on my own to either sink or swim. And with the purchase of Leo's company, I ended up doing a lot of dog paddling!

Becoming a small-business owner was a highly educational experience to say the least. Owning this company provided a crash course in the basics of business—everything from customer service to accounts receivable, from hiring new employees to making budget cuts. Although I didn't know it at the time, I was being prepared for what I would need to know with my next leap of faith.

I didn't have to wait long before I once again felt the itch in my soul to take an even bigger risk than I had taken by leaving FedEx. As the Internet and World Wide Web began infiltrating all aspects of our culture, I knew the impact of new technology on business could be dramatic if not limitless. And despite having little to no training with computer technology, I wanted to be part of that new frontier looming on the virtual horizon. So, I shut down my first businesses and prepared to take another crazy risk.

Actually, from my perspective the risk made total sense. My auditing company, which had used emerging technologies to create an early network thirty times faster than most in-house manual auditors, suddenly lost our biggest customer because they discovered how to use technology to accelerate their own internal auditing systems. The handwriting was on the wall: My auditing business would be going under as more and more clients followed suit. Then I realized that my passion wasn't providing auditing services—my passion was using technology to solve problems.

Unfortunately, many others—even friends and family—didn't follow my logic. I'll never forget someone telling me, "David, you're an African American with no computer experience in St. Louis! Why would you want to launch a technology company—and call it *World Wide Technology*?" I didn't have a good answer other than a quiet confidence God had instilled in my heart. Once again, serving a higher purpose meant stepping out in faith rather than playing it safe or doing what others considered logical.

The person whose faith in God and unwavering support of me enabled me to pursue God's vision for WWT is my precious wife. Thelma is my soul mate, and although she has a nursing degree instead of an MBA, make no mistake—she is the person most responsible for WWT's growth. Her deep understanding of God's Word provided me the firm foundation and encouragement needed to persevere and grow WWT through many challenging times.

Proverbs 18:22 says, "He who finds a wife finds a good thing and obtains favor from the LORD" (ESV). Occasionally, Thelma will reference this Scripture and ask me, "David, am I a good thing?" When she asks me this, tears often well up in my eyes.

"Yes! Oh yes!" I tell her, accentuating my answer with a gentle hug. The evidence is obvious as the Scripture says: I have clearly obtained favor from God. And I remind her that not only have I obtained His favor, but thousands of WWT employees past, present, and future, and their families and communities by extension, have received, are receiving, and will receive God's blessing and favor because of her unwavering support and encouragement rooted in God's Word. Literally every day, since before the inception of WWT, Thelma has enabled me to pursue God's vision. And from the beginning, it meant risking all we had to serve a higher purpose.

In July 1990 Thelma and I leveraged our life savings and ownership positions in our current holdings to seed WWT with $250,000, as well as to secure a $1 million line of credit. A quarter of a million dollars was a staggering sum of money to us—an amount beyond the imagination of my family when I was growing up. By the end of that year, WWT's revenues exceeded $800,000—which sounds like a promising start. But tech, especially in the early days, was a capital-intensive business, and while we managed—barely—to cover cash flow, I rarely took home a paycheck anywhere close to what I once made in my old corporate job. Sometimes I didn't take home a paycheck at all, but during those times, I made sure my employees got paid because God had called me to serve them first.

Those early days were tough as I have already mentioned, and they were about to get tougher—I'll tell you more about that in the next chapter—but I never changed my focus. When your leadership is driven by serving a higher purpose, then it's easier to persevere during hard times and to take a leap of faith during good times. You remind yourself that God is in charge and that His purposes are divinely appointed and eternally focused—which means we don't always get to see or understand what He is up to.

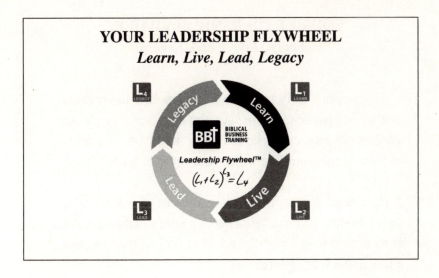

YOUR LEADERSHIP FLYWHEEL
Learn, Live, Lead, Legacy

The BBT *Leadership Flywheel*™ is a relational process focused on increasing an individual leader's spiritual growth in Jesus Christ with the goal of encouraging and equipping the development of other spiritual leaders. At the end of each chapter, you will find questions for you to think about and apply to your own life and leadership. If you're reading this book with a group and completing the companion BBT study, you can include your responses there. Learn more about the Leadership Flywheel at the end of this book and at www.B-B-T.org/LeadershipbytheGoodBook.

After you've spent a few moments engaging with these questions and considering your responses, I encourage you to spend some time talking to God about what's going on inside you. Don't worry about using fancy language or doing it a certain way; simply talk to the Lord about what's on your mind and heart. Make sure you spend a few moments listening for His response as well. To facilitate this conversation, you'll find a short prayer at the end of each chapter to help get you started.

YOUR LEADERSHIP FLYWHEEL:
Learn, Live, Lead, Legacy

1. Being completely honest with yourself, what presently motivates your leadership? As you consider your answer, think about how coworkers, family members, and others on your team would describe your style of leadership.

2. How does your motivation emerge in your leadership style? In other words, what do you tend to emphasize the most as you lead others? And what do you tend to minimize, deflect, or ignore?

3. What kind of leader would you like to be? Similarly, why are you reading this book and perhaps participating in a BBT small group to discuss Biblical leadership principles? What expectations and personal goals do you have for this process of reading and reflecting on the message in these pages?

Dear God, thank You for the opportunity to learn from the eternal wisdom of Your Word, the Holy Bible. Help me to open my mind and heart to the lessons You want me to learn and practice from Your Word. I want to be a better leader, one who serves and inspires others, one who follows the example of Jesus. In His name I pray, amen.

CHAPTER 2

SERVE THOSE
AROUND YOU

Be shepherds of God's flock that is under your care, watching over them—not because you must, but because you are willing, as God wants you to be; not pursuing dishonest gain, but eager to serve; not lording it over those entrusted to you, but being examples to the flock.

1 Peter 5:2–3

Did you hear the one about the chicken and the pig going into business together? They agreed to open a restaurant and then had to come up with a name. The chicken said, "I know the perfect name—let's call it Ham-'n'-Eggs!" The pig thought for a moment and then replied, "I don't think so. I'd be a hundred percent committed, but you would only be part-time!"

It's corny, but I love the point it makes. When you're committed to leading by serving a higher purpose, you naturally serve the people around you. When you begin with this commitment to servant leadership as your foundation, you create a domino effect. When you're all in, the people you serve are all in!

You not only model the kind of attitude and work ethic you expect in others, but you also attract new employees with the same sensibilities. These new hires reinforce the example of servant leadership while also attracting similar people to join their teams and their departments. People who aren't motivated to serve naturally don't stick around. Like the chicken, they're not committed 100 percent!

SOURCE OF SERVICE

Putting those entrusted to your care first is the wisest investment you can make in any business. When you serve them and look out for their best interests, over time you build up a level of trust that you can't get any other way. Over the years, I have learned that people want to work for and do business with people they trust. Once they trust you, the return on your investment is manifold.

This isn't a business strategy—it's a fundamental principle of human relationships and a commandment from our Creator. In the Bible we find a scene where Jesus is asked, "Teacher, which is the greatest commandment in the Law?" Jesus replied: "'Love the Lord your God with all your heart and with all your soul and with all your mind.' This is the first and greatest commandment. And the second is like it: 'Love your neighbor as yourself.' All the Law and the Prophets hang on these two commandments" (Matt. 22:36–40). As if the example throughout Jesus' life isn't enough, I'm not sure He could have been any clearer in His answer!

This is the same message we see throughout the pages of the Good Book and one of the key reasons its timeless wisdom remains so relevant to leadership today. The Bible is God's love letter of guidance to us so we can fulfill His purpose for our lives here on Earth. And one of those primary purposes is to serve. This servant leadership is how I operate and work with people—not just in business but also in every interaction and every relationship. Any time I'm standing in front of another human being, I am representing God. Whether I'm in the workplace or the marketplace, talking to a barista or the board of directors, I want to serve them.

Again, there's no better model of this kind of servant leadership than Jesus. We've all heard the slogan "What would Jesus do?" We've seen it virtually everywhere—on T-shirts, bumper stickers, and bracelets—to the point that it's become a cliché. Yet, it addresses a valid question. How should we lead? What does it look like to serve others through our leadership? The obvious answer is to lead and serve the way Jesus did. This isn't complicated or difficult to grasp.

No matter the situation, Jesus' ongoing message was to love each other. Even when facing arrest on the night He was betrayed, Jesus modeled this as He admonished a disciple who tried to protect Him, " 'Put your sword back in its place,' Jesus said to him, 'for all who draw the sword will die by the sword. Do you think that I cannot call on my Father, and he will at once put at my disposal more than twelve legions of angels? But how then would the Scriptures be fulfilled that say it must happen in this way?' " (Matt. 26:52–54).

Christ made no effort to save Himself. He was willing to give His life to save our souls, and He did. This is the ultimate lesson in serving those around you. Jesus said, "I am the good shepherd. The good shepherd lays down his life for the sheep" (John 10:11). He made it clear that we are to lead and serve in the same way: "My command is this: Love each other as I have loved you. Greater love has no one than this: to lay down one's life for one's friends" (John 15:12–13).

As a person of faith, as someone committed to following Jesus, your leadership must reflect this kind of love to everyone around you. When you choose Jesus as your example and God's Word as your guidebook, these values, principles, and commitments are essential. You can't apply them in one part of your life but not another! You don't have an option as to whether you apply them in business.

This standard of servant leadership has nothing to do with your job title. From a Biblical standpoint, leadership is not about personality, position, or title. It is about character. It is about serving others just as Christ did and as He instructed His disciples to do. One of the many things I love about Biblical Business Training (BBT) is the way it helps so many people apply these kinds of principles at work. It informs and educates leaders on their responsibility to not only know the Word but also live it out through their relationships.

IMPORTANCE OF INTEGRITY

When God entrusted me with His vision for WWT, I knew I was accountable to Him, and all who joined WWT, to be an ambassador for Christ. I believe that one's ability to lead, serve, and trust ultimately comes down to one's character. The word I like to use is *integrity*, which evolved from the Latin adjective *integer*, meaning whole or complete. Integrity refers to a person's inner sense of "wholeness," deriving from qualities such as honesty and consistency of character. People with integrity maintain a consistency of character.

While we will never reach perfection, we are each called to emulate Jesus' example to live with wholeness. We are told to live a life of integrity and follow the principles of God, which we find outlined in His Word. Living a life of integrity is a 24/7 undertaking. True leaders *never* compromise their integrity.

Unfortunately, many leaders attempt to compartmentalize their lives and conveniently forget to implement what they often claim to believe. They may go to church often, read the Bible, and pray on a regular basis, but during the week they fail to exercise integrity in their business practices. They think God's teachings are not applicable in business. They lead as if Jesus had a different set of rules to be applied on and off the job. Sometimes, the more successful they become, the more they exempt themselves from Biblical standards and Jesus' example of complete integrity.

Sadly, many leaders assume Jesus' teachings do not apply to

them. They convince themselves that their situation is unique, special, and exempt from the standards of integrity set in the Bible. Their egos have become so oversized that they believe they no longer have to hold themselves to the standard that often advanced their careers in the first place.

Of course, this is not true! Treating people according to Biblical teachings doesn't fluctuate depending on the day of the week or where you are. Leaders, of all people, must maintain their integrity. Even when circumstances try to fragment their lives and they're tempted to compromise and compartmentalize their faith, those leading by the Good Book never give in.

A good leader becomes known as a person who never compromises their integrity. It's often said that it takes a lifetime to build a good reputation, yet it can be lost overnight. This is why you must always treasure it! As Scripture reminds us, "A good name is more desirable than great riches; to be esteemed is better than silver or gold" (Prov. 22:1).

The more a leader succeeds, the more people he or she will be in a position to serve. This increase in responsibilities requires greater dependence on God, which in turn requires even more humility. God is the only reason we have been blessed to lead WWT to the heights where He has taken us. My focus is endeavoring to remain faithful to His Word and to the guidance I receive from His Spirit. I'm very far from getting it right every time, but I am committed to remain willing and able to serve those around me. Even today, there's no job, role, or responsibility that I would not do if needed by our company.

When you're climbing a corporate ladder, it's sometimes challenging to keep your service to others ahead of your ego. However, I'm convinced that in the long run, servant leadership will advance your role in ways that office politics and promotions never can. Any time I've been tempted by the spotlight shining my way, I've done my best to remind myself that the source of light in my life is Jesus Christ.

FLIP YOUR PYRAMID

Leadership fueled by serving those around you not only gets better long-term results than hierarchical leadership, but it also produces greater success for more people and provides a less stressful work environment. I knew that a traditional pyramid-style organizational chart wouldn't work for me. So, from the beginning at WWT, I flipped this pyramid structure. My highest priority, as well as that of all our leaders, is to serve everyone else, not get on a power trip to feed my ego.

I take Jesus very seriously when He said, "Whoever wants to become great among you must be your servant" (Mark 10:43b). This means that as a leader, I work for my people. My job is to serve them. Likewise, they serve those people who report to them. Everyone at WWT serves everyone else. As our attitude of leading by serving has permeated our organization, our customers have experienced it, which I'm convinced accounts for our success.

When people ask me the secret to WWT's success, I tell them, "As corny as it sounds, that's easy—we serve a higher purpose." *Leadership is at its best when a leader believes his or her job is to serve others.* A servant-hearted leader knows that it's impossible to serve other people unless they focus on serving God first.

Unfortunately, few business schools and corporate orientations train leaders to serve. For many, the paradox of a servant-leader is so counterintuitive that it doesn't make sense. But I cannot stress the vital importance serving a higher purpose makes if you want to lead and succeed.

If you truly want to be a better leader, then you don't have a choice about whether you become a better servant—of God and of those you lead. From a Biblical standpoint, leadership is not about personality, position, or title. It is about character. It is about serving others just as Christ did and as He instructed His disciples to do. The most effective, most fulfilled leaders serve a purpose higher than their own.

Sitting in the dark in 1993, I could not have imagined that WWT would be exceeding $12 billion in revenue, representing more than six thousand families and their communities globally, or that I would be writing a book about business and leadership principles. But that's the beauty of leading by the Good Book. When success blossoms from your service, you realize that God's higher purposes are at work. You realize that it's not about quarterly reports, profit margins, and bottom lines. Leading by serving others *is* the bottom line!

No matter how large your company grows, maintain your desire to serve. As I have sought to be a good shepherd and look after people, they, in turn, have done the same for others. God's vision of WWT inspires us to keep building a company that constantly gives back to its employees and customers, as well as others in our communities and around the world. But there's also another responsibility that comes with our mandate to lead: serving those in need.

YOUR LEADERSHIP FLYWHEEL:
Learn, Live, Lead, Legacy

Similar to the questions for reflection at the end of the last chapter, the following questions are designed to help you process the importance of leading by serving others and to help you consider what this looks like in your own life and leadership. Once again, you don't have to write down your responses, but it might be helpful and allow you to look back at what you've written and compare it to your other responses later in the book. If you're participating in a BBT group study of this book, these questions will help get you started.

1. On a scale of one to ten, with one being "rarely" and ten being "almost always," how would you rate yourself as a leader on how often you serve others? If we asked those you serve to rate the same thing, how would their score compare to yours? How would you explain the difference, assuming there is one, in your answers?

2. In what areas do you need to improve in order to serve better and strengthen your leadership? Check all that apply from the following list and feel free to add your own.

_____ Frequency of your communication with those you serve

_____ Ability to listen more closely to those you serve

_____ Responsiveness and ability to follow through

_____ Accessibility to those you serve

_____ Ability to solve problems and resolve frustrations for those you serve

_____ Issues of character and integrity you need to address within yourself before God

_____ Other areas:

3. How can Jesus' example help you in these areas? What specific encounter, or conversation did Jesus have that you can use as a model for growth? Based on your selection, choose one phrase or verse from the Bible to use as a reminder of the kind of servant-leader you want to be.

Dear God, I want to serve others the way Jesus served during His life on Earth, with strength, mercy, and humility. Give me the power and patience I need to remain accessible and humble. Open my heart to the needs of those I serve and reveal the wisdom required to help them grow. Help me to be a leader of integrity who remains committed to Your ways, Lord, no matter whether I fail or succeed. Let my leadership reflect Your light in all that I do as I seek to serve the people whom You have placed in my charge. Amen.

CHAPTER 3

SERVE THOSE IN NEED

And do not forget to do good and to share with others, for with such sacrifices God is pleased.

Hebrews 13:16

Over the years, in tough times as well as good times, my motto has never changed: I don't work to make a living—I work to make a *giving*! Leading by the Good Book means not only serving a higher purpose and the people around you. It means looking for opportunities and being aware of moments when you can fill the needs of others.

Being blessed with so much, I am now in a position to change people's lives in meaningful ways. Now well into my sixth decade of life, I will continue to give until I am unable to do it. My ministry is about changing lives for Christ, and this is what I was put on this earth to do. God has blessed me so much, and with that comes responsibility. I don't feel it is a burden, but instead, it is a wonderful opportunity of stewardship and a way to honor God. The Lord trusts me with what He has given me so I may do His will.

Jesus was the most generous person who ever lived, and with His last breath on the cross, He said to the criminal beside Him these comforting words: "Truly I tell you, today you will be with me in paradise" (Luke 23:43). Even in the agony of an excruciating, torturous death, Christ saw an opportunity to serve someone else in need and bless them. Of course, the reason He gave up His life was so we could have life everlasting. He served the greatest need of the human race—paying the debt for our sinful, rebellious natures.

Like Jesus, I want to give until I can no longer give. Retirement has never appealed to me, because my ministry is never done. This is the calling God places on all our lives, and we are blessed by serving Him rather than making our comfort our primary goal. As Jesus explained to His disciples, "From everyone who has been given much, much will be demanded; and from the one who has been entrusted with much, much more will be asked" (Luke 12:48b). I take this statement very seriously.

Giving is something we all can do no matter our season of life or stage of our career. Therefore, I don't believe in the classic definition of retiring and playing golf all day, because we will always have opportunities to serve those in need around us—in our workplace, our neighborhoods, our communities, churches, and schools. Our contribution is not limited to monetary giving. Everyone can volunteer to give his or her time. You can also give your talents, abilities, and expertise and find ways to serve others.

People often ask my coauthor Brandon and me, "How did you two meet?" They are usually surprised to learn that we did not meet through business connections or working together through our various companies. The Lord brought us together because we had both volunteered to mentor the African American owner of a small technology business in the early 2000s. This founder and owner was looking for Christian mentors with skills and experiences from larger businesses to help him grow and scale based on Biblical principles. Brandon and I were both very busy in our respective companies and careers, and we could have easily bypassed this opportunity to serve. However, speaking for both Brandon and myself, we are very thankful that the Lord connected us through this mentoring opportunity.

No matter how busy you are in building your career, you can

make time to apply your work skills to the needs of your community. If you're a carpenter, a plumber, or house painter, you can volunteer to help low-income people with their house repairs. Teachers can tutor children in the summer, an accountant can assist elderly people with their tax returns, and attorneys can volunteer at free legal clinics. All of us can find a way to use our God-given resources to help folks in need: "Each of you should use whatever gift you have received to serve others, as faithful stewards of God's grace in its various forms" (1 Peter 4:10). Therefore, our ministry is never done!

GIVING ALL FOR ALL

Giving to others has been deeply ingrained in my brain ever since I was a child. My mother used to say, "It isn't the amount you give, because generosity differs from one person to another, depending on his or her circumstances." To reinforce her point, she'd recall how Jesus and His disciples witnessed a poor widow who gave her last two coins there in the temple (Mark 12:41–44). Jesus said, "Truly I tell you, this poor widow has put more into the treasury than all the others. They all gave out of their wealth; but she, out of her poverty, put in everything" (vv. 43–44). Her gift came from a more generous heart than those who gave more money.

My mother also loved to remind us of Jesus' parable of the Good Samaritan (Luke 10:30–37). In response to a scholar's inquiry about what it means to love our neighbor and who our neighbors actually are, Jesus presented a parable about a man who was attacked by robbers when he traveled on the road from Jerusalem to Jericho. Severely beaten, robbed of his money, and stripped of his clothes, the traveler was left for dead there on the side of the road.

Soon a priest came by and crossed over to the other side of the road to avoid the bloodied, naked body in the ditch. Another religious leader, a Levite, responded the same way. But then along came a Samaritan, a foreigner generally disliked by Jews at the time, who stopped in his tracks at the horrific sight of another human being in need: "He went to him and bandaged his wounds, pouring on oil and wine. Then he put the man on his own donkey, brought him to an inn and took care of him. The next day he took out two denarii and gave them to the innkeeper. 'Look after him,' he said, 'and when I return, I will reimburse you for any extra expense you may have'" (Luke 10:34–35).

Jesus then asks, "'Which of these three do you think was a neighbor to the man who fell into the hands of robbers?' The expert in the law replied, 'The one who had mercy on him.' Jesus told him, 'Go and do likewise'" (Luke 10:36–37).

Our Lord's command does not provide conditions, requisites, or excuses. He doesn't say, "Go and help neighbors if you have the time" or "Go and serve those in need if you're not too busy or don't have more important things to do." No! The Good Samaritan parable teaches all of us a lesson about having compassion and giving to *all* in need.

Jesus taught us to love others regardless of their race, religion, or ethnicity. During Jesus' lifetime, Jews disliked Samaritans for many reasons, including their history of marrying non-Jews and the fact that they didn't follow all of the law. Presumably, the injured man was a Jew, so for Jesus' audience the thought of a lowly Samaritan stopping to help someone who despised him would be unthinkable. But it didn't matter to the Good Samaritan, who only saw someone in desperate need of help. He went above and beyond the call of duty by paying for the man's lodging and other expenses.

The power of this story is undeniable. We are put on this earth to help others who are in need, to serve them as Jesus would do without judging their circumstances. In our hectic, hustle-and-bustle world today, no one has time to get involved. We don't even see the needs of others so often because we've become accustomed to ignoring them in order to focus on our own agendas. But Jesus makes it clear that if we love Him, we have an obligation to get involved. You and I are both called to be the Good Samaritan to those around us, every single day.

ALL THAT JAZZ

Seeing the joy on another person's face when he or she receives something from you is one of life's greatest rewards. This includes when you give anonymously, and the person will never know that it was you who blessed them. To know that what I was able to do made a difference, had an impact on someone, or might have changed his or her life, even in some small way—that feeling means the world to me. I look at them and love to see their expression when they realize I expect nothing in return from them. In an instant, there's a connection between us, a bond—even if it's only for a moment—of peace and love. Anyone who's ever watched me in a situation where I have the privilege to meet the needs of others knows I light up.

Whether you give a buck or a billion—it doesn't belong to us anyway. The old cliché is true—you can't take it with you! We are merely stewards of all the resources God has entrusted to us. When the time comes that I face the Lord, if He asks me, "Well, what did you do with what I gave you on Earth?" I want to be able to say, "I gave to others in need. I used it to show people Your love. To help them understand who Jesus is. To invest in eternity for Your kingdom." I want to hear Him tell me, "Well done, good and faithful servant," and not, "Why didn't you give more?"

Of the many charities, nonprofits, and organizations my family has been blessed to serve, one of our favorites is the Harold and Dorothy Steward Center for Jazz. You see, my mom and dad loved music and always made it a part of our lives. Jazz was always playing in our home when we were growing up. Like New Orleans, St. Louis is known for its jazz, and when my wife, Thelma, and I saw an opportunity to help renovate this historical theater and honor my parents and their love of music, we jumped at the chance!

The jazz center features the Bistro, a club with seating for 220, and a jazz lounge, a more intimate venue with seating up to 75. In addition to staff headquarters, the center also houses the Centene Jazz Education Center, an educational practice space for budding musicians from across the greater St. Louis area.

Naming the center after my parents was a big thrill for my mother, and I'll always remember the big smile on her face on opening night. I remember telling her how much it meant to me to be able to see our love of music passed on to future generations. And I'll never forget what she said as she gently squeezed my hand: "Thank you, son. Proverbs 13:22 tells us, 'A good person leaves an inheritance for their children's children.' Your children's children and their grandkids will enjoy this jazz center for years to come."

THE SPIRIT OF GIVING

From the beginning, World Wide Technology was established as a community, an extended family of people who not only work together but care about one another's lives outside the office. And when a tragedy or crisis strikes, we try to look out for our own just as any family would. If one of our people is going through a difficult time, whether it's a major illness or a personal financial problem, the company will be there for them to help them get through it. We might pay for a funeral, make a tuition payment, or cover a medical expense—we are there for them. There is a spirit of giving at WWT, whether it's giving to the customer, the community, or to each other. Everyone here has the same goal, which is to serve others.

WWT has always actively encouraged our team members to give back, and we created our "Day of Giving" as a way for employees to work in the community while receiving their usual pay. No matter how much our company grew or the responsibilities pulling at me, I have always made sure to give back by serving personally, as well as corporately.

WWT's senior managers as well as entry-level team members are encouraged to do the same. We will also donate the use of our company suites for professional football, basketball, and hockey events. While these suites are generally used for entertaining customers, when there's an open date or cancellation, we call local groups so they can bring young fans who otherwise might not have the opportunity to see a professional sports event. We love giving them the royal treatment with catered food and beverages and great seats for the game.

While we give generously, both within WWT and beyond, we've discovered that our attitude of serving is also good for business. This benefit is not what motivates us, but we're grateful that our customers and others like how they're treated and become loyal partners. Most people trust good corporate citizens and want to do business with them. This kind of customer base also has a positive effect on employee morale and retention. It's easier to serve customers who like the way you treat them and conduct your business.

Our experience is not an exception. America's Research Group conducted a recent survey that revealed some compelling results. Their findings determined that 61 percent of Americans trust a company who is active in the community. Of the people surveyed, 41 percent said they would drive ten minutes out of their way to buy from a retailer with a good reputation for serving the community. This study also revealed that 54 percent of American shoppers are willing to pay more for a product associated with a good cause.

When you serve those in need, it's also good for business. But that's not why you do it. You do it because God commands you to serve. He blesses us so we can bless others. Whether it's time, money, talents, expertise, or materials, our resources are God's riches to share with others.

YOUR LEADERSHIP FLYWHEEL:
Learn, Live, Lead, Legacy

1. When was the last time you spontaneously helped someone in need? What motivated you to stop and serve in this situation? Would this experience make you more or less likely to help someone in a similar situation in the future? Why?

2. What obstacles do you face when you consider serving those in need around you? Too many needs pulling at you? Not enough time for your priorities? Exhausted from too many responsibilities? Something else?

3. How do you balance generosity with discernment? How do you serve those around you while also maintaining sufficient resources to achieve future goals?

Dear God, I know how You have so faithfully met my needs. Please use me to bless others by giving of my resources as I seek to share all You've entrusted to me. All I have is Yours, Lord, and I want to be Your conduit of generosity. Empower me to be the kind of leader that always gives to those I'm blessed to lead. May my leadership reflect the sacrificial love of Christ and the attitude of the Good Samaritan. Help me to see and serve my neighbors, today and every day. In the name of Jesus, amen.

SECTION 2
Love

CHAPTER 4

LOVE WHAT YOU DO

Whatever you do, do it all for the glory of God.

1 Corinthians 10:31

Biblical Business Training had a modest start. In early fall 2008, Brandon, his coleader, Greg Schuster, and a small group of coworkers held its first weekly Bible study meeting before work. This gathering differed from what they might have experienced at a church because they were colleagues coming together in an office environment. The participants of these first meetings, however, quickly realized that they were involved in something quite special.

"Each of us realized our small group meeting created a bond," Brandon told me. "We viewed each meeting as a refueling opportunity. We studied Scripture that applied to what we were facing at work, we talked about it, and the message stuck with us. We felt recharged, reminded of what we wanted our priority to be no matter what our role might be in our company—serving others."

From that first group, BBT began to grow and flourish as more and more individuals, leaders, and companies discovered the power from meeting together to study God's Word. Within a short time, Brandon soon faced a dilemma. BBT's continued growth and expansion required more time than ever before—just as his company was also exploding and requiring more from him. He loved doing both jobs and knew God would provide the perfect full-time leader for BBT. When Brandon's wife, Lisa, shared with him that she sensed God calling him to leave his corporate job to lead BBT, Brandon initially resisted. Had God equipped him with so much talent and so many experiences for business only to ask him to walk away?

Plus, Brandon and Lisa were well aware there would be a significant decrease in their family's annual income. Still, the more Brandon prayed about it, the more God confirmed this new, unexpected direction. When Brandon came to meet with me for one of our mentoring sessions and shared this potential move, I immediately confirmed it as a wonderful idea. I could see God's hand at work and trusted that Brandon's love for the mission of BBT, coupled with his unique leadership skill set, made him the perfect person for the job.

"This move didn't make sense to a lot of people in my office, but I knew it's what God wanted," explained Brandon. "I was willing to commit to this new direction so that BBT could help others grow in their relationship with God, bring their faith into the workplace, and become stronger leaders. I have a strong passion for helping others become empowered servant leaders."

PAY ATTENTION

It's easy to have passion for a new company, new venture, or new product when you first start out. But can you continue to love what you're doing when you face challenges and obstacles? Like any other start-up enterprise, BBT has had its ups and downs. Brandon and I knew this going in. Nobody said it would be easy. But it is something God has called us to do. It's a big part of living out our purpose in a way that honors Him and serves others.

This calling was why World Wide Technology's culture and values are what they are today. I passionately wanted to build a company based on the teachings of the Bible and sincerely believed if we built a company dedicated to serving others—just as the Bible instructs—it would succeed. And I had no doubt about doing what I loved to do and felt called and uniquely equipped to do—lead the company by serving others. Their needs had to take priority above my own. As the company owner, the needs of employees, associates, and customers would come before mine. I remember saying to my wife, Thelma, "A company that treats people like that—wow, that's the kind of company I would love to work for!"

For three decades, I knew that if I abided by the teachings in the Bible, our company would succeed in pleasing God—which matters more than any profit earned. I believed with all my heart and soul that God would be with us and He would guide us. God's message in Deuteronomy made so much sense to me: "Take care to follow the commands, decrees and laws I gave you today. If you pay attention to these laws and are careful to follow them, then the LORD your God will keep his covenant of love with you, as he swore to your ancestors" (Deut. 7:11–12).

While my passion was strong, it was faith in God that fueled building WWT. The two—faith and passion—go together. I am reminded how the two go hand in hand from Paul's letter to the Romans: "We boast in the hope of the glory of God. Not only so, but we also glory in our sufferings, because we know that suffering produces perseverance; perseverance, character; and character, hope" (Rom. 5:2–4). Passion is not jumping up on a table, and perseverance is not refusing to try something new. Both rely on faith to take risks and follow God's calling. Keep in mind that it's not necessarily what we do, but how we do it.

Paul's writing reminds me that it's our impact on people's lives that makes a difference. One of the primary ways we influence them is through our attitude. If we love what we do, then we can bear to suffer along the way. For example, you can go to work disinterested and tired—and most likely, you're going to have a bad day. Your negative mind-set soon becomes the way those around you see the workplace.

Or you can go to work with energy and passion with the mind-set, "I'm going to make everybody's day better that walks in that door today. That's my job." When you do, you will have a better day. You will feel better. Others around you will be drawn to you and feel better, too. Helping others, giving to others, and serving others give us the deepest satisfaction. Being vigilant and persevering requires a passion and faith—passion for what you're doing and faith in God.

MOVE WITH A MISSION

One fundamental way to combine your passion and your faith is to express them through a mission statement. A strong leader knows the purpose for his organization, and he articulates it with a mission statement. While all major companies have a mission statement, relatively few small businesses and start-ups do. Some entrepreneurs find them old-fashioned, and other leaders prefer the freedom to wing it. I'm not implying that they don't know what they want to accomplish. Most do, or at least have a vague idea in mind.

Having worked in corporate America for many years prior to becoming an entrepreneur, I was exposed to several mission statements, so from the beginning of WWT, I knew our purpose: people, quality, and technology. My first priority was assembling the best possible people, and this extended to customers and vendors, not just employees. I let everyone know that my job would be to serve them. I also made it clear that our company was dedicated to providing the highest level of quality to our customers through exceptional service and the use of state-of-the-art technology.

As WWT has grown, we've made sure the expressions of our purpose remain simple and memorable. What's our vision? "To be the best technology solution provider in the world!" And our mission? "Create a profitable growth company that is also a great place to work." Both our vision and mission are supported and sustained by our core values:

- Trust—in character and competency
- Humility—stay grounded; never forget where you came from
- Embrace—change and diversity of people and thought
- Passion—maintain a strong work ethic
- Attitude—be positive and open-minded
- Team Player—proactively share ideas
- Honesty—demonstrate honesty and integrity

Collectively, we refer to them as THE PATH because these core values are the path to employee and company success. We prominently display both our mission and vision statements along with our core values in every one of our buildings as well as on our website and all company brochures and materials.

When Brandon started Biblical Business Training, he knew the extreme importance of having a mission statement. He told me, "Ours is seven words: 'Helping people apply Biblical principles at work.' We deliberately wanted a one-liner so everyone could remember it. Then we condensed it to three words, 'Faith for Work,' so we could include it with our condensed vision statement, 'Leadership for Life,' in our BBT logo!"

FOCUS ON THE *REALLY* BIG PICTURE

Our emphasis on loving what you do and distilling it into a corporate mission is nothing new. Great leaders have always relied on their sense of purpose and calling to guide them. The Bible has many concise mission statements, and some of the most noteworthy ones are only a sentence or two. God makes His instructions clear for His people so they can lead effectively. He wants us focused on the big picture—the *really* big picture: His eternal purposes!

For example, in Exodus 3:10 God says to Moses, "So now, go, I am sending you to Pharaoh to bring my people the Israelites out of Egypt." And in Jonah 1:1–2 we find, "The word of the LORD came to Jonah son of Amittai. 'Go to the great city of Nineveh and preach against it, because its wickedness has come up before me.'" Later, we read about another brief yet crystal-clear mission statement in Matthew 28:19 when Jesus instructs His disciples: "Go and make disciples of all nations." Each of these examples illustrates the importance of having a clear, concise mission statement. You don't need a long, flowery mission statement to make your point. On the contrary, a long, flowery mission statement can adversely affect what you want to accomplish because the core message and primary purpose get diluted.

In 2014, Microsoft CEO Satya Nadella sent a company-wide email to employees laying out a broad agenda for the company's new fiscal year, setting the stage for the upcoming Windows 10 launch by revealing the company's new, official mission statement: "To empower every person and every organization on the planet to achieve more." While that's a tall order, it's memorable and leaves a clear, lasting impact for the company's more than one hundred thousand worldwide employees.

Strong leaders constantly and consistently communicate the organization's mission statement to employees, customers, and vendors so everyone is on the same page. Otherwise, even the best leader succumbs to what I call "mission drift." Regardless of whether the organization is small or large, the subtle shift away from the entity's mission can happen even when the company seems to be thriving. Ironically, experiencing success and implementing innovation can sometimes throw a team off track and off mission.

As a result, key people start losing focus as they're pulled in directions unrelated to their core strengths and expertise. For instance, at BBT, we focus on helping people apply Biblical principles to their work. While these principles are focused on application in business, they also apply to other areas of one's life, such as personal relationships and parenting. BBT leaves it up to other organizations and ministries, however, to address those applications in non-business-related areas.

Even great Biblical leaders can lose sight of their God-given purpose. Solomon was known to be the wisest person who ever lived, yet he, too, was not immune to mission drift. While he did great things during his forty years of leadership, Solomon strayed from his mission by not keeping God's command that no one should worship false idols. Under the influence of his wives, Solomon began practicing idolatry. When a leader does not pay close attention to developing and reinforcing an effective mission statement, the long-term legacy of the organization is jeopardized.

MIND THE MISSION

Even once you have a mission that reflects your primary purpose and passion, you have to instill it throughout the entire organization. If you don't love what you do, then it's tough to articulate a mission statement that you can execute and sustain. And loving what you do is not just about loving your products and services or excelling at sales and marketing. It all comes back to how you treat others. Are you willing to serve them in pursuit of serving your customers and other team members?

If you don't already have a written mission statement, I encourage you to build from a Biblical foundation by considering the Golden Rule: "So in everything, do to others what you would have them do to you, for this sums up the Law and the Prophets" (Matt. 7:12). This fundamental principle of servant leadership has been around for more than two thousand years and remains one of the most quoted Scriptures. Just remember: It's easy to quote but not always easy to practice!

In addition to the Golden Rule, another foundational verse for Biblical leaders comes from Colossians 3:23: "Whatever you do, work at it with all your heart, as working for the Lord, not for human masters." In fact, this is actually *the* foundational Scripture for BBT. To provide a bit of context, the apostle Paul was writing a letter to the church at Colossae to refute the heresy that had started to sprout like weeds. Composing his message from a Roman prison, Paul drew his readers' attention back to Christ, the Son of God, the Creator, the head of the church, the first to be resurrected, the fullness of deity in human form, the one who reconciles all things to God. With the example set by Jesus as our compass, we lead and serve out of our passion to please God, not just to turn a profit or please others. This verse captures the passion it takes to be a good leader. When we work with earnest dedication to please God, we can anticipate success.

We find this message echoed in another letter Paul wrote to the early Christian church in Rome: "Never be lacking in zeal, but keep your spiritual fervor, serving the Lord" (Rom. 12:11). Clearly, living passionately with purpose was vitally important to this man. In fact, Paul's story is fascinating because prior to being baptized a Christian, he considered himself "a Hebrew of Hebrews" (Phil. 3:5) and actually persecuted the followers of Jesus. Then known as Saul, he dramatically encountered Christ while on his way to arrest—and possibly kill—these early followers:

> As he neared Damascus on his journey, suddenly a light from heaven flashed around him. He fell to the ground and heard a voice say to him, "Saul, Saul, why do you persecute me?"
>
> "Who are you, Lord?" Saul asked.
>
> "I am Jesus, whom you are persecuting," he replied. "Now get up and go into the city, and you will be told what you must do." (Acts 9:3–6)

This heavenly light blinded Saul for three days, and once his sight was restored, he gave his life to Christ and committed the rest of his days to spreading the good news of the gospel, especially to non-Jewish people. Paul basically became the first missionary and was eventually recognized as the most significant one in the history of the church. He made four missionary trips throughout the Mediterranean region, addressing Jewish people who used to regard Jesus as he once did, as well as Gentiles.

Following the teachings of the Bible is a noble enterprise, and the reward can be beyond your imagination. Our purpose in this book, however, is to encourage you to look beyond the normal indicators of success and status. You cannot measure personal success with the size of one's bank account or the company's profit margin. Our motivation should be to receive God's blessing—and not necessarily a financial blessing. In fact, it is not even a here-and-now blessing. The bigger picture in terms of the reward is that you will receive an inheritance blessing from the Lord.

Passion is a powerful force that all great leaders seem to possess. Can it be acquired and cultivated? It can, but only when it comes from your heart. You can't fake it; therefore, to possess it, you must find something you believe in so passionately that it consumes you. You must love what you do—and more importantly, why you do it. Which means for those of us who follow Jesus, we do it to honor HIM!

those you lead and serve. As leaders at WWT, we love others by giving them opportunities for advancement, paying fair and competitive wages, contributing to their 401(k) plans, providing a wonderful environment in which to work, and making sure they feel respected and valued.

When a leader genuinely loves others in this sacrificial, servant-hearted way, the love spreads to others throughout the organization. They follow the example that you set for them. As a leader, you have the privileged responsibility of setting the tone for the rest of your team. We have been blessed to see the impact our love has on our company's culture. WWT is regularly on the *Fortune* "100 Best Companies to Work For" list, usually ranking in the top half. We're consistently highly ranked in Glassdoor's "100 Best Places to Work," and we've received the Glassdoor Employees' Choice Award multiple times. I'm especially proud that WWT is consistently named on other national lists chosen by minorities and women as a great place to work.

CLEAN FEET AND A HUMBLE HEART

Without a doubt, one of the greatest challenges to loving others is keeping our ego in check. Too often, others may tell us what they think we want to hear in order to keep us happy. Dramatic growth and unexpected increases in profits can also tempt us to take the credit instead of thanking God for His generous gifts. The more you make your leadership about yourself and your achievements, however, the harder it gets to love others and to keep serving them with humility.

When we don't depend on God, then inevitably we become the biggest tree in our little forest. We all know leaders whose success goes to their heads. You know the type—high achievers from humble beginnings who forget their roots and begin to think they are superior to other folks: the corporate executive who moved up the corporate ladder and fails to remember his supporters who contributed to his rise, or the self-made entrepreneur who has accumulated substantial wealth and becomes enamored with his sense of importance. The list goes on and on. Behavior of this nature damages morale and discourages teamwork.

It also goes against the teachings in God's Word. The Bible consistently condemns arrogance and pride, and it reminds us of the virtue of humility. The wisdom of Proverbs declares, "Pride goes before destruction, a haughty spirit before a fall" (16:18). We're also warned, "Do not think of yourself more highly than you ought, but rather think of yourself with sober judgment, in accordance with the faith God has distributed to each of you" (Rom. 12:3).

Jesus became the living embodiment of this truth by leaving the glory of heaven with His Father and coming to Earth as a baby in a manger. The King of kings humbled Himself to the point of living and serving as a mortal man, never demanding the attention and worship that He alone is worthy to receive. Instead, Jesus always served those around Him, whether they were fishermen and tax collectors or kings and priests. He healed lepers, welcomed little children, and loved those that society deemed unlovable and unimportant.

Among Jesus' many displays of humility, perhaps none is more striking than His symbolic act performed during the evening meal of Passover with His disciples, known as the Last Supper. After pouring water into a basin and preparing to wash His disciples' feet,

> He came to Simon Peter, who said to him, "Lord, are you going to wash my feet?"
>
> Jesus replied, "You do not realize now what I am doing, but later you will understand."
>
> "No," said Peter, "you shall never wash my feet."
>
> Jesus answered, "Unless I wash you, you have no part with me." (John 13:6–9)

Later, Jesus explained to His disciples, "I have set you an example that you should do as I have done for you. Very truly I tell you, no servant is greater than his master, nor is a messenger greater than the one who sent him. Now that you know these things, you will be blessed if you do them" (vv. 15–17).

By washing the feet of His disciples, Jesus taught a meaningful lesson on humility. Washing someone's feet has never been an enviable task, especially in Biblical times, when most people wore sandals if they wore anything on their feet at all, often walking countless dusty miles each day. Flecked with mud, sand, and animal dung, their feet quickly became dirty and crusted. By cleaning His disciples' feet, Jesus demonstrated that even the highest-ranking, most powerful leader should always be willing to serve at the lowest levels.

Another example of Jesus' humility emerges in His request for a donkey to ride into Jerusalem (Matt. 21), which fulfilled the prophecy about the Messiah: "See, your king comes to you, righteous and victorious, lowly and riding on a donkey" (Zech. 9:9). Unquestionably, Christ could have orchestrated an elaborate, grand entrance fit for a king, which would have been more than justified. After all, He's the Son of God! Such a display would have been a big crowd-pleaser for the Jewish people who had grown resentful of the way Roman leaders at that time traveled from village to village accompanied by legions of armored soldiers mounted on huge horses. As conquerors of Israel, they intentionally made a dramatic entrance to signify their authority and power.

In contrast, Jesus' demeanor was unassuming and meek. He was quite the opposite of a leader who sat perched up on a throne, far removed from the people. His manner of dress resembled a commoner, and He regularly mingled with the masses. Jesus preached that the meek shall inherit the earth. If His presence had focused on wealth and power, He would have contradicted His teachings. He walked the talk!

COMMANDED TO CARE

Jesus' example made it clear we are to love others by serving them. Throughout the Bible, we are also told to love others as we would love ourselves. In the Old Testament, the people of Israel were instructed to "love your neighbor as yourself" (Lev. 19:18), and this command recurs throughout the New Testament (1 John 4:11, 20–21; Mark 12:3; Matt. 22:39; Luke 10:27; Gal. 5:14). When Jesus knew His death was imminent, He said, "A new command I give you: Love one another. As I have loved you, so you must love one another" (John 13:34). Clearly, loving one another was not a new command; however, loving one another as Jesus loved—humbly and sacrificially—took it one step further.

Although you won't hear this principle expressly taught in business schools, I sincerely believe it should be. Loving others is a crucial attribute in the practice of good leadership. When we love somebody, we place his or her best interest above our own. It's like a loving parent who makes sacrifices for her child by giving unconditional love. It's the single mother who works at two jobs so she can support her family; it's the father who lives frugally to put away money for his children's college education.

Likewise, as a leader and follower of Jesus, you have a responsibility to place the welfare of your employees, coworkers, and customers above your own. It's rarely easy, but nothing communicates to people how much you value them than caring for them during tough situations. Back in 1992, our company experienced severe financial problems. Even though we were struggling to meet our weekly payroll, I made sure everyone received his or her full salary. In fact, the company's checking account balance dipped so low that some weeks I was unable to take a paycheck home for my own family. But I knew what I had to do.

As a young boy, I witnessed the love my father had for our family and the long, hard days and nights he endured for our benefit. He and my mother followed Christ's example in putting us before themselves, and now I wanted to do the same for my employees. Whether you are a head of a household or a head of a company, when we love others as Jesus tells us, we place their interests above our own. As I see it, when Jesus said to love each other (John 13:34), He made no exceptions, so it applies to the workplace as well as all other areas of our life. And please keep in mind it wasn't a suggestion—it was *command*.

DIFFERENT PARTS, ONE BODY

Jesus also commanded acceptance for those who are the most unloved, the most discriminated against, the most forgotten in our community and in our world. God's love doesn't discriminate, and neither should we in how we love coworkers, employees, clients, and customers. Naturally, some people may be easier to love than others. Without even realizing it, you may find yourself gravitating to others who share your skill set, enjoy your sense of humor, or go out of their way to express their appreciation. But don't overlook those who are different than you. They have just as much to contribute as your closest protégé. In fact, you may actually learn more from those individuals who are most distinctly different from you.

In any organization, some roles may be more visible, and some customer accounts may be larger and more lucrative than others. But the team members out front are just as important as the team members behind the scenes. The programmer and software engineer are just as important as the janitor and the warehouse worker. Everyone contributes and works together to serve each other—and our customers.

One way to maintain this equitable perspective on how we love others is by focusing on unity and diversity. We're told in Scripture, "There are different kinds of gifts, but the same Spirit distributes them. There are different kinds of service, but the same Lord. There are different kinds of working, but

in all of them and in everyone it is the same God at work"
(1 Cor. 12:4–6). The Bible goes on to compare how we love
and serve one another to a body made up of different parts
but working in harmony toward the unified goal of sustaining
life and health:

> The eye cannot say to the hand, "I don't need you!" And
> the head cannot say to the feet, "I don't need you!" On the
> contrary, those parts of the body that seem to be weaker
> are indispensable, and the parts that we think are less hon-
> orable we treat with special honor. And the parts that are
> unpresentable are treated with special modesty, while our
> presentable parts need no special treatment. But God has
> put the body together, giving greater honor to the parts that
> lacked it, so that there should be no division in the body,
> but that its parts should have equal concern for each other.
> If one part suffers, every part suffers with it; if one part is
> honored, every part rejoices with it.
>   Now you are the body of Christ, and each one of you
> is a part of it. (1 Corinthians 12:21–27)

This passage puts our leadership role in perspective. No matter how long we've served the company, how much profit we've
added to the portfolio, or the size of our bank account, as a
human being created in the image of God, we are never more
important than the entry-level person on their first day on the
job. If you expect them to love, serve, and respect everyone
around them, then you set the example, just as Christ set the example for us.

AMBASSADORS OF APPRECIATION

Loving others means it's always about them—not about you.
This is especially important with first impressions. We make

sure visitors are always treated warmly at WWT. Our reception-ists are our guests' first and last impressions when they visit here, so when we hire them, we make sure they naturally en-joy being friendly and warm. They are goodwill ambassadors for our entire organization. In fact, every good leader's job de-scription is to serve as a goodwill ambassador, an ambassador of appreciation, to others around them. I love stopping to talk with employees and teammates when I walk across our com-pany campus. I may be a couple of minutes late for a meeting, but I let those individuals I encountered know how much I value them by taking a moment to engage with them.

This kind of relational focus may come natural to some lead-ers and have to be cultivated by others. But connecting with people, really loving them and not just pretending to care, is the greatest way you serve them on a daily basis. I'm reminded of a story Brandon told me about a college business professor with a rather unique final exam. This professor would hand out a single blank piece of paper and then say, "I have one ques-tion for you, and how you answer it is the most important thing for you to know about managing people." Obviously, the entire class would hold their breath in anticipation of such a crucial question, unprepared when it finally came. "What is the name of the person who cleans this building we're in? You've all passed by her. Now I want to know who has taken the time to at least ask her name."

How often do we treat other people as individuals and not just someone filling a function? Do you know the name of who cleans your office building? Do you take the time to learn the name of a waitress, server, nurse, or dry cleaner? Do you know anything about the sales rep you just talked to or what their life is like? A small personal touch makes everyone feel impor-tant. Simply using and remembering their first name can change the entire dynamic of a business conversation. It's such a small thing—and one that is overlooked again and again.

LOVING THE UNLOVABLE

The easy part is loving those who love us and who are naturally "lovable." What about those people we encounter in our work, our families, and our communities who are not so lovable? How do we love them? For some time now, I have found myself using the phrase *loving them through it* to remind myself how to love the unlovable.

The first word of this phrase is *loving*. It is an action word. Love is often thought of as simply an emotion. However, the agape love that Christ has for us is based upon His actions, sacrificing Himself for our sins. "Dear children, let us not love with words or speech but with actions and in truth" (1 John 3:18).

Which leads me to the second word—*them*. This type of love is not about you or me, but the other person. Too often we may be tempted to think, *I'll love them if I can get something in return*. This is conditional love. But again, that is not what Christ modeled for us. "This is how we know what love is: Jesus Christ laid down his life for us. And we ought to lay down our lives for our brothers and sisters" (1 John 3:16).

Now let's look at the third word—*through*. Relationships are a journey, not a destination, and that includes difficult seasons through which we must walk with others. Reconciliation takes time. As Christ-centered leaders, we are called to develop and cultivate God-honoring relationships. Often, we are tempted to take a detour to avoid those who are unlovable, but Jesus did the opposite. He met them exactly where they were and walked with them.

The final word, *it*, is perhaps the toughest because *it* describes what they have done, will do, or may keep doing that makes them unlovable. For me, I have experienced my share of disappointments in others' behaviors and insults. Those can be challenging enough for me to love someone through *it*. However, when my family or others close to me are experiencing *it*, the challenge of loving the unlovable rises to another level. In those moments where I feel the need to reply or retaliate, I am reminded, "Do not repay evil with evil or insult with insult. On the contrary, repay evil with blessing, because to this you were called so that you may inherit a blessing" (1 Pet. 3:9).

If you want to lead like Jesus, then you will always love those around you, including the unlovable.

YOUR LEADERSHIP FLYWHEEL:
Learn, Live, Lead, Legacy

1. What does it mean for you to love others, especially people in your workplace, in your current season of leadership? What are some appropriate ways you can show more love to those you currently lead and serve? Choose at least one of these ways and practice it today.

2. What obstacles and challenges often prevent you from loving others the way you know God wants you to love them? How many of these barriers come back to your ego, self-image, and personal pride?

3. What body part best represents the role you're currently serving in? Why? How does this part—and your leadership role—relate to the rest of the body? How can you be more accepting and loving toward other parts of the body?

Dear Lord, I'm so grateful for the way You first loved me and sent Your Son, Jesus, to die for my sins so that I can be forgiven and have eternal life with You. Thank You for the people You have placed in my life, especially those with whom I'm blessed to work. Help me to love them as You love them. Give me patience, kindness, and wisdom so that they may see Your loving character reflected in all that I do. Protect me from temptations to take all the credit or deflect all the blame. Help me to stay humble and focused on how I can lead best by serving more. In the name of Jesus, amen.

CHAPTER 6

LOVE GOD AND HIS WORD

Love the LORD your God with all your heart and with all your soul and with all your strength.

Deuteronomy 6:5

We love others because God first loved us, and He sent us a love letter, called the Holy Bible. This isn't just my perspective—it's what we find in His Word: "Dear friends, let us love one another, for love comes from God. Everyone who loves has been born of God and knows God. Whoever does not love does not know God, because God is love" (1 John 4:7–8). If you want to be a leader who follows Jesus, if you want God to guide you every day, if you want to treat others like you want to be treated, then loving God is not optional. God's love is the source, the foundation, upon which everything else falls into place. "And so we know and rely on the love God has for us. God is love. Whoever lives in love lives in God, and God in them" (1 John 4:16).

If you want to love God, then, like any other important relationship, you need to spend time with Him. The two best ways I know to do this are through prayer and by spending time reading, memorizing, and meditating on His Word—ideally, on a daily basis, even several times throughout the day. Too often, prayer and Bible study can become two items to check off your list as a dutiful Christian, but that approach won't help you grow in your love for the Lord. Loving God through prayer and Bible study require openhearted, full-minded engagement.

When I read the Bible and pray about seeking first the kingdom of God and all His righteousness and trusting that everything else will be added unto me (Matt. 6:33), these words come alive. They remind me that when I make decisions, I should think eternally, and when I think with this mind-set, I am seeking God first, and what I do has no time frame because right is always right. I am comforted knowing that the Holy Spirit is always with me and is my connection to God's love.

With the Holy Spirit as my guide, I want my life to produce the fruit of the Spirit: love, joy, peace, patience, kindness, goodness, faithfulness, gentleness, and self-control (Gal. 5:22–23). These qualities all contribute to how we think when we are truly having a filled and blessed life. But the starting and ending point for this process is clear: "And now these three remain: faith, hope and love. But the greatest of these is love" (1 Cor. 13:13).

To love God, I need to talk to Him.

SAY A LITTLE PRAYER

We often get so caught up in our hectic, busy lives that we tend to forget what the Lord does for us every day, day after day. Every single hour blessings and miracles are happening all around you. His miracles are so many that they seem routine. The sun comes up every day in the east, and it goes down every evening in the west. As I see it, just the fact that we get up each morning is yet another miracle. We are surrounded by miracles, and there are so many to which we become oblivious and that we take for granted. Too often, we fail to honor and credit God for these everyday miracles. Every prayer I say is intended to praise God and give Him glory.

Success makes some people arrogant, and after their prayers have been answered, instead of glorifying God for His blessings, they pride themselves for their achievements. They are tempted to no longer give praise to the Lord, nor do they acknowledge Him for what He has allowed them to accomplish. Their unchecked pride can quickly become self-destructive. This is not the way I want to react when God blesses me. Instead I want my response to be thanking Him for honoring me with a wonderful opportunity to honor His Word. I want to always glorify and praise Him for it.

When I speak publicly, I use discretion on whether to pray and how I pray, depending on the audience. On such occasions, I'm always in the mind-set of ministry and know that others are often prepared and ready to share in my prayer, aware of the spirit in which it's given. Others, however, may not recognize my motive or intention in praying, so I try to discern whether it's the right time to pray. The right time could be at the beginning of a meeting, or perhaps at its end. I try to read my audience and get a sense of how receptive they will be. Most of all, I base my discernment on the leading of the Holy Spirit and know He will guide me to make the right call.

Before a meal, I always pray. It doesn't matter who is present, because I'm going to pray—there is never an exception. I've done this all my life, everywhere and with everyone, including CEOs of the world's biggest corporations, as well as heads of state. So far no one has ever expressed his or her disapproval. Regardless of their own beliefs or religious practices, people seem willing to accept my desire to offer a prayer of thanksgiving to God.

Occasionally, someone will hear me pray and want to know more about prayer. I encourage them to simply talk to God like they would talk to anyone else. I also encourage them to check out the Good Book for examples, especially the model for praying that Jesus Himself gave to His followers. Known as the Lord's Prayer, it can be found in Matthew 6:9–13, but in the preceding verses, it's noteworthy that Jesus first cautioned His followers about how *not* to pray:

And when you pray, do not be like the hypocrites, for they love to pray standing in the synagogues and on the street corners to be seen by others. Truly I tell you, they have received their reward in full. But when you pray, go into your room, close the door and pray to your Father, who is unseen. Then your Father, who sees what is done in secret, will reward you. And when you pray, do not keep on babbling like the pagans, for they think they will be heard because of their many words. Do not be like them, for your Father knows what you need before you ask him. (Matthew 6:5–8)

In other words, we don't need to pray in some formal, perfectly spoken, TV-anchor voice. We don't need to worry about having the "right words" or caring what others think of what we say. We should focus on opening our hearts before God, not trying to impress others, demonstrate our piety, or practice for our next Toastmasters. Instead, Jesus told us to pray like this:

Our Father in heaven,
hallowed be your name,
your kingdom come,
your will be done,
on earth as it is in heaven.
Give us today our daily bread.
And forgive us our debts,
as we also have forgiven our debtors.
And lead us not into temptation,
but deliver us from the evil one. (Matthew 6:9–13)

While we call this the Lord's Prayer, it's really *our* prayer because Jesus instructed us to use it as our model for how to communicate with God. Notice how the prayer is structured: by first honoring God, praising and thanking Him, then asking for provision for that day, followed by asking for His forgiveness and stating our commitment to forgive those who have sinned against us, and concluding with protection from the enemy of our souls. This structure is clearly intentional and helps us prioritize our conversations with God.

Many people use this prayer daily, either praying it word for word as rendered here in Scripture or using its categories in their conversation with the Lord. I like both ways and find new depths to this beautiful prayer every time I pray it. It reminds me that God is my loving Father, the Source of all life and Giver of all good gifts, that He graciously forgives me and commands me to lovingly forgive others the same way, and that He protects me from evil in this world.

WITHOUT CEASING

The Bible tells us, "Pray without ceasing" (1 Thess. 5:17 ESV). When I was a small child, I watched my parents pray, and our entire family—all ten of us—always attended Sunday morning services. We were also involved with church activities during the week. Each night before bedtime, my mother reminded me, "Don't forget to pray to the Lord, David."

While prayer has always been a significant part of my life, I can't recall a time when I've ever prayed like I did back in 1993 when WWT was on the brink of bankruptcy. It was one of those times when you get down on your hands and knees and pray, "Dear Lord, if you will get me through this..." I suppose all of us have been there at least one time in our lives. It's a time when your problems seem insurmountable and you feel as if your whole world has come crashing down on you.

I cannot imagine being in the position I was and not feeling assured God was hearing my prayers. When we opened our doors in 1990, I made a few sales, and we were off and running. Things were looking up and then—boom!—just like that, it was as if the roof caved in on us. One of our people, whom we viewed as a trusted employee, misstated financial information and misappropriated funds. Like most start-up companies, we were undercapitalized, and we didn't have a contingency plan in the event of an unexpected setback.

As a result, the company had difficulty paying our vendors, and consequently, our ability to respond to our customers' needs suffered. While nobody on the company payroll ever missed a weekly paycheck, some weeks I was unable to draw out money to pay our household bills. Consequently, my car was repossessed, and bill collectors were pounding on our door, sometimes threatening my wife, Thelma, to foreclose on our house and take away everything we had. It didn't matter that for years we always paid our bills promptly. Once we got behind, they showed no mercy.

Looking back, our problems were not related to providing value to the customer. What was missing was a lack of a set of values. I repeatedly prayed, "Lord, please get me through this, and when You do, I'll know that it was only You. I will give all praise, glory, and acknowledgment for what You do." Today, I am blessed to share my story in this book with you. As I write this, WWT will generate more than $12 billion in revenues this year. We have become a global player, a systems integrator, and we are considered best in class for what we do. Today, WWT shapes and defines what technology looks like in the market-place. This is a testament to God. It is not a testament to any individual here, especially not to me! I know exactly where all of this comes from. I pray to the Lord, constantly thanking Him for all He has blessed us with.

I also study His Word as I try to know and love Him more.

WORD TO THE WISE

A few years ago, I was blessed to receive St. Louis' Citizen of the Year award. In my acceptance speech, I made it clear that

I didn't deserve the award—the accomplishments they cited in giving me such an honor were only because of God. I told those present that my greatest comfort, most powerful motivation, and most profound inspiration comes from my practice of committing Scripture to memory. Thelma not only shares this habit with me, but I can't tell you how often she has lovingly quoted just the right Bible verse, or prayed truth from God's Word, just when I needed it most.

I love to read the Bible because it helps me learn more about the God I love, who first loved me (1 John 4:19). I always try to commit my favorite Scripture passages to memory. These verses are so rich, and eloquent, that I know of no better way to express my views with such clarity. I have repeated these meaningful verses enough times that these thoughts are now deeply embedded in my heart. Consequently, when I say them or share them with others, they come out naturally and blend in with my conversation. As the Good Book says, the Word of God does not return void, but it accomplishes the purposes for which God sent it (Isa. 55:11).

I would be hard-pressed to choose only one verse or passage as my favorite in the Bible, but Psalm 91 surely has to be one of them. It's relatively short with only sixteen verses, and the first two often come to mind almost every day: "Whoever dwells in the shelter of the Most High will rest in the shadow of the Almighty. I will say of the LORD, 'He is my refuge and my fortress, my God, in whom I trust'" (vv. 1–2). Then, like a perfect bookend, in the last two verses God reminds us, "He will call on me, and I will answer him; I will be with him in trouble, I will deliver him and honor him. With long life I will satisfy him and show him my salvation" (vv. 15–16).

I view this psalm as an opportunity to commune with God, and I do not need to be in a physical place such as in church. I am able to find rest in God by reading His Word anywhere I am. As I shared in the first chapter, back in 1993, I was at my wit's end from dealing with all the enormous stress and turmoil from the challenges I faced. In the midst of each day's stormy battlefront, this psalm provided me with peace and rest. I was able to think more clearly and logically. We're told that faith comes by hearing the Word of God (Rom. 10:17), and this is certainly true for me. When I meditate on His Word, it invigorates me, and I feel stronger and calmer. At first, it's internal, and then I find myself speaking those words of faith, both to myself and to others as well. These life-giving words uplift and nourish others, particularly in the midst of the depletion of difficult times.

Thelma also has several verses she reads and recites regularly. One that she treasures is also one that frequently speaks to my heart:

> Do not be anxious about anything, but in every situation by prayer and petition, with thanksgiving, present your requests to God. And the peace of God, which transcends all understanding, will guard your hearts and your minds in Christ Jesus.
>
> Finally, brothers and sisters, whatever is true, whatever is noble, whatever is right, whatever is pure, whatever is lovely, whatever is admirable—if anything is excellent or praiseworthy—think about such things. Whatever you have learned or received or heard from me, or seen in me—put it into practice. And the God of peace will be with you. (Philippians 4:6–9)

Thelma once explained to me, "This Scripture lets us know that the Lord will often answer our prayers with what we think we need but also with what we don't even know we need—He provides *all* we need. He is our Father and we are His children. He loves us so much."

The Bible truly has something for everyone. It offers an enormous selection of powerful verses that have specific appeal to a diverse group of readers across cultural, social, historical, and temporal lines. Often, people tell me, "Reading the Bible is such a personal experience for me. It strengthens my relationship with God and helps me understand Him and His love for me—and for everyone." Sometimes others tell me how they read a certain passage that spoke directly to their needs, their circumstances, or their feelings, almost as if it had been written just for them. No wonder the Bible remains the best-selling book of all time, acclaimed for its power, history, truth, and revelation.

Through prayer and Bible study, leaders grow closer to God and experience new depths of His love. As we mature in our faith, our wellspring of divine love benefits everyone around us. We can only love our employees, clients, and customers—along with our competitors and even our enemies—when we grow in love with God.

YOUR LEADERSHIP FLYWHEEL:
Learn, Live, Lead, Legacy

1. What are three times in your life when you have experienced the love of God in a major way? When was the most recent time you were reminded of how much He loves you? What was your response?

2. How would you describe your prayer time with God right now? Momentary and on the fly? Dedicated and contemplative? An ongoing conversation throughout your day? What's required for you to spend more time talking with God?

3. What's one of your favorite verses or passages of Scripture? Why? How does this verse, either directly or indirectly, remind you of God's love?

Dear Father in heaven, I praise Your name and give You thanks! I pray that I may advance Your kingdom here on Earth as I rely on You to guide me each day. Help me to trust You completely and to surrender my agenda today to Your perfect will. Give me what I need to get through this day. Thank You for forgiving my sins—I want to show others the same compassion and grace in forgiving them when they hurt or offend me. Allow me to lean on Your strength when temptations come my way. Protect me from the devil and his attempts to distract and derail me from Your purpose. I love You, Lord, and want others to know Your love through me. In the name of Your loving Son, Jesus, amen.

SECTION 3
Imagine

CHAPTER 7

IMAGINE YOUR
VISION REALIZED

Where there is no vision, the people perish.

Proverbs 29:18 KJV

If you serve God and lead others, then you must be willing to exercise one of His greatest gifts to us—our imaginations. So much emphasis is placed on intelligence, technical ability, social aptitude, and organizational skill. But the human imagination is bigger than any of these. The imagination encompasses all you know and connects your head with your heart and soul. When God speaks to us, He often ignites our imaginations as we envision what He is asking us to do and how we will go about it.

Once the imagination looks ahead, a good leader has a vision of what will be, and he shares it with others to know what to expect in the future. And please understand that a leader's *God-given* vision should not be confused with that of the person who envisions his future with a life of riches and luxury. Such self-centered thinking is not big enough to serve others. Imagining must be the catalyst for acting. A leader's vision should not focus on personal gain. When you succeed at serving others, you will be amply rewarded.

A business leader's vision anticipates, as specifically as possible, the place and time when the vision will be actualized. While the leader views the dream as a faith-based expectation, others may not get on board and may, in fact, dismiss the vision as grandiose, unfeasible, or pretentious. But strong leaders pursue their visions with passion, patience, and perseverance. They can imagine their dream and know how to build the structure to support its reality. Their belief in such a pursuit often inspires others to rally around and share in its completion.

Once your dreams are in motion, you don't want others slowing you down.

SHARE YOUR DREAM

Great leaders are able to clearly communicate their vision with others. If the vision is not clear enough, it is unlikely to ever happen. When one dream is brought to life or one milestone reached, visionary leaders expand their vision to reach even more audacious heights of success. In 1995, we celebrated WWT reaching revenues of $74 million. Instead of resting there and seeing how long we could enjoy such a lofty plateau of success, God scaled my dream to giant proportions!

Once we reached that once-unbelievable goal, God then raised my vision for an even more audacious milestone and let it be known that WWT would have $1 billion in revenues by 2003. "The reason why we will do it," I announced to our people, "is because we are building something extraordinary that will provide outstanding services to people for generations and generations. This is only our beginning." This wasn't inflated, pie-in-the-sky talk to push them harder and spotlight our achievement—I meant exactly what I said. For this past year, our annual revenues were more than $12 billion. And as I've shared with you, and will likely tell you again, we can only credit God for this level of unbelievable success!

When I knew God was guiding me, others began to share my vision. They realized that our endeavor was bigger than us, that our success wasn't about money or fame or any of the typical business goals. Instead, we were part of something God was building and using to minister to people's lives.

Sure, there were setbacks along the way. Yet even during those times, I never lost faith in my God-given vision. I kept praying and reminding myself of the truth of God's Word: "So do not fear, for I am with you; do not be dismayed, for I am your God. I will strengthen you and help you; I will uphold you with my righteous right hand" (Isa. 41:10). With God's guidance, I knew the vision He had given me was attainable, and as leader, you can also model this for others entrusted to your care, inspiring them to have the same mind-set.

GUIDED AND GIFTED

Brandon concurs that God inspires a person's vision, and then it becomes a leader's responsibility to communicate it to others. Our visions can be God inspired, and we should then share them with others to discern what God is calling us to do. I'm not the only one to experience this belief, because this is exactly what happened to Brandon when he first started the Bible study that would eventually grow into Biblical Business Training. And the original message God gave him made it clear that this was not just a one-time event.

Brandon recalls,

> Back in 2008 when I was still in corporate America, I was praying one morning before work. As part of my prayer, I simply asked God what I could do for Him that day. His response came through loud and clear to my listening heart. I was told to start a Bible study at work. I went to the office and tried to focus on my work, but His message was so intriguing to me that I thought about it all day. I didn't realize that if I started a Bible study at work, it would be just the beginning. God of-

ten reveals His plans in phases. Frankly, had I known the initial Bible study would lead me to resign from my executive position and to start and serve a nonprofit, I may have been more apprehensive about studying God's Word with colleagues. But, with God's leading, that is exactly what happened.

Eventually, my mission would be to enable opportunities for work-related Bible studies all over the world. If this vision were to be realized, then it might even require me to quit my job in order to bring this God-given dream to life. At the time, I was blessed to be on the fast track at my firm, and this vision wasn't what I expected. What God was telling me could vastly change the direction of my career and the lives of my family. Yet, it was undeniable. I had heard my calling from the Lord, and I knew it was something I must do.

Even when God gives you such a vision, it can still be quite daunting. Brandon shares,

The next morning, I got on my knees, and again I received a Word from God. It was like the previous day's message. It wasn't this audible, booming voice that caused the lights to flicker. But it was clear. And I simply couldn't reconcile this vision with my present circumstances, abilities, and schedule. So, my conversation with God that morning was more or less about how I tried to convince Him that I wasn't the right person for the job! I even told God what He already knew and talked about how my career was going so well, and how He made it possible. "Surely, dear Lord," I prayed, "You don't want me to waste the great opportunity You have provided to me?" Can you imagine? It seems comical now. I was trying to talk God out of the vision He had for me!

But Brandon discovered what all leaders know once they align their path with God's calling.

By the third morning, I picked up on my conversation with God to where it had left off. I told Him I would do it but that I didn't know how. Then to my surprise, the Lord said, "Ask Greg Schuster and he will help you lead it." I was surprised to say the least. Greg was also on the fast track with our firm. We were in the same division of the company, but I hardly knew him. I couldn't even re-member if he was a Christian! Then I recalled that Greg once invited my son and me to a father-son banquet at his church. My son was so young at the time that he was barely walking. So maybe Greg was a follower of Jesus. But still, I barely knew him. How awkward it would be to bring up this vision and the way God prompted me. But I knew I had to talk to Greg.

On my way to work, though, I decided to take my time. I figured now that I had some clarity, I could just let this thing play out and not try to force anything right away. I would likely bump into Greg in the coming weeks and the timing would be right. Just after I arrived at the office before work that morning, I went to the break room to get my usual cup of coffee, but the coffee machine was out of order. A creature of habit, I had to have my morning coffee and hurried over to a break room in another part of the building. As I started to fill my cup, I heard someone walk in behind me. Somehow, I knew who it was even be-fore I turned: Greg Schuster. We exchanged pleasantries and then I nervously said, "Say, Greg. Mind if I ask you a question?"

"Sure, Brandon."

"Have you ever thought about starting a Bible study at work?"

As soon as I heard the words come out, I froze—it was

as if time suddenly stopped. I had no idea how he might react, and I was so nervous.

"I thought I was supposed to ask *you*," he said, chuckling.

I looked at him in astonishment.

"Let me explain," he continued. "My wife and I recently returned from a one-week mission trip, and I have prayed that God would give me an opportunity to do something for Him during the other fifty-one weeks. The Lord told me that I should talk to you."

We both looked at each other in amazement and were momentarily at a loss for words. Then I told Greg about my conversations with God and again we were speechless. We agreed to meet so we could make the vision that God had implanted in our minds become a reality.

When you allow God to expand your imagination, you can expect others to share in His vision. He will guide you and gift you with all you need to bring the dream He has planted in you to life.

GROW WITH GOD

From the God-given vision to start one Bible study at work, thousands of people have participated in BBT groups throughout the United States and around the world! The vision statement for BBT is "To see people grow in their relationship with Christ and expand God's kingdom through their leadership." It is what we call "Leadership for Life!"

When Brandon and his wife, Lisa, discussed him walking away from his successful corporate career to train others to apply Biblical teachings to their work, she certainly had some reservations. "I could see God working in him for a while, and I had been praying about it," she says, "but I was worried about how we'd be able to survive financially." At the time, they had three small children and knew how expensive it would be to raise and educate them. When she talked about it with some of her friends and family, their response was, "Are you saying that Brandon talked to God and was told to quit his job to do this? Lisa, you're not going to let him do this, are you? Perhaps he should go for some counseling."

Lisa knew they meant well and wanted to help, but they were unable to reconcile their expectations for Brandon and his family's future with what God was asking him to do. Some would also say, "Lisa, Brandon is so successful, and his future looks so bright. Don't let him quit his profession to serve the Lord. Tell him to tithe—even double tithe if he wants! But remind him that his wife and children come first." Other times, some friends and family members didn't say anything, but their silence spoke volumes. They were totally shocked. Instead of being supportive, they thought Brandon had gone off the deep end.

Lisa may have been apprehensive initially, but she says, "I had no doubt that it was a call from God. Still, I wasn't sure how we should move forward. Just because you get a call from God, it doesn't mean it's going to be easy. My husband is very smart, and he was aware of how hard it was going to be to leave a successful career to serve the Lord. It was really not something either one of us wanted to do. We were so comfortable and content with how his career was progressing, and we were enjoying our lives. We definitely did not want this change. However, when you get a calling from the Lord, if it's what He wants you to do, you have to do it."

As she looks back on those years during this transition, Lisa admits that they were undoubtedly the hardest five years of their married life. Both of their mothers had significant health issues, and there were other challenges, too, but that time was also very rewarding, because they knew they were doing what God asked them to do. Romans 8:28 was an anchor verse for Brandon and Lisa during those challenging years and continues to be.

After BBT was up and running, Brandon and Lisa were not surprised when God asked him to partner with me to create Kingdom Capital. It overlaps God's calling on Brandon's life and exercises his leadership skills and financial expertise. But making that move required faith as well.

SOUL SOLUTIONS

If you're struggling in your ability to reach your present organizational goals, I encourage you to dream bigger. Too often, when we face setbacks or challenges, we retreat and hit pause in our pursuit of the original dream God gave us. While you don't want to be reckless or uninformed in your risk taking, many problems can be solved by returning to the original God-given vision and sharpening your focus. Sometimes you simply need to analyze the obstacle or problem more closely to see what's really going on. Whether it's a relational issue, a technical challenge, or a mechanical glitch, once you grasp the essence of the issue, you can then imagine potential solutions.

This process is basically at the heart of how WWT often serves our customers. They come to us with a need, a problem, a concern about efficiency, or growing pains and want help with utilizing technology. Our team members study their business model, look at their client base and past history, and then come up with ways they can overcome their present hurdles to grow and thrive. Whether it's an app so their customers can order online instead of waiting in line at their brick-and-mortar shop or a complete overhaul of their hardware and software systems, we focus on the problem in order to imagine solutions.

Our life goals and divine dreams work the same way. Once you've clarified the vision to which God is calling you, then use your imagination to create your path forward, trusting Him to guide you each step of the way. I like to think of these revelations as soul solutions or "soul-utions!" After all, as His children we are created in the image of our Father, the ultimate Creator. He has given us imaginations to use as a compass on our adventure of faith.

If you can imagine it with God's vision, you can do it with His guidance!

YOUR LEADERSHIP FLYWHEEL:
Learn, Live, Lead, Legacy

1. How would you express your God-given vision in one sentence? Write it here. How are you fulfilling this calling God has placed on your life in your present role of servant-based leadership? How are you bringing your divinely inspired dream to life?

2. Who are the people who currently share your big dream? How do they contribute to its fulfillment? How could you work more closely and cohesively with them?

3. When was the last time you prayed, "Lord, what can I do to serve You today?" When will be the next time?

Dear God, You are Creator of heaven and earth, sea and sky, people and planets, grass and galaxies. Thank You for creating me in Your image and instilling in me my unique imagination. I'm so grateful for the dreams You have given me and the dreams yet to come. Give me strength and courage to risk security and comfort in order to bring to life the dreams You've planted in me. Expand my vision and empower my mind so that I may find solutions where others see problems. Help me to be an innovator, Lord, in order to advance Your kingdom. In Jesus' name, amen.

CHAPTER 8

IMAGINE YOUR
FUTURE SUCCESS

*Truly I tell you, if you have faith as small as a mustard seed,
you can say to this mountain, "Move from here to there," and
it will move. Nothing will be impossible for you.*

Matthew 17:20

Prior to launching WWT, I had developed two freight-auditing businesses, so I knew that the investment Thelma and I made was like a tiny seed. I had no real tech experience or expertise. I had no backers or investors underwriting my family's life savings that we were investing into WWT. Other older and more established companies were already ahead of where we would need to be in order to compete in this new field.

But starting small didn't stop me from thinking big and believing we would become the company we are today. We rented space in a modest four thousand–square-foot warehouse, which is now dwarfed by WWT's campus of buildings. I hired four people. The sign on our door revealed just how big we were thinking: WORLD WIDE TECHNOLOGY. "World Wide?" a friend said to me skeptically. "You've got to be kidding!"

"Give us some time," I told him. "We're just getting started. Someday we'll do business around the world, and when we do, we won't have to change our name!"

He thought I was joking or being incredibly naïve or both. But you see, I knew that someday we really would be doing business around the world. It was never "if" in my thinking but "when" we would serve clients around the globe. After all, one of the incredible benefits of technology, then as now, is how it connects us all in a global village of communication, information, and commerce without limits of time zones and geographic distance.

I remember the first time I took Thelma to show her our new sign on the building. She looked at it smiling and said, "It's red, white, and blue—very patriotic. I like it." When I reminded her that we were World Wide Technology—not US Technology or North American Technology—she just nodded. Remembering some papers I wanted to bring home, I asked Thelma if she minded waiting just a moment while I ran in. Less than five minutes later, I got back in the car, and now she really had a big smile on her face. "You chose the right name, honey," she said. "God just gave me confirmation. I have a real peace about this new company you're starting."

MOVING MOUNTAINS

Thelma confirmed what I already knew to be true. I had complete faith in God, and knowing that He was on my side gave me confidence. Of course, I also knew I'd have to put in long hours, work smart, take risks, and surround myself with good people. I also realized that along the way I'd have my share of setbacks. There were days when it was much more difficult and challenging than I had even imagined. But that's when you have to exercise faith, trust in God, and imagine your future success.

For guidance during those tough times, I read Scripture, of course, and often I found encouragement in this story about Jesus' encounter with a fruitless fig tree:

The next day as they were leaving Bethany, Jesus was hungry. Seeing in the distance a fig tree in leaf, he went to find out if it had any fruit. When he reached it, he found nothing but leaves, because it was not the season for figs. Then he said to the tree, "May no one ever eat fruit from you again." And his disciples heard him say it....

In the morning, as they went along, they saw the fig tree withered from the roots. Peter remembered and said to Jesus, "Rabbi, look! The fig tree you cursed has withered!"

"Have faith in God," Jesus answered. "Truly I tell you, if anyone says to this mountain, 'Go, throw yourself into the sea,' and does not doubt in their heart but believes that what they say will happen, it will be done for them. Therefore I tell you, whatever you ask for in prayer, believe that you have received it, and it will be yours." (Mark 11:12–14, 20–24)

This story encouraged me deeply because it reminded me that no matter how daunting the problem or how overwhelming the circumstances, I was not hopeless or powerless. With the faith that God has blessed me with, I knew that He would be able to move any mountain. And we all have mountains in our lives. Sometimes they're only molehills, and other times they're the Himalayas, but no mountain is too big for God. To overcome our mountains, we must believe and have the courage to speak out to that mountain, act in faith, and trust that it shall be removed. You can move any obstacle in your way if you believe it and you say it. God's Word is that powerful.

Another truth from Scripture that has become deeply ingrained in my thinking reminds us, "Now faith is the substance of things hoped for, the *evidence* of things *not seen*" (Heb. 11:1 KJV, my emphasis). Here we are told to look beyond our circumstances and present reality and gaze into the future at the fruit we will bear. At the time we started WWT, I looked at it as planting a seed. It takes faith to sow a seed. I trusted that God would use the efforts of our team to produce a harvest for His purposes, but

I had no idea how long it would take to bear fruit. I simply had to keep looking to the future while staying engaged with what I needed to do in the present.

GIANTS AND GRASSHOPPERS

By no means was WWT an overnight success story. It reminds me of that old quote, "Everyone's overnight success started more than a decade ago!" We had to overcome many mountains to keep this start-up enterprise afloat during its early years. Unquestionably, a positive attitude coupled with an unwavering faith contributed to its success. Another way I often dispelled negative thoughts was to reread the story of how Moses sent twelve scouts to explore the land of Canaan, the Promised Land that was occupied by fierce inhabitants. Moses instructed, "See what the land is like and whether the people who live there are strong or weak, few or many. What kind of land do they live in? Is it good or bad? What kind of towns do they live in? Are they unwalled or fortified?" (Num. 13:18–19).

When the scouts returned, their report identified both the bounty of the land as well as the major obstacle in settling there. They told Moses, "We went into the land to which you sent us, and it does flow with milk and honey! Here is its fruit. But the people who live there are powerful, and the cities are fortified and very large. We even saw descendants of Anak there" (Num. 13:27–28). When Moses asked them if the Israelites should take possession of the land, as God had instructed them, the spies cautioned, "We can't attack those people; they are stronger than we are.... All the people we saw there are of great size.... We seemed like grasshoppers in our own eyes, and we looked the same to them" (vv. 31–33).

This is a timeless lesson on how negative thinking is self-defeating and self-fulfilling. These men assumed there was no way for them to overcome such formidable adversaries. Two of the twelve, however, dared to trust that God had not led them there only to be defeated. Caleb and Joshua said, "The land we passed through and explored is exceedingly good. If the LORD is pleased with us, he will lead us into that land, a land flowing with milk and honey, and will give it to us. Only do not rebel against the LORD. And do not be afraid of the people of the land.... Their protection is gone, but the LORD is with us. Do not be afraid of them" (Num. 14:7–9).

Despite this faith-based assessment of the challenge they faced, Moses was unable to convince the Israelites to move forward. Instead, they were paralyzed by logic and the odds against them. They felt as inferior as grasshoppers before these mighty giants occupying the land. Even though God had promised the people of Israel this land, they could not see themselves taking possession of it. They were doomed to defeat. Keep in mind, also, that these are the same people who knew God had already done the impossible for them numerous times—including their exodus from Egypt and the Red Sea parting.

When you undertake a new venture, you must think big and *know* that you will succeed—not in your own power but in God's power. Consuming yourself with doubt severely handicaps you. Focusing only on what you're capable of doing by yourself will always limit you. Listening only to negative, critical people who tell you that your big dreams are unattainable limits you as well. These "doubting Thomases" won't necessarily be your adversaries or competitors hoping to see you fail; sometimes, they will be well-meaning family members and friends trying to help you, at least as they see it.

Others may simply lack the faith and maturity to take such big risks. They may lack the spiritual foundation needed to trust God and to follow His guidance toward what appears impossible to our human eyes. Some people may envy your big thinking and secretly resent the possibility that your dreams may become reality. I'm reminded of Jesus' warning to His followers: "Do not give dogs what is sacred; do not throw your pearls to pigs.

If you do, they may trample them under their feet, and turn and tear you to pieces" (Matt. 7:6). This verse advises us to be wary of people who do not share your faith in the Lord or understand your trust in His Word. That's why I'm convinced we will usually accomplish more for God's kingdom when we are "equally yoked" to those people of like faith.

FAITH IN MOTION

There are many people who think big and they have big ideas. They can talk big, too. But that's often the problem—they're all talk! As a friend of mine once told me, "Ideas are a dime a dozen, but the men and women who implement them are priceless." His maxim reminds me of what they say in Texas about people who talk big but do little. They're described as being "all hat and no cattle." I suppose people aren't any different today than they were back in Biblical days. After all, we're told,

> What good is it, my brothers and sisters, if someone claims to have faith but has no deeds? Can such faith save them? Suppose a brother or a sister is without clothes and daily food. If one of you says to them, "Go in peace; keep warm and well fed," but does nothing about their physical needs, what good is it? In the same way, faith by itself, if it is not accompanied by action, is dead. (James 2:14–17)

That's a powerful observation, and I can't stress the vital importance of its truth. Faith is not enough if it's not deep enough to compel you to act! Success only comes when you put faith in motion. When you're willing to put your investment on the line, along with your resources and reputation, then you're taking your faith seriously. Not that you should do this recklessly or impulsively. But when you know without a doubt what God has instructed you to do and where He wants you to go, then you step out in faith no matter how many giants loom ahead of you.

You must have faith in God when you think big, but you must also work hard to turn those big thoughts into action! Imagine your future success and move toward it with confidence. Step out in faith and follow the Lord. Because He always honors His promises. Ultimately, after wandering in the desert for forty years, the people of Israel, of course, defeated the Canaanites and took possession of what God had promised them. They might have felt like grasshoppers, but they were more than conquerors!

God empowers us the same way today. He asks us to plant seeds, to nurture and tend to our growth, and to keep trusting Him for all we need. He reminds us, too, that when we have the faith of a tiny mustard seed, we can not only move mountains—we can watch that seed grow to epic proportions: "The kingdom of heaven is like a grain of mustard seed which a man took and sowed in his field; it is the smallest of all seeds, but when it has grown it is the greatest of shrubs and becomes a tree, so that the birds of the air come and make nests in its branches" (Matt. 13:31–32 RSV). Our seeds may seem small, our growth may appear limited at times by weeds and drought, but we imagine our future success as a tree of life. God is the source of our growth! When we serve those we lead, we keep our eyes on Him.

YOUR LEADERSHIP FLYWHEEL:
Learn, Live, Lead, Legacy

1. What major goal or accomplishment needs to happen in order for you to consider yourself successful one year from now? What stands in your way to achieving this success? What actions do you need to take in faith toward this future success?

2. When have you experienced God's power in doing the seemingly impossible? When has He empowered you to conquer giants in new territories? How do these experiences help you face new challenges?

3. Imagine yourself five years from now. What does success look like by then? Will you be in the same role of servant leadership? If so, how will you have improved your team and organization? If not, where do you see yourself serving in five years? What needs to happen for you to get there?

Dear God, You have already given me an abundance of blessings in my life. Please continue to provide me with direction and a clear vision for how You want me to serve and to lead. Help me to measure success on Your terms, not my own. When problems develop and giants seem to loom ahead of me, please give me the courage and the strength to step out in faith and trust You to guide me. I know that nothing is impossible for You, Lord, no matter how it may appear to my human senses. I trust You for the future success that I know is ahead of me, whether it be great or small in the eyes of others. In Jesus' name, amen.

CHAPTER 9

IMAGINE YOUR ETERNAL LEGACY

Very truly I tell you, whoever believes in me will do the works I have been doing, and they will do even greater things than these, because I am going to the Father.

John 14:12

A good leader must think long-term. Every decision I make is based on what its significance will be, not for today, but for many years to come. As I've shared, this future-focused thinking led to choosing to call my start-up *World* Wide Technology. I wasn't thinking about the company in its infancy, but the company it would someday be. From an early age, I've tried to focus on the big picture for the long run.

Several years ago, however, I sensed God compelling me to invest in eternity at a whole new level—He gave me a vision of WWT's success being used as a seed for His kingdom, producing a bountiful harvest for heaven's purposes. I was more than willing but unsure what form this new investment might take. As I reflected on this message and continued praying about it, I also shared it with Brandon. He and I believe that capital is a force that can do more than yield a financial return; it can also influence culture and core values of organizations. So, we discussed ways to plant capital in start-ups and companies, as well as ministries, nonprofits, and philanthropies, to have the greatest impact.

Exploring many ideas, we began to realize God was leading us toward eternity.

KINGDOM CAPITAL

During our conversations, Brandon shared that he had recently felt God pulling him to consider new directions as well. He knew many of his business and financial skills and previous experience were not being utilized fully. While Brandon remained deeply committed to BBT, it had reached a point of stability and growth. He asked me to pray about what was next for him just as he was praying for me and the new direction God was calling me to take.

As Brandon and I continued praying and discussing these matters, it became clear that our new directions intersected. Then one day we were driving to the airport to fly to an event together, when the idea for a values-driven private investment and philanthropic firm dawned. On that flight we created a model, and the basic framework for Kingdom Capital took shape. Our new venture would serve investors who share our values and want to make a positive difference in the world. It would manage capital in accordance with a set of core values rooted in our Christian principles, and it would invest this values-driven capital in companies with cultures and leadership committed to these same core values.

With our shared vision for Kingdom Capital clearly in place, we agreed Brandon would transition over time from BBT to serve as CEO and managing partner of this new firm. He would still be actively involved at BBT as its executive chairman, but relieved of daily operational duties, he could focus on creative, entrepreneurial opportunities for partnering with like-minded investors with a kindred spirit and shared values.

Today, Kingdom Capital's mission is to invest values-driven capital that maximizes financial return and eternal impact, which reflects our belief that we are stewards entrusted by God with various resources through which we can bless lives around the world. We claim a key verse of Scripture, Matthew 6:33, as our lodestar: "But seek first the kingdom of God and his righteousness, and all these things will be added to you" (ESV). Our vision is to transform the world through a virtuous cycle of capital.

ETERNAL RATE OF RETURN

While still in development, Kingdom Capital's visionary platform connects its values-driven investors and investments in a comprehensive ecosystem that enables the flow of capital to its philanthropic community via the Kingdom Capital Foundation. Consequently, investors, investments, and philanthropic partners all benefit from this strategic integration. Returns from investments can then be reinvested into a Kingdom Capital fund, creating a virtuous cycle of capital that catalyzes real impact and blessing in the world.

We continually look for investment opportunities that are uniquely better, address unmet or underresourced needs, and profoundly enhance standards and outcomes in specific industries. For example, Kingdom Capital's Health & Medical Group focuses on transforming the healthcare ecosystem by investing in innovations that have the potential to dramatically improve patients' quality of life. Today, we invest across the spectrum of healthcare technologies, including therapeutics, devices, diagnostics, healthcare IT, and life science tools.

In order to advance our mission and fully serve our investors and other stakeholders, we also created the Kingdom Capital Leadership Institute. Because our values-based model of leadership is central to creating positive change in our world, we want to invest in equipping, empowering, and enhancing leaders driven by the desire to transform lives. The Leadership Institute partners across our community of investors, investments, and philanthropies to bring a values-driven, thriving future to life.

While Kingdom Capital, like all private equity and venture capital investment firms, focuses on a cash-on-cash return, or an internal rate of return, or IRR, we also pursue what we call an eternal rate of return, or ERR. As you might guess, this is simply a way to try to measure the often invisible or intangible impact we want to have through Kingdom Capital. This is the same impact we want WWT to have in the business world and BBT to produce in business leaders. Kingdom Capital, however, can focus both deeply and broadly at using as many resources as possible to maximize an eternal return on each and every investment.

RISK AND REWARD

While Kingdom Capital is squarely focused on creating an eternal legacy, every successful organization envisions an end result it wants to realize. History bears out this way of imagining the legacy you want to leave in order to fulfill it. For years, IBM dominated the computer industry. Its mainframe computers were an incredible product. They were also very expensive and were affordable mainly to government agencies, large corporations, banks, insurance companies, and large institutions such as universities and hospitals. When the mainframes were first introduced in 1943, they were so costly that IBM founder Thomas Watson said, "I think there is a world market for maybe five computers."

This assumption about the role of computer technology remained pervasive for many decades. In 1977, Ken Olsen, founder of Digital Equipment Corporation, said, "There is no reason anyone would want a computer in his home." Back in the early eighties when IBM came out with the IBM PC, it was considered a joke—even IBM thought so! Compared to the big, huge mainframes of the day, a PC did very little. In 1983, only six years after Ken Olsen's 1977 statement, Steve Jobs, a young man in his twenties, made a speech at the Design Conference in Aspen. He envisioned a future where technology was a vital part of everyday life—much like our world today.

Another of today's best-known long-term thinkers is Warren Buffett, CEO of Berkshire Hathaway. Buffett's long-term investment strategy has made him one of the world's wealthiest persons. The multibillionaire has often described his investment holding strategy as "forever." An article in the *Wall Street Journal* summarized Buffett's strategy quite well: "He has a long-range perspective in a short-term world. Since 1965, Berkshire's book value per share has grown by nearly 800,000%, compared with an 11,355% gain in the S&P 500 stock index" ("Buffett: Politicians 'Dead Wrong' on Economy," February 28, 2016).

This kind of long-term strategy often requires harder work in the short term. There has to be some risk for the reward. At the end of 1991, following WWT's first full year in business, its revenues were $3 million. This is when I decided to focus on doing business with the federal government. My reason was that the federal government was spending $25 billion on technology at that time. To enter this competitive business arena meant that we would have to invest considerable time and energy into learning the ropes, building relationships, developing political contacts, becoming knowledgeable about government procedures, and learning the culture.

Most companies, particularly small ones, won't take the time and put in the effort required to get federal contracts. When they learn about all the rules and regulations that must be followed, the seemingly endless amount of paperwork, and how it's a long, tedious process, the government sector is viewed as much more trouble than it's worth. The process is so overwhelming that many companies are unwilling to get into it. And it's true that to be in compliance with the government's rules and regulations, a contractor must be willing to constantly adapt.

Nonetheless, my team and I could see where we wanted to go. We determined that with the government's potential to do high-volume business with WWT, it was a worthwhile market.

Landing a government contract takes months, or longer, from when you first approach an agency or department to the time a deal is closed. This long time period before any revenue is realized can be a killer for small start-up companies because they don't have the cash flow, let alone the patience and staying power. In our case, in addition to the usual overhead such as rent and utilities, we had to spend money on technology; plus, we had a payroll to meet. Basically, we had a lot of bills that were due without a steady flow of revenues coming in. All the while, we were bidding against other competitors with no assurance we'd even get the contract. While it was an arduous process that discourages most people, we relentlessly pursued it, and I had complete faith we'd prevail.

My advice to an owner of a start-up company is you must commit yourself and your resources to your long-term goal and concurrently avoid temptations of short-term profits that could sidetrack you. In my case, this meant passing up some smaller contracts that would have generated immediate revenues but would have also sapped our energy and focus. We were committed to give up short-term gains to achieve our long-term gains. Needless to say, when you operate a neophyte company that's strapped for cash, it takes discipline. We refused to let short-term profits throw us off track.

LIVING YOUR LEGACY

The same could be said about leaving a spiritual legacy. As followers of Jesus, we choose to follow His example of suffering and sacrifice for a higher purpose. We live out our legacy every day. We want others to know His love and have a personal relationship with Him as we do. Even in the most difficult circumstances, we must not lose sight of the impact our thoughts, words, and deeds have on everyone around us.

At a time when he faced many obstacles, Martin Luther King Jr. always reminded his followers to think about the future. "I just want to do God's will," Dr. King said. "And He's allowed me to go to the mountain. And I've looked over, and I've seen the Promised Land! I may not get there with you, but I want you to know tonight that we as a people will get to the Promised Land." Dr. King imagined the eternal legacy he wanted to create and emulated the example set by Christ.

Jesus lived a perfect life and He committed no sin, yet He went to His crucifixion for our future. Referencing the prophecy of Isaiah, Peter emphasizes the way Jesus fulfilled it as He forever changed history: " 'He himself bore our sins' in his body on the cross, so that we might die to sins and live for righteousness; 'by his wounds you have been healed' " (1 Pet. 2:24). Throughout His mission to serve humankind, Jesus always thought long-term, knowing His deeds would determine how we lived generations and millennia to come. God's Word makes many references to the eternal legacy of Jesus Christ.

From the beginning in Genesis, we see how God has always had a plan for His creation. Our Maker did not create the universe and have humankind inhabit the Earth for a brief period of time. Our Creator was thinking long-term, even after Adam and Eve rebelled and went their own way and had to leave the Garden of Eden. Omniscient and timeless, God, of course, knew the choices His first two creations would make and had a long-term plan for redeeming humankind. Our Father never stopped loving them—or us—just because they turned away from Him. Sending His Son, Jesus, was the ultimate redemption plan on our behalf!

Jesus instructs us to follow what He taught us so that His works will forever be His legacy. Emulating Jesus is an ongoing lifetime endeavor because He was the only perfect person. While we can never achieve perfection, we are to give God our best efforts and resources. Just before Jesus ascended to heaven, He stood on the Mount of Olives and said, "But you will receive power when the Holy Spirit comes on you; and you will be my witnesses in Jerusalem, and in all Judea and Samaria, and to the ends of the earth" (Acts 1:8). We have a call to carry on with His legacy so that His Word lives everywhere and forever.

Jesus loved us so much that He gave His life for us, and He told us to resume the legacy of His love, His forgiveness, and His grace. His Word endures forever—everywhere—in the home, the community, and the workplace. My mission is to live my life according to the Word, 24/7. Living—and leading—by the Good Book is not reserved for church on Sundays. We're called to obey God and to follow Jesus' example in all facets of our lives, all the time.

While in prison, Paul wrote, "And the things you have heard me say in the presence of many witnesses entrust to reliable people who will also be qualified to teach others" (2 Tim. 2:2). Paul understood his mission was to ensure Jesus' legacy lives forever. For this to happen, he told his protégé, Timothy, to follow his footsteps by seeking dependable people—leaders who can develop other leaders.

Starting two thousand years ago with a small group of disciples, Jesus influenced them and that has led to there being more than two *billion* Christians in today's world. We perpetuate His legacy by living according to His teachings, and in turn, it becomes our legacy.

EMPOWERED BY EXAMPLE

My parents blessed me in so many ways, setting an example for what it means to invest in the lives of others for eternity. They gave me the Word of God as my life's instruction manual, which remains my ultimate source to this day. Thelma and I have tried to pass down the same kind of legacy to our own children. Once we decided to begin our family, my wife made the sacrifice of giving up her nursing career to stay at home to raise our son and daughter. Even when WWT was struggling, Thelma and I were committed to investing in our children before anything else. Even during those tough times, we never stopped tithing. I wanted our kids to see the same example in us that I saw with my parents.

My wife and I also sacrificed to send our children to the best schools in St. Louis, even when we were struggling to get ahead. Education is such a huge investment in an eternal legacy. We always tried to help our kids see the big picture and to realize the relationship between their actions, the consequences, and their future.

Whenever David II or Kimberly didn't perform well in school, I would remind them that they should never allow a low score, mediocre assignment, or failed test determine who they were going to be in life. I stressed that it's a big world out there and that one bad grade or poor performance was only a tiny part of who they were becoming. Thelma and I tried to help them see how much we believed in them.

An entrepreneur at heart like his father, my son is involved in a number of acclaimed media and entertainment projects. My daughter has a successful career as a movie producer, including the Academy Award–winning film *Manchester by the Sea*. Thelma and I couldn't be prouder of them!

Throughout their lives, we wanted them to know we loved them unconditionally, not because of the grades they made or how well they conformed to any of our expectations. I wanted them to know that they're still growing, changing, and becoming more and more of who God made them to be. That's what I believe for all of us! Our growth never ends until the day we leave this earth.

We also made sure our kids realized the importance of perseverance and tenacity. When Kimberly was in middle school, around seventh and eighth grade, she played basketball, so I volunteered to assist the coach. Knowing that I played college basketball, the coach—and Kimberly—welcomed my assistance. The team had been suffering a losing record, and I was determined to try to turn that around. Not because winning was so important, but simply because I knew they could do better. So, I focused on fundamentals, like being a good free throw shooter, doing layups—the basics. I can remember staying after practice to work with Kimberly on her free throws until she felt confident about her ability. I also tried to connect the skills we were honing with life skills by talking about how I used them at WWT. Throughout life, you always have to focus on the fundamentals of character: discipline, honesty, compassion, integrity, and service, just to name a few.

SERVE TO SUCCEED

Following my eternal investment in my family, my career has been the greatest catalyst to facilitate my mission to serve the Lord. Our success at WWT has enabled us to provide wonderful opportunities for the thousands of people who work there and, in turn, for them to be able to provide for their families. The company has also tried to be a strong model for others to witness how treating people with love and respect is a viable way to succeed in business. I want everyone there to see that, contrary to what some people think, you don't have to step over people on your ascent up the corporate ladder.

We are here to serve each other, and if I serve my people, and this serving philosophy permeates the organization, and they serve each other and our customers, we will be successful. This way of doing business is deeply ingrained in the company's culture, and I pray it will endure long after I'm no longer with the company. I know that virtually everything in a company is subject to change—except its core values. Company names change, people replace other people, locations change, buildings are torn down and new ones are put up, products and services change—the only anchor that must remain constant is a company's core values.

In addition to the lasting legacy of WWT, I pray that my legacy will continue to echo through eternity by how Thelma and I are blessed to give to others. We truly love to give more than to receive. God has blessed us with a thriving company, and its success provides us with the privilege to give to a multitude of diverse charities in St. Louis, across the nation, and around the globe.

As with all Christ followers, my calling in life is to emulate Jesus, and I am always thinking about what God has put in my heart to do. I often meditate on a passage of Scripture that has deeply influenced the way I think about my legacy: "Now to him who is able to do immeasurably more than all we ask or imagine, according to his power that is at work within us, to him be glory in the church and in Christ Jesus throughout all generations, for ever and ever! Amen" (Eph. 3:20–21).

These verses help me think differently and to make decisions differently. I'm reminded that the power at work in me is beyond the limitations others want to impose on me or that I may impose on myself. I'm reminded that everything I do will have an eternal impact. This is the legacy that I constantly consider, the one I imagine with each decision on a daily basis, the one I want to pass on to others for generations to come.

YOUR LEADERSHIP FLYWHEEL:
Learn, Live, Lead, Legacy

1. At the end of your life, what do you want your legacy to be? How do you want others to know you made a difference in their lives? How will they know God by what they witnessed in your life?

2. What fundamentals do you need to focus on and practice more in order to leave the kind of eternal legacy you know God has called you to create? How can you practice one of these fundamentals today?

3. What favorite Bible verse or passage gives you strength and power as you look at the long-term, big picture of your life? Read through it again today and make it your prayer for the coming week.

> *Dear God, I want my life to make a difference for eternity. I want to use my gifts, talents, abilities, and resources as Your good steward, following the example of Jesus who gave everything so that I can experience the fullness of Your love and grace. Help me to see the connection, Lord, between the decisions I make each day and the ultimate legacy I want to leave. When my life here on Earth is completed, I want to hear You say, "Well done, my good and faithful servant!" In Jesus' name, amen.*

SECTION 4
Invest

CHAPTER 10

INVEST IN YOUR VISION

"For I know the plans I have for you," declares the LORD, *"plans to prosper you and not to harm you, plans to give you hope and a future."*

Jeremiah 29:11

As WWT began to develop, I truly believed that it was going to be something extraordinary beyond anything I could think, dream, or pray for (see Eph. 3:20). But I also knew I would have to invest in my vision and continue to work hard while relying on God if this new venture was to get off the ground. The primary way I continued to invest in this God-given vision was simply by growing in my faith and learning to completely depend on the Lord.

At the risk of repeating myself from an earlier chapter, I believe that it is critical for Christ-centered entrepreneurial leaders to hear this message...Throughout all the obstacles we faced at WWT, I never once stopped believing that God would guide me to overcome any and all challenges I faced. With strong faith combined with hard work and tenacity, I refused to let cynics discourage me. Even today, knowing I can trust Him regardless of my circumstances still furnishes me with a contagious attitude of expectancy.

However, leaders must be self-starters. We must first demonstrate our ability to lead ourselves before we should attempt to influence and lead others. Being on my own early on meant that no supervisor would ever be looking over my shoulder to approve or disapprove a decision I made. The umbilical cord was cut, and I was on my own to either sink or swim. Until I stepped out on my own, I had been the beneficiary of other leaders and organizations for my entire life. I worked my way up the corporate ladder, and I took as many opportunities as my employer gave me. I was grateful, but I felt that it was time to *give* those same kinds of opportunities to others. In John 3:16, Jesus said, "God so loved the world that He *gave...*" (emphasis mine)! And I was determined to build a company that would give back to the community. I realized a vacuum existed in the young technology sector, and it was a void that I knew I must fill. This was my calling.

This calling was the impetus to build a company on the premise that it would give to others. I wanted to provide my employees and team members with unique opportunities to be all that God made them to be. And I knew that when they succeeded, our company would thrive and give back even more to the community. Others sometimes tell me how noble and altruistic my motivation sounds. Skeptics occasionally criticize my attitude as naïve, old-fashioned, or idealistic. But all I can tell them is that it is Christ in me at work.

My security is in God and Him alone. He made me and loves me and has saved me from my selfish, sinful natural tendencies. I'm blessed to pass on His blessings to others. It's that simple. If that makes me old-fashioned or out of touch, then so be it. I just wanted to be obedient to God and to treat others the way I wanted them to treat me. I hoped they could experience God in real ways that demonstrate how much He loves and cares about them. I wanted to build a company from the ground up unlike any other.

GROWTH REQUIRES CHANGE

Brandon also wanted to build something unique when he started that first Bible study that would lead to Biblical Business Training. He walked away from a successful career that was going great because he had a vision bigger than his own personal gain. Simply put, he wanted to help others. His mission was to start a small group and see it spread out. He was called by the Lord to help people grow in their relationship with Christ and to expand His kingdom through Biblical leadership in the workplace.

As a result, BBT's vision is to see people grow in their relationship with Christ and expand God's kingdom through their leadership. Consequently, our ministry model starts by putting them in autonomous small groups. They get to know one another and become comfortable discussing God's Word in a natural, conversational way. There's no rigid model for how a group leader has to act other than in a way that honors God and is consistent with His Word. People can be who they are and lead in their own unique way.

Keep in mind that BBT is not about financial profit; in fact, it is a nonprofit. So, no one has ever been paid to lead a BBT group. In fact, it is quite the opposite. At our suggestion, they make donations to cover the cost of the resources that we provide to them so that they can focus on leading, not creating curriculum.

There are numerous event-based ministries with an array of platforms to promote leadership. People can always attend a prayer lunch, Bible study, or church small group. Seminars are readily available. They can enroll in Sunday school classes. Churches often have leadership events and encourage members to actively participate. In fact, if you ever want to see an entire congregation duck under their seats to avoid eye contact, just have someone up front announce, "Who will volunteer to lead this new group or ministry?" You would think everyone had lost a contact or dropped an earring by the number of heads bowed so low!

I knew from the start that getting people to join a small leadership group would not be easy. Our calling at BBT is focused on the development of leaders via small groups. It is much different than inviting people to attend a seminar to hear a gifted speaker who motivates his or her audience at that moment. While I have enjoyed listening to many motivational speakers who challenged or inspired me, when I walked out the door, it was difficult to follow through. It was easy to continue living, working, and leading as I had been before I heard the speaker.

Real change requires more from us.

Real growth relies on change.

DO THE RIGHT THING

BBT has a different model that we refer to as a "leadership laboratory." In this environment, participants are face-to-face with others, all of whom have received the Bible study lesson in advance. The meeting opens in prayer, so participants share their requests and concerns as everyone listens to what's on each other's hearts. Qualifying and revealing questions are asked, and over time members grow into their natural leadership sweet spot.

You don't have to leave corporate America to start a company like I did or to launch a ministry or nonprofit like Brandon. You don't need to be at the top of the corporate hierarchy or be the founder who initiates each and every aspect of growth. It's not necessary to own your own business or be a CEO to be a leader. You can have a leadership role in your current position. The Bible tells us, "When the righteous thrive, the people rejoice; when the wicked rule, the people groan" (Prov. 29:2). We want to cultivate righteous leadership.

The Good Book tells us that no matter where you work or what your job description may be, when you see immoral or unethical conduct, you can take a leadership role and begin doing

something about it. You must not look the other way and con-
done it. As the Bible says, by disregarding bad behavior, people
will groan. Unethical acts in the workplace run the gamut. It
could be small stuff such as the office staffers gossiping around
the watercooler or certain workers habitually coming in a few
minutes late and leaving work a few minutes early. It might be
the undermining of a coworker to win a promotion, the padding
of an expense account, or stretching the truth to a customer.
Sometimes it can be difficult to determine the boundaries in so-
called gray areas. For example, I know a company that won a
contract by promising products that had not yet been developed.
Its management had confidence that its engineering team would
come through, and if so, all would be well. If the products were
not developed on time, was the company deceitful to customers?
Or was it simply taking a necessary risk?

Then there are the bigger bad deeds such as embezzlement
and "cooking the books." Sometimes an entrepreneur who is
desperate for cash might cover up a failure by exaggerating or
misrepresenting the facts to a bank or investor. There are times
when an employee must speak out and reveal these transgres-
sions. If you do, however, you might jeopardize your career—
especially when you expose the misconduct of your boss or a
senior executive. Do you blow the whistle and hope for the best?
Or sit tight and hope the problem goes away or gets reported by
someone else?

In situations such as these, doing the right thing may carry serious consequences. I can't tell you what to do other than know
and obey God's Word and trust His Spirit to guide you. We're
told, "Trust in the LORD with all your heart, and do not lean
on your own understanding. In all your ways acknowledge him,
and he will make straight your paths" (Prov. 3:5–6 ESV). This
truth and many other lessons in the Bible instruct and encourage us to recognize that situations arise when we will be faced
with difficult choices, and we are capable of knowing right from
wrong. These are the times when we must always do what we

know is right. As Martin Luther King Jr. said, "The time is always right to do what is right."

EMBRACE CHANGE

One of the most important ways to invest in your future success is by embracing change. Too often, I see companies and organizations reach a goal and then plateau until they stagnate. They're so fearful of losing business that they resist addressing changes in the marketplace, in technology, and in their customers' needs until it's too late.

Change is a natural occurrence, and rather than resist it, we should embrace it. In the competitive world of business, you must anticipate change because those who resist it are doomed to fall by the wayside. A good leader either goes forward or backward but can never remain stationary.

Many leaders fail to invest in their future growth and success because they fear making the wrong decision. They procrastinate because they believe it's safer to do nothing than to risk failure. While I'm a firm believer in due diligence and not making impulsive decisions, I'm also convinced that good leaders must be unwavering in the face of change. Lack of deliberate direction is worse than choosing a path and then hitting a dead end, because at least you learn something about where that direction leads. When you fail to choose, you're bound to lose!

Decisiveness is a virtue, and good businesspeople understand that procrastination is also a decision—it is a decision to do nothing, which can be a poor decision. Other times people refuse to make a decision because they don't have enough facts to make a reasonable decision. Being well-informed is part of the decision-making process, and strong leaders collect the information they need to move forward and always do their due diligence. But they also know enough to listen to their instincts, to notice signs of change in the market, and to risk rather than miss a big opportunity. Conversely, weak leaders might collect too many facts and numbers that clutter their mind with trivial information. They suffer "paralysis by analysis" as they over-think situations and lose sight of the big picture.

As I considered what it would take to launch WWT in 1990, I understood the challenges that faced a start-up entrepreneur in the ever-changing high-tech industry. While I considered my-self up for the task, there was no way at that time I could have fully anticipated the enormous role technology and the Internet would play in our lives. Nobody could have forecasted how it would touch the lives of billions of people around the world and forever change most ways of doing business. However, those who were able to embrace this change and develop new business strategies as a result would help shape the future.

You'll recall that in 1990 the Internet was still in its infancy and relatively few people even knew what it was. Well aware that the high-tech industry was highly volatile, I plunged into the field eyes wide open. Nonetheless, there was no way I could have envisioned that once the Internet took off, it would grow so rapidly. In 1994, only about three million people in the en-tire world were online. It was not until 1995 that millions more jumped on the Internet, in large part thanks to Amazon and eBay. Arguably the online retail market maker, Amazon led the way for online shopping while eBay created a platform that eventually introduced its auction mechanism into mainstream retailing.

By 1996, the year Hotmail started, we could now communicate through email with anyone anywhere in the world at any time. Microsoft then acquired Hotmail in 1997, the same year that on-line services were made available around the world and global Internet usage doubled, with 1.7 percent of the world population now online. The term *weblog* was coined, which later became simply *blog*. Flash forward two decades later and the number of Internet users totals more than three *billion* worldwide.

The magnitude of the Internet's rapid growth might best be realized when compared to changes in yesteryear's technology. It took thirty-eight years after radio came out until there were fifty million listeners. It took television thirteen years to hit the fifty million mark. The number of Internet users to total fifty million took only four years. I quickly realized that technological changes occur exponentially, and those who fail to keep current are certain to lose ground to their competition.

KNOWLEDGE IS POWER

What continues happening with the Internet and online technology dwarfs the Industrial Revolution. What an exciting time to be alive! When we started WWT, it would have been hard to imagine the efficiency with which we now are able to move information—anytime, anywhere, and to anyone in the world. The vast opportunities that have opened are mind-boggling. Knowledge is power because knowledge initiates change.

The Bible tells us, "My people are destroyed from lack of knowledge" (Hosea 4:6). Without knowledge, a company, an organization, or an individual is destined to go the way of the dinosaur. In order to compete in today's business environment, a company must be technology driven in order to realize certain efficiencies. This demands a significant commitment to investing in equipment, hiring highly skilled people, as well as spending money training people to keep ahead of the competition.

The real business that we are in at WWT is changing the status quo. Our job is to improve the lives of families, children, and the community to make it a better place than it was before we came along to help them. We want to serve our customers by putting them in a better situation because we added strategic value to their businesses. We have created Advanced Technology Centers (ATCs) in St. Louis and in Washington DC, which allow us to replicate a client's technological environment, thereby enabling its people to make better decisions about the blend of technologies it utilizes. WWT is in the solutions business. We've invested hundreds of millions to ensure our customers make well-informed decisions. We want our customers to feel comfortable that their technology infrastructure will be secure.

Some companies and cultures, however, are simply not receptive to change. It's just not in their DNA. When we meet with potential clients, and we sense that they're not receptive to fresh, new ideas, we realize that they would be hard people for us to work with. And although we're certainly not in the habit of turning down customers, we won't do business with them. We want to work with companies that are like us—ones willing to work hard in order to be competitive as they serve their customers. They're willing to make scary decisions about the future and won't shy away from making changes.

This compatibility is why we select our clientele very carefully. We have a special relationship with our customers, and in order for WWT to effectively serve them, they have to become a partner in collaboration with us. Only then do we bring additional value to the table.

FAITHFUL AND FLEXIBLE

While adapting to change is essential, the changes themselves are not always positive. The business community has become conditioned to believe change is absolutely essential and positive to the point that some business leaders are too quick to make unnecessary changes. They're so married to change that they don't always allow enough development and incubation time for new products, systems, and procedures to work. While striving for excellence is a positive trait, changing for the sake of changing does not always represent an improvement over the old way.

At the risk of being tagged as a person who resists change, a good leader must be convinced that the change is true progress, and if it cannot be quantified, he rejects it.

Some aspects of the company should never be subject to change. When it comes to matters like a company's mission, values, and core beliefs, we should stick to our principles. Similarly, we see how Jesus makes it clear that His intention was not to change what had been written in the Old Testament: "Do not think that I have come to abolish the Law or the Prophets; I have not come to abolish them but to fulfill them. For truly I tell you, until heaven and earth disappear, not the smallest letter, not the least stroke of a pen, will by any means disappear from the Law until everything has been accomplished" (Matt. 5:17–18).

Often a leader is given suggestions that do not completely harmonize with the company's mission and vision, and in those situations, he should not submit to change. An organization's bedrock beliefs never change. The Good Book reminds us, "Do not conform to the pattern of this world, but be transformed by the renewing of your mind. Then you will be able to test and approve what God's will is—his good, pleasing and perfect will" (Rom. 12:2). This admonition from Paul is as relevant today as it was two thousand years ago when he wrote it. We must keep our firm foundation in Christ while adapting to the winds of change that blow around us. We must be both faithful to what is eternal and flexible in what is temporary.

When you lead by following God's ways, then your faith, conviction, tenacity, and courage inspire those around you to invest in your vision with you. People tend to want to emulate the leadership style they experience from above. If they see their leader embrace change as he or she trusts God for the outcome, then they, too, become inspired to make bold, faith-based decisions. Rather than shy away from change, they embrace it. Invest in your vision, and others will, too!

YOUR LEADERSHIP FLYWHEEL:
Learn, Live, Lead, Legacy

1. How have you invested in your vision in the past year? The past month? Week? What investment could you make today to help your team, department, and company grow?

2. How would you describe your general attitude toward change? Are you an early adapter and enjoy changing as soon as possible? Or do you tend to procrastinate and delay deciding how to move forward in the face of change? Or something in between?

3. What have you refused to alter or compromise in the face of changes around you? How do you remain anchored by your faith in God when change overwhelms you?

Dear Lord, thank You for providing me with opportunities to demonstrate and strengthen my servant leadership. Please continue to give me strength, courage, and tenacity when I'm faced with new changes and shifting norms. Remind me that You are always the same—yesterday, today, and tomorrow. You are my rock and my foundation, my constant in a world where change is inevitable. Grant me wisdom to lead in Your direction and discernment about when to risk. When I rely on You, I have nothing to fear. In Jesus' name, amen.

CHAPTER 11

INVEST IN YOUR PEOPLE

A generous person will prosper; whoever refreshes others will be refreshed.

Proverbs 11:25

If you want to lead and serve like Jesus, then you must consistently invest in the people around you. Christ always addressed people's immediate needs as a means of touching their underlying spiritual need for God's grace. He provided wine at a wedding party, healed the lame, restored sight to the blind, fed the multitudes, cast out demons, and comforted those in turmoil. He also touched on their hearts' deepest needs for healing, forgiveness, purpose, hope, and renewal.

As servant-leaders today, we have access to this same kind of divine power to help, heal, and offer hope to all those we serve. As entrepreneurs and leaders in the workplace, we invest in our team members by showing them love and respect in how we relate, making it clear that relationships ultimately matter more than productivity and profit margins. While our shared goal is to fulfill our mission by working hard as a team, we must also honor God in the process.

DARE TO DELEGATE

While good leaders invest in their people in a variety of ways, none is more important than delegation. It sounds obvious, but it continues to be a struggle for so many leaders I encounter. In order to invest in people, a good leader must be willing to delegate. It's not only a source of frustration when a leader micromanages others, but it also deprives them—and the company—of the resources waiting to be unlocked within them. Trust and responsibility are essential if you want to bring out the best in others and see them grow in their own leadership capacities.

One of my favorite examples of delegating appears in the story of Moses, charged by God with leading the people of Israel out of Egypt and into the Promised Land. Only, instead of a linear, straightforward journey, they wandered in the wilderness for forty years. During this circuitous journey, Moses was holding court for his people from morning to evening when his father-in-law, Jethro, advised him: "You and these people who come to you will only wear yourselves out. The work is too heavy for you; you cannot handle it alone" (Exod. 18:18). Jethro instructed Moses to teach his decrees and instructions to capable, trustworthy men who could become officials and judges, freeing up Moses' time and energy. Explaining how this system would operate, Jethro said, "Have them serve as judges for the people at all times, but have them bring every difficult case to you; the simple cases they can decide themselves. That will make your load lighter, because they will share it with you. If you do this and God so commands, you will be able to stand the strain, and all these people will go home satisfied" (vv. 22–23).

This situation reminds us of a vitally important truth: If we attempt to do everything by ourselves without delegating to others, we limit our productivity. This may seem obvious, and yet so many leaders fail to practice this Biblical principle. Instead, they hold tight to every aspect of their organization rather than empowering others to invest their own talents and abilities.

Everyone must do his or her share in order to maximize productivity.

A successful enterprise cannot be a one-man band—that's when one person bangs away and makes a lot of noise, but when he stops playing, then the band stops playing. Successful organizations operate like an orchestra, synchronized in rhythm to produce harmonious results. Good leaders, like the conductor of an orchestra, get a lot more done because they coordinate the synchronized efforts of others. They learn how to invest in their people with exponential results. And the more a business grows, the more its leader must empower people. Otherwise, to paraphrase the wise Jethro, the workload becomes overwhelming and too much for an individual to manage.

NO SELF-SERVICE

As WWT began to grow, it quickly became apparent that I could not touch every area of the company. It's simply not possible for me to be involved in all the things that happen here. It's not humanly possible because there are simply not enough hours in the day. Such an endeavor would not only exhaust and impede my ability to lead, but it would also cripple the growth of the company.

When we started out, I could tell you the names of every employee and members of their immediate family. Today, with thousands of employees, such a feat would be a full-time job in itself! We're too big, and it would not be the best use of my time or theirs. Instead, I had to learn to delegate by design. So many things must be done by individuals with expertise in specific areas of our business, so I let them make decisions that I'm not equipped to make. And I work hard at making sure I don't interfere with their decision making. WWT has some of the smartest technology people on this planet who are making major decisions, and I let them know how much I trust their judgment.

I believe this builds their confidence and makes them better at their work.

For example, a few years ago, WWT upgraded its enterprise resource planning (ERP) system, a monumental task that cost tens of millions of dollars and hundreds of thousands of hours. This new system integrates the company's customer management systems, accounting and receivable systems, forecasting and planning, human resources, and other vital operations. Basically, the new system provides procedures that permit all areas of the business to interconnect with each other.

It took more than a year for our team consisting of hundreds of people across the spectrum of our company to implement this enormous change. It was a massive undertaking but something that had to be done because as our company grew bigger, the old system no longer had the capacity to support our needs. Had we not changed, our business would have been at risk.

A prerequisite for this new system's implementation involved asking our people throughout the company to think differently about how we operated and worked together. Naturally we made a few mistakes along the way, but all in all, the implementation was seamless. While I'm the founder and majority owner of WWT, there's absolutely no way this transition could have ever happened without the leadership of others. It was a big team effort, and many major decisions had to be made on a daily basis.

I couldn't do it alone.

And neither can you!

CHOSEN TO SERVE

It's natural for an entrepreneur who puts all of their money into a start-up company to make all the decisions. And why not? It's their business and their money that are on the line. An entrepreneur who fails to empower people, however, will not be able to make the transition from a small start-up company to a large enterprise. They must realize that it takes a different set of skills to operate a big company than it does to manage a small one.

If a leader wants to do business on a large scale, they have to learn to delegate to others and trust they will make the right decisions. They have to be comfortable knowing that eventually others' authority in their areas of expertise will equal or surpass their own. In other words, good leaders let go!

In fact, I have a special word for those with the attitude that they can do everything by themselves. I call it "ego," meaning to "edge God out." We're told in Proverbs 16:18, "Pride goes before destruction, a haughty spirit before a fall." At some point, you have to let go and trust your people. If you're not willing to sow seeds of truth and water them with delegation, then you limit the growth of your company. Only when a business owner loosens their tight grip is it possible for the small mustard seed to grow and branch out.

This servant style of leadership is the essence of what we see in the life of Jesus. His ability to empower others to work with Him exemplifies His extraordinary leadership skills. Jesus told His disciples, "Very truly I tell you, whoever believes in me will do the works I have been doing, and they will do even greater things than these, because I am going to the Father" (John 14:12). Curiously enough, Jesus selected twelve key followers who all shared a common denominator: None of them had any religious training or stature. None were involved in leadership roles at the temple. None had a rabbinic background. They were average, working-class people. But Jesus recognized their willingness to follow Him and to serve others as they grew in their faith.

It is said that these twelve disciples were a motley crew—a group of seemingly unlikely, disparate individuals assembled by Jesus to carry out the eternally significant work of furthering God's kingdom. Most of His disciples came from communities around the Sea of Galilee, which explains why more than half their number were fishermen. The rest were not held in any higher esteem. Matthew, a Jew, was employed by the Roman government to collect taxes, a lowly, scorned-upon profession. Simon was a zealot, committed to the vehement belief that the Jews should rebel against the Romans and overthrow the Roman Empire's occupation of Israel. Philip, James, and Judas are believed to have been tradesmen, but their specific trades are unknown. Once recruited by Jesus, however, it no longer mattered what their previous professions were. The disciples each gave up everything to follow the Master. With the exception of Judas Iscariot, who would betray Jesus, these were the people the Messiah, the Son of God, hand selected to invest with His power. Jesus told them, "You did not choose me, but I chose you and appointed you to go and bear fruit—fruit that will last" (John 15:16).

This is the team charged with sharing the good news of the gospel, the greatest story ever told!

WISE INVESTMENTS

As His disciples followed His orders, Jesus gave them more responsibilities. We're told in Matthew 10 how Christ delegated them to cast out unclean spirits and cure the sick. He told them not to solicit Gentiles or enter any town of the Samaritans, but instead to go to the lost sheep in the house of Israel. Jesus instructed them to proclaim the good news that God's only Son, the Promised One, had arrived to save people from their sins once and for all. The disciples' mission required them to serve in the power entrusted to them by the Living God—to cure the sick, raise the dead, cleanse the lepers, and cast out demons.

Jesus told them, "Whoever can be trusted with very little can also be trusted with much" (Luke 16:10). This principle of successful delegation has withstood the test of time. This same truth must be applied by effective leaders today. God gives wonderful gifts and talents to all of us, and a good leader is able to recognize individuals with special skills and accordingly dele-gate responsibilities. A God-dependent leader empowers trusted people and believes in them. For the most part, when you trust people, they will do their best not to disappoint you, and they will endeavor to be worthy of your trust. You may make some mistakes or errors in judgment, but that's where opportunities to practice forgiveness and grace emerge. No one is perfect.

As leaders committed to following Jesus Christ, we have the privilege of investing in the people we have been chosen to serve through our leadership. We must never lose sight of this pre-cious responsibility and the power we have to influence others for God's kingdom. We will always get back more than we give when we invest in the lives of others. It's just the way God op-erates. Investing in the lives of our people is never a burden and always a blessing!

YOUR LEADERSHIP FLYWHEEL:
Learn, Live, Lead, Legacy

1. Who has invested time, energy, and resources in you? How has their investment paid off in your present leadership role?

2. How are you currently investing in the people God has entrusted to your care? What are some other ways you can honor them and show them you value their contribution?

3. On a scale of one to ten, with one being rarely and ten being almost always, how frequently do you delegate to others? What prevents you from delegating more responsibility to others more often? How can you overcome these obstacles and personal barriers?

Dear God, I am so blessed to serve and lead the wonderful people You have placed in my care. I give You thanks for each individual and their dedication to our shared goals and ultimate mission. Help me know how best to serve people and to invest in their leadership abilities by delegating to them. Protect us from any dissension or division that the enemy might try to sow among us. Give us Your power and wisdom to work harmoniously as a team so that others might know You, Lord, by the way we love each other, our customers, and those in our communities. In the name of Jesus, amen.

CHAPTER 12

INVEST IN GOD'S KINGDOM

Do not store up for yourselves treasures on earth, where moths and vermin destroy, and where thieves break in and steal. But store up for yourselves treasures in heaven, where moths and vermin do not destroy, and where thieves do not break in and steal. For where your treasure is, there your heart will be also.

Matthew 6:19–21

We must recognize our time in this life is limited. When I look at my hourglass, I readily detect that the sand at the bottom exceeds what remains at the top. Because there is so much more to do, I feel a sense of urgency. The Bible assures us, "Jesus Christ is the same yesterday and today and forever" (Heb. 13:8). Only He can continue to make a difference in our lives. Just the same, I aspire to emulate His teachings as best as I can, and as long as I have the energy, I will always aspire to invest in His kingdom by developing and serving people.

INTEGRATED MANAGEMENT AND LEADERSHIP

I am often asked, "How did WWT maintain its core values and preserve its culture over the course of three decades of rapid growth?" The answer is this: by investing in what matters most—our people.

From the beginning of WWT in 1990 to the present day, attracting the best candidates and then investing in their development has been a top priority for our leadership team. Our umbrella term for this process is *integrated management and leadership*. It is our investment in this "secret sauce" that ensures long-term organizational health and success.

World-class leadership is the key driver to developing WWT's greatest innovations: our people and culture. We believe the tone of the culture is set at the top of an organization by the executive leadership, and it needs to be reinforced at every level. Our focus is to ensure there are great managers at every level of our organization who will engage and inspire their employees, who in turn will engage and invest in our customers, partners, and community.

Not investing in leadership and management training is the quickest way to erode our culture, core values, and organizational health. We expect every employee to have a great manager, and we devote considerable financial and organizational resources to ensure that is the case. When you invest in people through developing them to their fullest potential, you are investing for eternity!

LOVING GOD = SERVING OTHERS

Jesus maximized His impact in such a short time. We're told, "Now Jesus himself was about thirty years old when he began his ministry" (Luke 3:23). Beginning at this young age, in just a matter of three years, He made a difference for humankind that is unparalleled. No mortal person can ever accomplish what He did. All we can do is strive to conduct our lives in a way that follows His example. Ever since I experienced God's calling to advance His kingdom through relationships in the workplace, I've focused on creating something that does more than provide jobs, sell services, and improve technology. As wonderful as those goals are, I know that none of them matter if people do not have a personal relationship with God through the sacrifice of His Son, Jesus Christ. We serve so that others might want to know God.

Jesus made His mission clear: "For the Son of Man came to seek and to save the lost" (Luke 19:10). And the motivation behind His mission was just as apparent: "For God so loved the world that he gave his one and only son, that whoever believes in him shall not perish but have eternal life" (John 3:16). Here we are told that His work is an eternal, lifesaving mission.

God calls each of us to do our part in fulfilling this same mission. Christ told His followers then as well as now, "Let your light shine before others, that they may see your good deeds and glorify your Father in heaven" (Matt. 5:16). This reference to good deeds is how each of us can make a positive difference in the lives of others. Jesus' good deeds in serving others were many, including healing the affirmed, the blind, and the suffering. He taught His disciples to serve others by how He served them. And as we explored in a previous chapter, perhaps the most striking example was how Jesus washed the feet of His disciples at the Last Supper (in John 13).

The washing of His disciples' feet is an example of leadership that we can easily emulate in today's workplace. There are so many ways we can convey humility, kindness, and goodwill to our coworkers and customers. A few examples off the top of my head include the following:

- volunteering to assist a team member who is swamped with a heavy workload
- mentoring a less experienced coworker
- visiting a colleague who has been hospitalized
- congratulating a colleague on his or her promotion
- encouraging and guiding a teammate whose performance is not up to par

If you love God, then you will love others by investing in them.

It's that simple!

BECAUSE YOU CARE

Everyone wants to feel that what he or she does makes a difference. How would you feel if your boss told you, "Anyone could do your job, so it doesn't matter if you or someone else does it"? So many companies communicate that their employees are expendable and interchangeable. But good leaders do just the opposite!

Top leaders in all fields know that when people feel they are making a difference by improving the lives of others, they become more productive. When our people are able to see how the excellence and high quality of their work translate into doing something that truly matters and has a global impact, it does wonders for their self-esteem. Combine this with the praise they receive, and they go home at night feeling good about themselves, knowing that they are making a difference.

When I started Transport Administrative Services (TAS) in 1987, the Union Pacific Railroad contracted us to audit $15 billion of rate information. We received the contract by finding a new way to audit rates that was better than the way the railroad companies had been doing it for 150 years. We were able to make a difference that was faster and cheaper! In this particular incident, we came up with a new process, but it isn't always necessary to conceive a new product or service in order to succeed. Most often, successful people prosper because they are willing to work harder and smarter than their competition. The difference they make is by going that extra mile. This is something that everyone can do. You don't have to reinvent the wheel! Because you care, others will be blessed and catch a glimpse of God's goodness.

All of us can make a difference, and the good news is we don't have to wait until we're head of the company or launching our own business to begin. We're all capable of doing good deeds—and throughout our lives we can do many of them. While these kind, thoughtful deeds, each seemingly insignificant, may not be known to the world, you will make a difference many, many times.

When an investment banker cooks the books on Wall Street, it makes the evening news. But when a middle manager on Main Street stays late at the office to help a coworker with a heavy workload, it doesn't get picked up by the media, and few people may ever even know it happened. Eventually, though, some people will notice. Not only has this made a positive difference to that struggling coworker, but leadership of this nature has a ripple effect. And this ripple of serving others will inspire others throughout the organization to do similar good things that will make many positive differences.

When you invest in what matters most, you reflect God's goodness to those around you! No one else has ever made as great a difference as did Jesus. His time on Earth changed the world forever. He lived a perfect life, and using Him as our role model, we can invest our time, energy, and resources into God's kingdom by serving others.

YOUR LEADERSHIP FLYWHEEL:
Learn, Live, Lead, Legacy

1. When was the last time you went the extra mile to serve one of your coworkers, supervisors, clients, or customers? What motivated you in that situation? What were the consequences of your willingness to serve above and beyond?

2. What are you creating, sharing, or contributing to that will endure after your career has ended? How can you pour more of yourself into serving, teaching, and mentoring others?

3. What's one act of service you can do this week to "wash the feet" of those you serve? How can you demonstrate your commitment to them with unexpected humility and kindness?

Dear God, thank You for the many ways You remind me of what matters most. Help me to recognize opportunities where I can go the extra mile and serve in ways above and beyond what others expect. Give me the strength, stamina, and energy to invest in others' lives in ways that will bless them and allow them to see Your love for them. Guide me this week to someone who I can serve as Jesus served His disciples by washing their feet. In His name I pray, amen.

SECTION 5
Risk

CHAPTER 13

RISK YOUR HEART

Be strong, and let your heart take courage, all you who wait for the LORD!

Psalm 31:24 ESV

The greatest risk in any endeavor is not the investment of money, time, or what you do but the investment of *who you are*. If you want to be a servant-leader like Jesus, then you must risk your heart. And the greatest challenges when risking your heart involve trust.

Many leaders consider themselves good at reading other people and discerning others' characters. While it's necessary to try to assess if, and how, a potential team member might fit in your organization, you can't always judge a book by its cover. When God sent His prophet Samuel to search for the next king of Israel, He told Samuel to look beyond surface appearances: "The LORD does not look at the things people look at. People look at the outward appearance, but the LORD looks at the heart" (1 Sam. 16:7). And as it turned out, God's choice to be the next king was a young shepherd boy, the youngest in Jesse's family and therefore a selection whom others would have overlooked because of their own assumptions based on appearances.

Instead of wondering whom you can trust by how they appear, you must realize trust begins within your own heart. We're all familiar with the Golden Rule: Treat everyone as you would want to be treated by others (Matt. 22:36–40). But I would encourage you to consider this: *Trust everyone as you would want to be trusted.* To be an effective leader, you must be trustworthy—or to break that word apart, *worthy of trust.* A person with love and faith in God and an unselfish love for others is someone who can be trusted, someone worthy of being trusted. While other qualities are necessary, a leader's trustworthiness is essential. No matter how otherwise capable and dynamic a person is, if there is an absence of trust, their leadership will collapse upon their own dishonesty and deception.

As we have seen, this foundational trust begins with a leader's trust in God. In order to serve with humility, wisdom, and power greater than anything you could do on your own, you must rely on God and serve Him and only Him as your King. This pillar of leadership explains why Jethro advised his son-in-law Moses to delegate—but only to those who met certain criteria: "Select capable men from all the people—men who fear God, trustworthy men who hate dishonest gain—and appoint them as officials over thousands, hundreds, fifties and tens" (Exod. 18:21). This timeless advice is as applicable today as it was centuries ago.

It is not enough to assume you will be trusted because you are a designated leader. Being "the boss" doesn't qualify you as a leader. Trust must be earned. Then, you must keep earning it. Remember, it takes a lifetime to earn a good reputation, yet you can lose it overnight. As we're told in God's Word, "A good name is more desirable than great riches; to be esteemed is better than silver or gold" (Prov. 22:1). Others will trust you if you consistently prove yourself to be a person who tells the truth and aligns their actions with what they say.

GOOD AS YOUR WORD

In Biblical days, few people could read and write; therefore, verbal agreements were common. The old expression "You're only as good as your word" was literally true. Throughout the ages, honorable men and women told the truth and stood by what they said. They didn't change their words, insert deliberate ambiguity, or spin their message to mean something different depending on their audience.

While verbal agreements are still binding in a court of law today, without a reliable witness, the intent of the two parties involved and what was agreed upon can be difficult to prove. Nonetheless, written or unwritten, a good leader always does what she says she will do. In time, she is recognized as a woman of her word, and others view her as an honest woman. One's reputation is earned by one's actions.

While it's important to have contracts, orders, invoices, receipts, and necessary documents in writing, they become meaningless if the promise behind them isn't firm. I've made many deals on a handshake and a promise and worked hard to always follow through and honor my promise. We should always treat those we serve with respect and be focused on doing what's in their best interest. If we do what's right for them, they will do the same for our customers, our vendors, our partners, and everyone with whom we interact.

You have to remember that you're the same person in a crowded room as you are in an empty alley. You have to behave the same way when others are watching you as you do when no one else is around. Trusting yourself is the key to integrity. Risking your heart to trust God is at the core of obeying His commands.

TRUST IS CONTAGIOUS

If team members only comply because they are being measured and held accountable, then they likely won't last long. You can force yourself to do what you think others expect for only so long, and then your true colors begin to show. At WWT, we have always tried to build the company with people who treat others with love and respect because it's who they are and what they truly believe, not just because it's our company culture. We all make mistakes and have lapses of judgment, but the basis of our character reveals itself. We're either living for ourselves or for God. And if we're living for God, then we're serving others with honesty, integrity, and trust.

Trust also tends to be contagious. People with a like mindset were attracted to our company and our commitment to serve. They trusted me and our other leaders. Over time, more and more people became aware of the uncommon way we operate and wanted to experience our culture for themselves. Those in our workforce remain our greatest ambassadors, heralding who we are and what we're about through their actions, attitudes, and accountability. The more someone trusts you, the more likely they are to risk trusting their own hearts as well. When you believe in something bigger than yourself, something that's not just about profit or material gain or personal advancement or achievement, then others notice. My hope has always been that they catch a glimpse of who God is through their interactions with us at WWT.

When there's no trust, it has a domino effect—on relationships, on performance, on productivity, on everything. People who joined our company or did business with us but proved untrustworthy haven't lasted long. They get called out and called up to a higher standard, and if they're not willing to change and grow by being honest and earning trust, then they leave. It's a matter of culture. Over time, those people playing games or serving their own personal agendas get weeded out by their own behavior. They either choose to leave or fail to meet the standards clearly explained in order for them to stay.

THE LAST WORD

A good leader earns the trust of others by making it known that he or she trusts them. Time and time again, I've been blessed to hire talented people who have skill sets that I don't possess. So, I trust them to make major decisions that I can't make. When you trust people with a responsibility to make high-risk decisions, they don't want to let you down. Trusting people begets trust.

Empowering people also earns their trust. Empowering them doesn't mean that you back away from being involved or making decisions related to their area of responsibility. On the contrary, because we trust each other, we can communicate openly and honestly. If we disagree about something, then we discuss our views and try to understand what we're missing and how we can reach better decisions together than on our own. When there's trust, no one feels defensive or takes coaching as a personal affront.

At the end of the day, though, when I disagree with someone and haven't been convinced to have confidence in their point of view, it is my responsibility to make the final decision about the direction we take. Leaders must be willing to own the ultimate authority and responsibility for major decisions that will impact the entire company. Jesus taught us, "All you need to say is simply 'Yes' or 'No'" (Matt. 5:37), and His instruction to be decisive should remind us to embrace making the tough calls.

With Christ as our example, we must always do what we believe is right in God's eyes. People won't always agree with your decisions, but if they trust you and know your heart, then they will continue to respect you and follow your leadership. If they see your faith in God informing all your decisions and actions, then they will remain loyal. As I once heard someone say, if you want to have the last word, then make sure it's "AMEN!"

SHOW AND TELL

Trust is the currency of leadership. When you tell others that they can count on you, then you must be able to bear the weight of your commitment. You must be able to back it up. And backing it up requires consistently doing what you say you will do over and over again, every time. Showing others that you can be trusted tells them more about the kind of leader you are than simply telling them to trust you.

Showing tells more than telling shows!

Jesus earned the trust of people by His miracles, especially His acts of healing. He didn't claim to be the Messiah because He just performed one miracle. Christ consistently performed miracles and spoke truth everywhere He went so others could see He was the Son of God all the time, everywhere—not just in the temple or in front of a crowd. Jesus delivered on His promises then just as He continues to do today.

In time, people began to trust Jesus. They believed Him because He fulfilled prophecies made by prophets of past generations, which we now find in the Old Testament. What Jesus did backed up who He said He was! Nevertheless, many people did not accept Him as the Messiah, because He did not have the credentials or prerequisites according to their expectations.

Even in His hometown of Nazareth, people refused to accept Jesus as God's Son:

He went to Nazareth, where he had been brought up, and on the Sabbath day he went into the synagogue, as was his custom. He stood up to read, and the scroll of the prophet Isaiah was handed to him. Unrolling it, he found the place where it is written:

"The Spirit of the Lord is on me,
because he has anointed me
to proclaim good news to the poor.

He has sent me to proclaim freedom for the prisoners
and recovery of sight for the blind,
to set the oppressed free,
to proclaim the year of the Lord's favor."

Then he rolled up the scroll, gave it back to the attendant and sat down. The eyes of everyone in the synagogue were fastened on him. He began by saying to them, "Today this scripture is fulfilled in your hearing." (Luke 4:16–21)

Although the congregants praised His locution, they did not accept His claim to be the Son of God. They likely murmured, "Isn't that Joseph's son? Isn't he that little boy we used to see helping out in the carpenter's shop?" (see Luke 4:22). In their minds, Jesus was only a hometown carpenter. They had envisioned that the Messiah would be a glorious king, a conquering warrior like King David. Jesus simply didn't fit the image they imagined. He didn't arrive in town on a chariot pulled by a large white stallion or dress in fine linens adorned with jewels. Although He did miraculous things, His wonders were not what the people expected Him to do.

Jesus was trustworthy and provided ongoing evidence.

But others' expectations got in their way and blinded them.

Sometimes even when you do the right thing, others refuse to trust.

TRUE CONFESSIONS

Battling others' expectations remains a frequent challenge in today's world of business—at times a leader's strong performance may not be accepted by others simply because it's not what they wanted. For example, a CEO might sacrifice short-term gains for long-term gains and, as a result, disappoint certain investors, often those wanting to sell their holdings in the near future and cash out. At the risk of their disapproval, a good leader does not abandon what he believes is the right thing to do. He does what is in the best interests of the company.

As inherent risk takers, leaders must also know how to keep their heart engaged when they make a mistake or fail to achieve the desired goal. Good leaders make their share of mistakes without avoiding the necessary risks involved, but they never deny owning responsibility for their failures. I never have a problem letting our people know when I make a mistake, because the sooner I admit that I was wrong, the more likely others will accept it. Fessing up to a mistake builds trust. Denying it hinders a leader's credibility and may erode others' trust.

You would be surprised how powerful it can be for a leader to offer a sincere, humble apology. It shows others your humanity and reminds them that we're all a work in progress. Saying "I'm sorry" or "I made the wrong decisions" acknowledges that you recognize the impact of your choices and how they affect others, both inside and outside your organization. Apologizing or admitting your mistakes shows that your strength relies on God, not what others think of you. You're strong enough not to deflect blame or make excuses.

Apologizing as the leader also sets an example for your team to follow when they make a mistake. You will be disappointed many times with your team members. Everyone has a bad day or goes through a rough patch from time to time. Poor decisions will be made. Your trust in your teammates will be tested. However, I encourage you to see the God-given potential in every person when they disappoint you. Make that your first reaction. Then wisely assess whether they can be restored to the same responsibilities. Are they repentant? Are they committed to not making the mistake again? If so, outline a path for them to rebuild the trust they lost. When you do this, you are truly risking your heart to help them.

Also, as a leader, it is natural for scar tissue to build up around your heart because of these disappointments. Each time someone betrays your trust, your heart can become a little more hardened. Over time, this can lead to trusting people less and less. I encourage you to not let bitterness take hold and begin to limit your leadership. Instead, use the wisdom you've gained to lead more effectively for the Lord. Continue to risk your heart and trust those entrusted to your care.

Good leaders say what they mean and mean what they say— and always do what they promise to do. In order to lead like Jesus, they know they must go "all in" and serve wholeheartedly. The best leaders rely on God and invest all they've got—their time, money, energy, and their heart—in order to fulfill His calling on their lives to serve others.

YOUR LEADERSHIP FLYWHEEL:
Learn, Live, Lead, Legacy

1. Do you tend to trust others easily or are you usually more cautious or even skeptical about the motives of other people? How has this way of relating influenced your style of leadership? How does your ability to trust others affect your willingness to serve them?

2. How much of your heart have you risked investing in your current role of servant leadership? At least half? More than half? A full 100 percent? What gets in the way of serving wholeheartedly? How can you overcome the obstacles blocking your ability to risk all of your heart?

3. How often do you admit your mistakes or take responsibility for an outcome that misses the mark? When was the last time you apologized to someone you serve for saying or doing something that was hurtful or misguided? How have others responded when you have apologized for an offense or taken responsibility for a failed endeavor?

Dear God, You are my shelter in life's storms! I praise You and give You thanks for Your faithfulness, Your goodness, and Your holiness. Help me to trust You with my whole heart so that I may lead, serve, and give myself to those You have entrusted to my care. May I always reflect Your truth in all that I say and do. May others always be able to rely on my word and know that a promise made is a promise kept. In the name of Jesus, amen.

CHAPTER 14

RISK YOUR BEST EFFORTS

Never be lacking in zeal, but keep your spiritual fervor, serving the Lord.

Romans 12:11

As a young boy, I loved the story about David and Goliath and always felt honored to be named after the shepherd who slayed the giant. Going to church with my parents, I often heard people say, "Little David, play on your harp!" While David's skill as a musician and poet intrigued me, it was his willingness to risk his best efforts and trust God that inspired me. The Bible reports that Goliath, the Philistine warrior taunting the Israelites, was more than nine feet six inches tall. Just the iron head of his spear weighed 15 pounds, and his coat of mail weighed about 125 pounds (1 Sam. 17:4–7).

There wasn't a single warrior from Israel willing to engage in a fight-to-the-death combat with Goliath. Only David, a shepherd boy, volunteered. Most experts estimate that David was in his early to mid teens. He didn't even have a sword and couldn't stand up under the weight of the armor loaned to him by Saul, the king of Israel. So, David wore no armor and chose a surprising weapon: his trusty slingshot, used to protect his flock of sheep against wolves. We all know the rest of the story told in 1 Samuel 17—about how David fearlessly slayed the giant warrior who had bullied men much older and stronger than the shepherd boy. What boldness David had!

RISK BEFORE YOU REAP

When facing a new venture, we must approach it with the same boldness exemplified by David's life. Boldness does not mean you aren't afraid or uncertain about the outcome. Risking boldly simply means you're willing to do your best and trust God with the outcome. Many times when I face a situation in which I'm forced to risk boldly, I return to one of my favorite verses: "Now if we are children, then we are heirs—heirs of God and co-heirs with Christ, if indeed we share in his sufferings in order that we may also share in his glory" (Rom. 8:17). This verse reinforces my belief that as God's heir and Jesus' coheir, whatever I have been called to do, I can achieve through God's power.

When you undertake a mission that requires you to sail in uncharted waters, you must think of yourself as God sees you, not as you see yourself. Shifting your perspective forces you to think differently and view the situation from a different vantage point. This allows you to have confidence in God's power to see you through. Such confidence enables you to come up with solutions and strategies you might never glimpse otherwise.

Among the many attributes taught in the Bible, boldness is high on the list. Being a business owner or CEO of a publicly traded company is not for the faint of heart. Nor is it for a multitude of individuals who hold senior and middle management positions, men and women who also make decisions for which they are held accountable. In today's highly competitive environment, leaders must make bold decisions that expose them to dire consequences and could result in significant financial risk, loss of market share, employee layoffs, and even company bankruptcies. Bad decisions and poorly executed plans can also cause demotions and firings. Risks and bold decisions are required at all levels of leadership, especially if you want to lead according to the Good Book.

When a business leader makes long-term plans, he or she must be bold because there are no guarantees of what the future holds. They must risk their best efforts without holding back or trying to protect themselves from the fallout if their efforts fail. Now, risking boldly does not mean we should avoid thinking about what lies ahead or anticipating long-term consequences. While there's no crystal ball, every leader must constantly look forward. Depending on the cost and the amount of risk, the degree of boldness varies. Be assured, however, that success depends on making difficult decisions. You do it knowing the liability of possible loss in order to make the best calculated risk possible.

Most entrepreneurs know it takes courage to put themselves on the line by launching a new venture. It takes faith to walk away from a job with a guaranteed paycheck and company benefits. Your new start-up could go belly-up! Not only could you lose your source of income, but you could also lose years' worth of accumulated savings that you invested in your business. But you must never let fear prevent you from risking your best efforts when God calls you to step out in faith. Good leaders know risk taking and faith walking go together if you're going to produce your best results. You have to risk in order to reap the reward!

TEAM EFFORT

Most successful leaders know they must rely on their team to share in the risk taking. In fact, risking by faith is always a team effort. God blessed me with an exceptional wife who not only trusted Him completely but also had so much faith in me. It took incredible boldness on her part to support the risk I was taking to start WWT. But we both wanted to make a difference in other people's lives, and as partners, we were determined to succeed. In addition to not wanting to disappoint God, we didn't want to disappoint our children, David and Kimberly, by risking anything short of our best efforts.

Nor did I want to disappoint our extended family—the men and women with whom I worked who were taking risks to be part of my risk! Many had other job offers besides mine. They took a bold risk by accepting my offer, for which I am forever grateful.

Whenever fatigue or fear came after me, I armed myself with God's Word. I often repeated Joshua 1:9 when I faced an unexpected challenge or setback: "Have I not commanded you? Be strong and courageous. Do not be afraid; do not be discouraged, for the LORD your God will be with you wherever you go." Again and again, I repeated this Scripture when times were difficult, and it restored my courage and strengthened my faith.

God blessed us with living in the greatest country in the history of the world. Our bold ancestors, men and women of amazing courage and unshakeable faith, built this great nation for us. We are so blessed to be alive at this time in history. If we aren't thinking boldly and taking leaps of faith, then we're not only wasting the many opportunities God gives us, but we're wasting our most precious resource—our time.

TIME AND TIME AGAIN

In order to risk our best efforts, we must know how to make the most of our time. Among all the questions that other, often younger, leaders ask me, the one that recurs most often has to do with time management. "How do you know the best way to invest your time?" they ask. "What's the best way to schedule appointments with team members?" others add, and on and on the questions continue.

There are no easy answers other than to honor the gift God

has given you and invest it wisely as your most precious resource. Money and materials can be replaced. They often come
and go. But time rolls forward and stops for no one! Scripture
tells us, "Teach us to number our days, that we may gain a heart
of wisdom" (Ps. 90:12). And our days are definitely limited!
Our time on Earth is like grass withering or a shadow passing.
We must make risking our very best efforts an ongoing practice
if we are to make the most of our time.

I learned this practice by watching the example set by my parents. Back in the 1950s and '60s, job opportunities for African
Americans in small-town USA were limited, and Clinton, Missouri, was no exception. My father was the family's sole bread-
winner, and keeping food on the table and a roof over the heads
of a family of ten meant putting in long hours and working a
six-day week. Back then, as a person of color, he had to create
his own work. He couldn't afford to waste time when he could
be doing something to provide for his family.

As a jack-of-all-trades, my father worked as an auto mechanic
at a local Chrysler dealership and moonlighted by repairing cars
at night. He also hauled trash and did janitorial work, cleaning
offices some evenings. And somehow, he found time to do some
farming. We raised a few hogs and chickens on our six-acre plot
of land. Our property sat next to the railroad track just outside of
town. We had a couple of cows that provided fresh milk for us
every day. We had a vegetable garden that we all helped maintain. We were poor by other people's standards, but we never
considered ourselves underprivileged.

My mother worked just as hard. In addition to cooking, cleaning, and keeping our household running, she was very active at
our church and spent time there nearly every day of the week.
She taught Sunday school and Bible study classes and served on
just about every committee our church had. Most evenings after
dinner, she supervised us kids with our homework. My mother
was always there for us, and she made my siblings and me feel
like we were special.

How did she find the time to do so much? I can only answer by recalling the old adage, "If you want something done, then give it to a busy person." Obviously, she was very good at managing her time, just like my father. By watching them, I learned by osmosis how to manage my time. Not only did they teach me to study the Bible, but I learned about being a good Christian by watching them be good stewards of all they had, including their time.

TAKE TIME

In prioritizing how I use my time, and to avoid wasting it on minutiae, I focus on God's reminder that we live in various seasons: "There is a time for everything, and a season for every activity under the heavens" (Eccles. 3:1). Every successful business leader values his time. But we must be careful about allowing our awareness of time to pressure us in the wrong direction.

Making the most of our time is not always about productivity, at least not in the usual sense. We have to look at how Jesus maximized His time. His public ministry was about three years, and in this relatively brief period of time, He influenced the world more than any other person that ever lived. He was constantly on the move, preaching to congregations in synagogues and addressing crowds of people that assembled to hear His message.

Throughout it all, however, He also took time to pray: "Very early in the morning, while it was still dark, Jesus got up, left the house and went off to a solitary place, where he prayed" (Mark 1:35). He prioritized His time by keeping His focus on His relationship with His Father.

Even though spreading the Word to large numbers of people was the best way for Jesus to maximize His impact, He still set aside time for one-on-one interactions with individuals. This is witnessed by numerous stories in the Bible, such as when

He stopped to heal a blind man and a sickly woman and even restored life to a dead man. He also took time to single out individuals for counseling.

I constantly try to emulate the teaching of Jesus, so even when I'm short on time, I will stop to talk to WWT associates while I'm walking across our campus on my way to a meeting. It doesn't matter what role they serve in our company, because everyone is precious in God's eyes. I try to let everyone know I think this way. While it consumes time, I know it's productive according to what matters most. My mother often told me in her soft voice, "You may be the only Bible someone sees today."

Under pressure, people are sometimes tempted to cut corners or compromise their principles. Instead of pursuing God's will, they make quick decisions based only on what appears easy. Scripture warns, "Be very careful, then, how you live—not as unwise but as wise, making the most of every opportunity, because the days are evil. Therefore do not be foolish, but understand what the Lord's will is" (Eph. 5:15–17). While it may appear expedient to take shortcuts or go through the motions, we must keep focused on risking our best efforts if we want to please God and serve others well.

YOUR LEADERSHIP FLYWHEEL:
Learn, Live, Lead, Legacy

1. Do you usually enjoy taking risks, or do you tend to be more cautious by nature? How is your response reinforced by key decisions you've made in your life?

2. What risk is God calling you to take as a leader committed to following the example of Jesus? Where do you need to exercise boldness?

3. What fears or concerns do you have about taking this bold risk? What promise from the Bible will you claim to remind you of God's power and faithfulness?

Dear Lord, I'm amazed at how far You have brought me and the risks You've allowed me to take along the way. Thank You for giving me Your strength and encouraging my heart with Your presence and peace. Help me not to become complacent and make cruise control my default setting. Show me the risks You're calling me to take in order to make the most of my time here on Earth. In Jesus' name, amen.

CHAPTER 15

RISK YOUR REPUTATION FOR WHAT'S RIGHT

For God gave us a spirit not of fear but of power and love and self-control.

2 Timothy 1:7 ESV

The role of a leader is to make the best decisions, not the most popular ones. If you lead and serve long enough, you will realize that it's simply not possible to do what you believe must be done *and* please everyone. Like most leaders, I have made decisions that were not always welcomed unanimously. Ironically enough, several of these situations emerged in roles in which I had volunteered to lead.

Giving our time and talent is just as important as giving our treasure; consequently, I've always made time for serving worthwhile causes. In addition to being vice chairman of Biblical Business Training, I've also served on the board of directors of the University of Missouri and the Barnes-Jewish Hospital here in St. Louis. I've also served as an executive committee member and past vice president of the national board of the Boy Scouts of America. I served as chair of the board of United Way for several years and help shepherd their annual giving fund and also served back-to-back terms as chairman of Variety the Children's Charity of St. Louis.

During my time chairing United Way and Variety, some of my decisions disappointed some constituents. While we enjoyed record fundraising, some groups within each organization received increased funding while others received less.

Just as you have to make difficult decisions and take risks in business, you also face such challenges in the nonprofit sector. It's very difficult to reduce the amount of funding to a good cause, and everyone naturally believes his or her charitable organization deserves to receive the most funding. But when you assume a leadership role in the world of philanthropy, you accept the responsibility to do what you believe is the best use of available funds. While we endeavor to support many worthy causes, the need always exceeds the budgets. Inevitably, others disagree with certain allocations. While serving as past chairman in these two organizations, I focused more on a global perspective than a tactical one.

Some people vocally criticized me and my decisions because I was not directing funds to their specific causes. While I agreed wholeheartedly with their need for funds, it became a matter of having *many* good and deserving causes in need of United Way funding. As the first person of color to chair these campaigns, I attracted the attention of many within the African American community. My job, however, was to serve the entire community, not just the part reflecting aspects of my own demographic, and to do what I believed was for the greater good of all.

MINDFUL OF THE MIRACLE

This friction between a leader's decisions and others' responses is nothing new. Sometimes the backlash even occurs on the heels of a miracle. Jesus fed over five thousand people by blessing and distributing a boy's lunch of five small barley loaves and two fish.

The following day, people began grumbling, complaining, and doubting. How quickly they had forgotten! They were no longer mindful of the miracle they had just received. And the dissension continued to simmer for some time until the Festival of Tabernacles: "Among the crowds there was widespread whispering about him. Some said, 'He is a good man.' Others replied, 'No, he deceives the people'" (John 7:12). Jesus, the Son of God and the greatest leader of all time, was unable to please everyone!

In the Old Testament, Moses was the foremost leader of the Israelites but encountered resistance from his followers. It started shortly after the Exodus began and before they reached the banks of the Red Sea. The people of Israel complained, "It would have been better for us to serve the Egyptians than to die in the desert!" (Exod. 14:12).

Plainly, Moses was unable to please everyone. Still, he did not deviate from his mission and continued to pursue the vision God had for them. Even when the people of Israel later wanted to abandon his leadership and rebelled against God by creating a golden calf to worship as their idol (see Exod. 32), Moses focused on what God called him to do. Through good times and bad, Moses' reputation was not based on people's approval.

PRUNE FOR PURPOSE

We would be wise to remember that Moses and even Jesus, the Good Lord Himself, could not please all the people all the time. A leader is constantly facing challenges, and how he or she chooses to deal with them is unlikely to please everybody. For instance, during tough economic times, a decision may be necessary to reduce overhead that results in closing a business unit, therefore reducing the number of people on the payroll, cutting back on bonuses, and so on.

As hard as these decisions can be—and they are hard because you know they affect people's lives—you also must consider the overall health of the company. You must be willing to risk your reputation, knowing you will no longer be liked or popular with some team members, in order to preserve and maintain the health of the organization as a whole. You must be willing to prune for a higher purpose.

We're told in the Bible that God prunes branches that aren't bearing fruit in order for the tree to grow, flourish, and produce more fruit (see John 15:2). The same is true in business. You must sometimes trim back, and if you don't take definitive action, the entire company is in harm's way. These are often agonizing leadership decisions; however, if no action is taken, catastrophic consequences result that are even more harmful. For example, from 1984 to 1990, my company audited freight bills. Then, I planned to enter the fast-growing technology industry. As a result, I decided to shut down the transportation company so I could devote all of my energy into the new company. My decision to enter a new field in which I had no experience was poorly received. Many people said, "It's too competitive in tech! Focus on what you already know." Others said, "There are no African American business leaders in technology. You don't belong there!"

Transitioning from one business to another was not the only time I've made tough decisions that attracted a negative response. After WWT was up and running, I decided to pursue contracts with federal government departments. Some people criticized this direction and said, "It takes years to land those contracts. You don't have the staying power to finance your company in the interim."

But I've never shied away from risk when I knew the reason was right.

DINOSAUR OR DYNAMO

By definition, an entrepreneur must take risks, a requisite in our free-enterprise system. I have a high risk tolerance, which is likely greater than most leaders. Naturally, my willingness to take risks causes others to question, argue, or doubt my leadership at times. They resist what I believe must be done or can't see what looks clear when considering the big picture. If I relied on their support, approval, and affirmation as the source for my confidence as a leader, then I would feel forced to let them influence my every decision. That's why it's so vitally important to be a leader who relies on God and walks by faith—otherwise, the roller coaster of others' opinions will keep you going up and down on the same track over and over again.

Depending on your particular field, you may feel the pressure to risk more acutely than leaders in other fields. Today's technology is high risk. If we don't take some risks, we won't be relevant tomorrow. Technology is always changing so rapidly, which means that we have to be aggressive in order to stay ahead of the curve with the next generation of advancement. We must be assertive in learning about improvements in our ability to serve our clients and in educating others about it so we can be on the forefront in serving a wide range of industries. This is a constant challenge that we readily accept, and by doing so, I think it puts WWT in a special place where we will continue to grow in the long-term future.

In the IT industry, there is so much change happening that in order to be competitive, you cannot stand still. You must embrace change or become a dinosaur. The IT graveyard is filled with failed companies—ones that stopped taking risks and became complacent. Their failures are, in part, due to their leaders' inability and/or unwillingness to adapt to change. By its nature, change involves taking risks with no guarantees that the new way will succeed.

The bigger risk, however, is to resist change.

You can risk becoming a dinosaur or being a dynamo!

WWT's management team has shared in the calculated risks we've taken as a company, sometimes winning and sometimes losing. Fortunately, by the grace of God, our successes have outnumbered our failures. Over the years, I've tried to set an example of risking for the right reasons. My goal is not only for the desired outcome resulting from those risks but for WWT leaders to become more comfortable and confident making bold decisions.

We encourage them to take risks, and we do it by continually communicating with them. I frequently repeat, "Our future depends on your feedback!" We want them to take ownership, and we have built-in incentives to reward them for their successes. We let them know that no idea is viewed as a bad idea. We are eager to have their input, and they are constantly reminded that they are our source of innovation and that our growth depends on their ideas. We challenge ourselves to take risks, and we are constantly pushing the envelope.

Our Advanced Technology Centers are focused on experimenting and challenging our people to determine what the next generation of technology will look like. My job is to be a cheerleader, a support system, an investor, and the person who reminds them to challenge the status quo. My job is also to push the limits of possibility.

Sometimes a successful company founder will take a less aggressive approach in his later years. He becomes less risk prone for fear he might lose what has taken a lifetime to accumulate. Or, it might be that his company has become so big it becomes riddled with bureaucracy and is no longer agile and light on its feet. Consequently, it moves too slowly and is unable to continue at its former innovative pace. But either extreme becomes stifling. At WWT, we work overtime to make sure this never happens—that no matter how large we grow, we can still move quickly and responsively.

After all, our reputation is at stake!

YOUR LEADERSHIP FLYWHEEL:
Learn, Live, Lead, Legacy

1. When have you risked your reputation and what others thought of you in order to do the right thing? What were the consequences?

2. How important to you is it for others to like you and to enjoy your leadership? How has your need for others' approval gotten in the way of leading to the best of your ability?

3. How do you strike a balance between valuing the input of those you serve and allowing them to determine decisions that only you, as their servant-leader, must make? What does it look like for you to welcome others' buy-in without needing their ultimate approval for the decisions you make?

Dear God, I want only to please You and honor Your name as I serve in my current position of leadership. Remind me that my confidence comes from the strength, power, and wisdom I have in You—not my own abilities and what others think of me. Help me to remain humble and willing to delegate while also being bold and making the hard, unpopular decisions required for us to grow in the right direction—toward You and Your kingdom! In the name of Jesus, amen.

SECTION 6
Trust

CHAPTER 16

TRUST GOD FOR THE IMPOSSIBLE

Jesus looked at them and said, "With man this is impossible, but with God all things are possible."

Matthew 19:26

Shortly after launching WWT, I experienced one of the last things anyone wants to happen, especially in front of others. In 1993, we were struggling to get on our feet as a company, and I got behind on my car payments. As bills piled up, I made sure everyone else got paid, but I didn't always get to take home a paycheck myself.

That's my car! I remember thinking one morning while conducting a meeting. I had glanced out the window, which happened to be facing the parking lot, and saw a tow truck backing up to my 1991 Lincoln Continental. Of course, I was embarrassed to have this happen in broad daylight at work of all places! What would my team think if they saw their boss's car being towed? I immediately realized such a spectacle might understandably cause them to panic.

My mind raced with what to do. As calmly and casually as possible, I excused myself, saying that I needed to fetch my briefcase from the back seat of my car. A few minutes later, when I came back to the meeting, I nonchalantly tossed my briefcase beside my chair and went on with business as if nothing had happened. Nobody seemed to mind, but had they sensed my internal distress, they might have reacted quite differently! After all, if the boss isn't making his car payments, the company must be in dire shape.

When I told Thelma what happened, she calmly replied, "You can drive my car, honey."

We looked at each other as I smiled at the gracious, generous, loving response of this remarkable woman of faith. "I'm sure many other companies have had their ups and downs when they started," I told her, "and they had to overcome many challenges to get to where they are today. Besides, it's only a car, and it can be replaced. There are many worse things. Everyone in our family has good health, and we have so many blessings."

Thelma placed her hand in mine and said, "Someday when you're a big success, you can share this experience to encourage others who are down. It's a good lesson on tenacity. This is just a minor setback. The Lord will see us through this."

I started to laugh then as I described the scene that morning. "Honey, I acted as if nothing had happened at the meeting, and everyone in the room seemed oblivious. It was as if they didn't even notice. Or maybe, they just couldn't believe their own eyes! It was surreal—like I was acting in a skit on *Saturday Night Live!*"

"Years from now, David," my sweet wife said, "you'll have a wonderful story to tell."

LEARN TO LAUGH

She was right! I've gotten a lot of mileage out of this story, no pun intended. At the end of that miserable day, I struggled to imagine the future scenario Thelma described, but I've had more than one occasion to use that story as a way to frame God's ability to do what appears impossible to us. In fact, I was recently at a business dinner with a group of successful executives in Manhattan. We were in a private room at a fancy restaurant with white linens, crystal glasses, and fresh flowers on the table. Everyone looked so elegant and refined in bespoke suits and designer dresses—consummate professionals at the top of their game. I had asked to give thanks before our meal, which I proceeded to do right before we were served, but while I had everyone's attention, I decided to try to break the ice.

"Before we talk business," I said, smiling around the table at everyone, "I thought it would be nice to get to know each other better. Maybe we could begin by answering a question." I paused to rein in everyone's attention. "Who here has ever had your car repossessed?"

You could have heard the proverbial pin drop for about ten seconds, and then I raised my hand and laughed just as everyone else began to laugh, too. I proceeded to tell them my experience, and then several others chimed in about similar financial struggles and embarrassing incidents along the road of their current success. We connected as human beings and enjoyed laughing together, and any pretense of competitive jostling slipped away.

When I laugh about such struggles, it gives others permission to do the same. It's like when I tell stories about all the cows I milked and the hogs I slopped on our tiny farm while growing up. I often tell people that I'm not a rags-to-riches story because my family was too poor to have rags! I couldn't laugh about such struggles back then, but I sure can today.

DO YOUR BEST

If we want to be leaders who rely on the Lord as our wellspring, then we must do our part to be faithful by working hard and doing our very best. Brandon and his family have a saying: "Do your best, and let God take care of the rest!" Then we can experience peace knowing we've done our best and can leave the outcomes or results to God, trusting Him to provide for our needs and to guide us as He wills. Sometimes, we ask God for

His blessings before we've done our part to sow the seeds for the harvest we long to see.

God requires us to give our best, not just some of the time but *all* the time. My mother, a big believer in self-discipline, instilled this lesson in us kids from an early age. There was no room for excuses, because excuses could always be found if you weren't willing to invest your best efforts. She made sure we studied every night and completed our homework before we went to bed. Schoolwork didn't come easy for me, and as I look back, I often had trouble concentrating on my studies. With ten of us cramped into such tight quarters, our home was not an ideal study environment. It had dim lighting, and none of us had a desk. Only a few of us could do our studying at the dining room table—the rest of us spread out our books and papers on the floor.

I'm not making excuses for my average grades, but it sure would have been nice to have a bedroom that I could have shared with one or two of my brothers, a place to study in relative privacy. Plus, by the time I hit the books at night, I was exhausted because I had been up since the crack of dawn doing my chores before heading to school. Sometimes by midday, I could barely keep my eyes open.

I also participated in sports and loved basketball. While I eventually shot up to my present height of six foot five, I was short for my age while growing up. Until my senior year in high school, I mostly sat on the bench. But what I lacked in stature, I made up for in grit and tenacity. I was a scrappy player, and perhaps because I was so skinny, I ran faster than the bigger boys, so I was always going after the ball. I'd be embarrassed, but my coach would say to my teammates, "Look at the way Steward hustles! That's what I want the rest of you to do. If you all play with that kind of intensity, nobody will beat us."

I had a late growth spurt, and by my senior year, I was a starter. When I stopped growing, I was by far the tallest member of my family, including all my relatives. My mother used to say, "David wanted to play basketball so badly that he *willed* himself to grow!" My love of the game helped me get a partial athletic scholarship to Central Missouri State University (now University of Central Missouri). Once again, I was mostly a benchwarmer, but by my senior year, through sheer determination, I became a starter. We had a seven-foot center, but I would usually play that position when we had jump balls because I would be so fiercely determined to control the ball.

Looking back, I had to work extra hard to get by in the classroom and on the basketball court. But I can see now how those endeavors forced me to work harder and push myself further in almost everything I've attempted. Trusting God for the impossible requires regular leaps of faith along the way.

ALL THINGS ARE POSSIBLE

At times, however, we all struggle to keep going. Too many obstacles get in our way, and circumstances close in on us in ways that leave us feeling powerless to change them. Some battles seem more pervasive than others.

In 1954, the landmark Supreme Court case *Brown v. Board of Education* declared that state laws establishing separate public schools for black and white students were unconstitutional. The ruling provided a major victory for the civil rights movement and paved the way for integration. Actually ending racial segregation in schools, however, took time and provoked racial tension that lasted for years. Terrible riots resulted in the loss of innocent lives and the destruction of billions of dollars of property.

As the only African American boy in my class at my Clinton high school, many folks didn't like my being there, so consequently, I confronted bigotry in some form on a daily basis. Even in college, when I traveled with my basketball team, we were not permitted to eat at the whites-only restaurants or stay at the whites-only hotels. As difficult as those situations were, I recalled how my parents taught us never to resent people or to allow bitterness to take root. Following their example, I refused to let other people's prejudices discourage me.

Battling racism has helped me to be a catalyst for change instead of a casualty of defeat. As I approached graduation from college and began considering job options, I struggled to accept the picture of the corporate world painted for me in school. And as a business major, I couldn't relate what I learned in the classroom with what my father did as a small-time entrepreneur. I couldn't connect the relevance of the abstract principles my college instructors taught us with what I ultimately wanted to do.

This disconnect foreshadowed what proved true once I entered the business world: Textbooks overlooked the realities of relationships. Not to mention the vital importance of faith in God to do more than what you can do on your own! Of course, most of my college professors had never owned a business, nor, for that matter, had the authors who wrote the textbooks! And perhaps they knew the Lord, but it never came up in our discussions.

Once I got out in the real world, I realized that in school they were teaching us how to work for somebody else—just like they did. But I wanted to work for myself and to change the way employees were treated. Plus, immediately out of college, I found out very quickly that corporate America wasn't interested in hiring a person of color with mediocre grades. I would have to trust God if I wanted to create a business that operated on His principles and share them with others. While there were moments when such an endeavor felt like mission impossible, I never gave up believing that with God all things are possible (see Matt. 19:26).

While obstacles like racism and traditionalism appeared daunting, they were no match for human grit and God's grace!

FAITHFUL TO FRUITFUL

We've all been told that "the world is our oyster," meaning there are endless opportunities in a free-market, democratic society for those who work diligently. While I agree that America is the greatest land of opportunity on our planet, a college education is never enough to ensure success. One must possess grit to overcome the continual hurdles along the road to success.

I'm a firm believer that what doesn't kill you makes you stronger—as long as you have faith. Any success I have experienced resulted from divine refinement. Just as iron must be fired in a blast furnace in order to burn away dross and to produce steel, we grow stronger when we persevere and trust God in the process. Like most entrepreneurs, I faced many setbacks and early defeats, but I always focused on what could be learned from those disappointments. Obstacles and challenges are a given, so it becomes a matter of how to rely on the Lord to transform them into opportunities and strength builders. No matter how deep the disappointment, I never gave up or let hard times define me as a person.

As a youngster, the racial prejudices I faced didn't discourage me, because my parents believed that God could always do the impossible. I remember selling Christmas cards door-to-door and having doors slammed in my face because of the color of my skin. Those moments stung, of course, especially for a young kid unaware of the extent of some people's prejudices. But I refused to quit and just kept knocking on other doors until I had sold all the cards I had. In other words, I learned how to be a better salesman at an early age!

Trusting God to do the impossible is never easy. But this kind of faith is essential if you want to lead others by serving them. Remember, you can do all things—even things that appear impossible—through Christ who strengthens you. When we're faithful, the Lord is fruitful!

YOUR LEADERSHIP FLYWHEEL:
Learn, Live, Lead, Legacy

1. When have you been forced to trust God for something that seemed impossible to you at the time? What did you learn from this experience? How did it change the way you lead and serve? Why?

2. What are the largest obstacles you've been forced to confront as you lead and serve by faith? How has God empowered you to persevere in the face of such adversity?

3. What's one "impossible" goal, target, or milestone that you're presently trusting God to help you reach? How are you seeing Him already at work?

Dear God, thank You for being the God who makes all things possible, even when they appear impossible to my mortal eyes. Help me to trust You, Lord, for bigger dreams and greater goals than I can even envision on my own, let alone bring to life. Grant me both the courage and compassion of Christ as I seek to be more like Him today. In His name I pray, amen.

CHAPTER 17

TRUST GOD'S WORD
FOR GUIDANCE

Your word is a lamp to my feet, and a light to my path.
Psalm 119:105 NKJV

Making decisions as a servant-leader is rarely easy, but it's an essential part of spiritual growth. Only human beings, created in God's image, are blessed with the capacity to make complex decisions, create and express creativity, and reason and solve difficult problems. Our intellectual competence is not based on a whim or an impulse. Our Creator wants us to use our intellects, experiences, and instincts as we make important decisions. But *how* we make those decisions as servant-leaders often makes a big difference in our effectiveness as leaders.

Each of us makes many daily automatic decisions. In fact, the vast majority of our daily decisions are easy, mindless choices. Even many of the decisions we make in positions of servant leadership result from getting into a routine and doing what's been done before. As our responsibilities grow, we often delegate these, trusting that any number of other managers and leaders within our organization can handle them. Then, there is a small number of big decisions that are significantly more complex, and accordingly, the risks and the rewards are proportionately higher. In most institutions, leaders in higher positions are held more accountable for making these tough choices.

If WWT was going to succeed, then I knew I would have to make big decisions and, as outlined in the previous section, take bold risks. Only, my decisions would not be determined just from due diligence, numbers, and factual data. Nor would I set a course of action based entirely on gut instinct or unexpected hunches. While all of those variables might factor into my decisions as a leader, ultimately, I placed my trust in God's Word and His guidance to reveal our company's next steps.

From the beginning, I trusted the Lord's sovereignty and goodness to show me the way: " 'For I know the plans I have for you,' declares the LORD, 'plans to prosper you and not to harm you, plans to give you hope and a future," (Jer. 29:11). Without a doubt, I knew God had plans for me to do well, and the faith He gave me provided the courage to take big risks.

LISTEN BEFORE YOU LEAP

Another promise God gives us in Scripture has also strengthened my faith numerous times: "Have I not commanded you? Be strong and courageous. Do not be afraid; do not be discouraged, for the LORD your God will be with you wherever you go" (Josh. 1:9). Knowing that God is always with me forms the foundation of my strength and conviction. I can be strong and courageous and make the bold decisions necessary to lead and serve others as long as I remember that the Lord is with me.

Whenever I faced a decision with huge consequences for WWT, I prayed for the Lord to show me which way to lead. Still today, any time I must make a bold and audacious decision, I ask God for guidance and listen to what He tells me. He speaks to all of us if we're willing to listen. Like the proverbial light bulb going on above a cartoon character's head, ideas pop in my mind at times that I know come from God. Trusting Him, seeking Him, loving and praising Him, and studying His Word help attune the ears of my heart to God's voice.

Ultimately, the Word of God is brought to life by the illumination of the Holy Spirit. The Holy Spirit works within believers and helps us discern what is human intuition, which the Bible often refers to as the flesh, and what is God-given instruction. Sometimes, it may be difficult to discern between your own thoughts and communication imparted from God's Spirit.

Sometimes when I talk about obeying God's Word and following His direction, people might say, "David, it's easy for you to trust and have faith in God. You're so successful! Look at all He's done for you. Of course you trust Him!" Usually, I'll respond by telling them that God is there for them the same way He's been there for me throughout my life. Then I encourage them to listen, and not just to listen but to act on what God tells them. After all, the Bible makes it clear:

> But be doers of the word, and not hearers only, deceiving yourselves. For if anyone is a hearer of the word and not a doer, he is like a man observing his natural face in a mirror; for he observes himself, goes away, and immediately forgets what kind of man he was. But he who looks into the perfect law of liberty and continues *in it*, and is not a forgetful hearer but a doer of the work, this one will be blessed in what he does. (James 1:22–25 NKJV)

If you want God to guide you, then you must be willing to step out in faith and follow Him. Instead of trying to look before you leap, before making a major decision, try to stop and listen for God before you leap!

ALIVE AND ACTIVE

Too often, God speaks to us, but we refuse to listen. Then we complain because we fail or don't know which direction to go! It's been said that the definition of insanity is when you keep doing the same old thing the same old way and expect a different result. I've had my share of setbacks like everyone else, and each time, I've had to go back to my roots, to what has worked for me, for my family, and for others. I go back to my trust in the Lord and the foundation of my faith, which is anchored by God's Word. Then, I stand firm with His truth, regardless of what happens. Because I know that the Lord will never leave me or forsake me (see Deut. 31:8).

Scripture urges us, "Trust in the LORD with all your heart, and do not lean on your own understanding" (Prov. 3:5 ESV). Notice it doesn't tell us to trust Him half-heartedly! When you trust God's Word for guidance and you take God at His Word, then you can't go in halfway. You've got to be all in! You must believe in what you hear: "So then faith *comes* by hearing, and hearing by the word of God" (Rom. 10:17 NKJV). The Word of God is true. And it is a book of instruction. It is also a book of love. His Word is forever and does not change. This explains why I am focused on absorbing and receiving His Word, whether I'm making an important decision for WWT or seeking His guidance on where I can give and serve others. It is why I continue making decisions relying on the Word of God.

My story is living proof that God is faithful and always honors the promises in His Word. The Bible has stood the test of time and continues to impart the history, power, wisdom, and promises of the Living God. With all the advances in technology and discoveries in science, nothing has changed in this world to weaken the principles in God's Word. The timeless power of Scripture never changes. We're told, "For the word of God is alive and active. Sharper than any double-edged sword, it penetrates even to dividing soul and spirit, joints and marrow; it judges the thoughts and attitudes of the heart" (Heb. 4:12).

NO LUCK

Brandon has shared numerous times about his reliance on the Word and how God has communicated with him through it.

In 2008, long before he resigned from corporate America to serve BBT, Brandon and his coleader, Greg, were struggling to develop enough material for their first Bible study in their office. He said,

> One day, I closed my office door and prayed to God for guidance on how to solve this problem. Immediately, my eyes opened, and I saw a copy of *Doing Business by the Good Book* practically buried in a stack of books on the corner of my desk. I had read it several years previously when I first met David, and I had given it to many people. But its subtitle jumped out at me, as if I were seeing it for the first time: *52 Lessons on Success Straight from the Bible*. Smiling as I quickly pulled it out and thumbed through its pages, I knew it was perfect for our needs.

Brandon then came to me and shared his discovery, asking if his workplace Bible study could study my book. I was thrilled and asked him how many I could send over! The whole reason I wrote that book, and now feel compelled to continue exploring Biblical leadership in this one, is to equip people with principles that have been instrumental in my own life and that of others. As made clear in both books I've authored, my source is the Good Book!

When people ask me about my success and learn how I trust God's Word for guidance and listen to the Holy Spirit, they sometimes struggle to take me seriously. Then when I give them examples, such as the one with Brandon needing source material for his Bible study and seeing my book, they say, "Surely that's just coincidence!" Even after I share numerous other examples with them, they still try to find any reason except giving God the credit. These doubting Thomases either want a logical, rational example that can be made into a scientific system or formula, or they want to believe in coincidence. Some even attribute what God does to luck!

Those who follow Jesus and trust in the Lord, however, know there's no such thing as luck. In fact, a while ago Thelma and I, along with Brandon, were flying back from a conference when the two of them began discussing something one of the speakers there had said about "how lucky they were." We all chuckled, and then Thelma and Brandon got out their Bibles and started going through the concordance. Sure enough, the word *luck* is nowhere to be found in the Word of God!

TRUST AND OBEY

God often reveals His guidance at the most unexpected times. As I've shared with you in previous chapters, back in the early nineties, WWT experienced major financial problems and was on the brink of going out of business. That's when I made a promise to God that if I was able to survive those difficult times, I would always give the credit to Him. I vowed to spend the rest of my life reaching out to others, and in particular, those who needed encouragement. I promised to give them hope, faith, and the courage to walk boldly. My business would serve as my ministry and would bless as many people as possible for my entire lifetime.

As a result of my renewed vow to serve and honor God through WWT, I once again affirmed the power of trusting His Word to guide me. I continue to honor my commitment, and it is what inspired me to share what I've learned about leadership with you here in these pages. Just as the Holy Spirit serves as our guide, on a smaller scale I want to help you unlock the gifts of leadership God has created in you.

Ultimately, however, the best advice I can give you as you seek to lead like Jesus is simple: Trust and obey. Read the Bible and study God's Word. Obey His commands and seek to honor Him in all that you do. Trust the Lord to guide you as you lead others, providing illumination, clarity, and direction through the power of His Holy Spirit!

YOUR LEADERSHIP FLYWHEEL:
Learn, Live, Lead, Legacy

1. How would you describe your past experiences reading and understanding God's Word? How often do you read and study the Bible now? What obstacles currently prevent you from spending more time in the Word? Not enough time in your schedule? Difficulty in understanding the text? Something else? How can you overcome these barriers?

2. When has God most recently spoken to you, either in prayer as you listened for His voice, or through the power of the Holy Spirit as you read the Bible? What action did you take as a result of this communication? How does God continue to speak into your life and guide your decisions?

3. What verse or passage from the Bible gives you the most strength and courage as you make hard decisions or face tough challenges? Write it out or print it on a sticky note and place it in a spot where you will see it every day. Ask God to bring it alive for you in a fresh revelation to inspire your servant leadership.

Dear Lord, thank You for the gift of Your Word and Your many promises. As I seek to study the Bible and meditate on Your truth, may Your Holy Spirit guide and direct me. Give me wisdom and discernment so that I may lead with confidence founded on my faith in You. Attune my heart to Your voice so that I may trust You for each step I take and honor You all the days of my life. In Jesus' name, amen.

CHAPTER 18

TRUST THE PEOPLE
YOU LEAD

Be kind to one another, tenderhearted, forgiving one another,
as God in Christ forgave you.

Ephesians 4:32 ESV

When traveling to other countries, and even other parts of our own great nation, one of the greatest joys is experiencing different cultures. Whether it's enjoying an exotic meal, participating in a unique event, exploring local history, or talking with native inhabitants about their favorite pastimes, you quickly learn what they value most. Culture reflects the character of its people.

The same is true for any company and its corporate culture.

In recent years, management gurus have continued to emphasize the way an organization's culture contributes to its overall success—or impedes its progress toward realizing its full potential. Few people would argue with this observation. The problem with corporate culture, however, becomes how to identify, implement, and exercise the variables needed to create the kind of environment in which people thrive. And from my experience, both in practice and observation, corporate culture begins in the heart of the leader.

If you want your company to thrive, then you must trust the people you lead!

ATTITUDE AND ACTION

While many small-business owners may not think much about their culture because of their size, their company nonetheless has its own unique environment. Even a one-person start-up company has its own culture, whether much time or attention has been given to its creation or impact. Its culture emerges from the owner's work habits, the quality of her products or service, how she solicits customers, treats them, and so on. As a company grows and the owner hires employees, more people get involved and, consequently, create more variables.

Although a company's culture is always important, large companies usually place a higher priority on it than small mom-and-pop businesses. This happens because as the company grows, its owner/founder is unable to spend as much one-on-one time with individual employees and customers. So instead of his beliefs and behavior primarily shaping the company's culture, it is also being shaped by what other people do in the organization.

Rarely is a company's culture decided by a committee when somebody suggests, "Hey, we ought to have a company culture." On the contrary, it evolves over a period of time and becomes a product of attitude and action that makes the organization run smoothly—or not. It can be viewed as the personality of the organization, much like a person's character, and similarly, company cultures run the gamut.

Culture is a big and somewhat vague term. Some people might define it as "what happens when nobody is looking." In reality, it's much more complex. Culture is the set of behaviors, values, artifacts, reward systems, and rituals that make up your organization. You can "feel" culture when you visit a company because it is often evident in people's behavior, enthusiasm, and the space itself.

I invest a high percentage of my time visiting our customers and partners around the world, and I can sense a company's culture after being there only a short while. Many first impressions catch my attention as likely indicators of culture. For example, do the companies' employees start on time? Are people empowered to take charge or must they adhere to strict company rules? Is there a tense atmosphere of rigid control? Or a relaxed air of mutual trust and productivity? Do people seem comfortable because they've been equipped to do their best? Is there a sense of connection among team members? Are they a kind of family?

You would be surprised how even the smallest details can reveal the overall attitude and atmosphere of a corporate environment. Years ago, I was shopping in a large department store and found a suit I wanted to try on. As I wandered through the cavernous men's department, I stopped at the cologne counter and asked for directions to the dressing rooms. "I don't work in men's clothing," barked the associate behind the counter and briskly turned away. Wow, did that curt remark speak volumes about the culture there! Obviously, that experience left a lasting impression on me.

On the other hand, I recall a very different experience in another department store. Shopping for a gift for Thelma, I got lost in the cosmetics department and asked an associate if she could direct me to the ladies' handbags. She immediately smiled and told me she would be happy to help me. With a brief nod to another associate, which I assumed was a signal to let them know she would be right back, she then walked me to the other side of that floor of the store, pausing right in front of the purses and accessories. Again, our interaction lasted less than two minutes but revealed a year's worth of insight about the corporate culture there.

I'm sure it's a pet peeve of mine, but anytime you ask an employee a question and get the response, "That's not my job," it raises a red flag. In well-managed companies, everyone's job is serving customers. Just imagine if someone visited your home and asked for a drink of water. No one would ever dream of saying, "I'm sorry, but that's not my job!" Instead, you would get your guest a glass of water with the hospitality of any good host. Serving is always the hallmark of a healthy company culture.

CULTURAL COMPASS

Common courtesy and basic kindness also go a long way in shaping the kind of culture where people want to work and do business. We are made in the image and likeness of God. This fact should make it obvious how we should treat people! When leaders share this view with the people they serve, it becomes deeply ingrained in the company's culture. Keep in mind that a company's culture is determined by its values, which always start at the top with the founder and CEO.

When the people at the top are honest and caring, not only to their employees, partners, and customers but also to their community, it sets the cultural compass for the entire organization. Their attitude and actions demonstrate to everybody by example that it is an organization with caring, principled values— for leaders following the example of Jesus, Biblical values. This sets the company apart from the competition; its culture becomes a magnet for bringing out the best in others. This tone is what makes people want to work for your company. This energy is what makes people want to do business with you. In our competitive business world, a company's cultural compass determines the direction of employees and customers alike.

FAMILY PRACTICES

Prior to when a company acquires another company, it's essential to determine if their cultures will be compatible. Otherwise, the culture clash from incompatible systems undermines the merger. A company's culture is often clearest when compared to one that prioritizes a different set of values and practices.

Larger, more successful companies often have bigger budgets that allow them to provide higher salaries and better benefits than smaller companies. But offering these items does not ensure a positive, healthy work environment or a connection among the people leading and serving there. Many times, a closeness can exist in a small company that makes employees feel like family. And because a company is small, cultural intimacy gives it an edge over a large company. For example, a small-business owner can celebrate employees' birthdays—everyone's! In addition to taking breaks to serve birthday cake, he or she can send personal birthday cards or even give a gift. Leaders in smaller, more relational companies can keep up with their employees' personal milestones, such as births, anniversaries, their kids' achievements and graduations.

In smaller businesses, it's often easier for leaders to socialize with their employees, whether that means enjoying a meal together or taking in a ball game, concert, or community event. These leaders can bowl or play golf with those they serve, invite them to dinner at their home, have company cookouts, company picnics—the list goes on and on. Some small companies even develop traditions and rituals that everyone enjoys and counts on, such as gathering around a big table once a week for lunch. Some days they talk about business and other days they just talk like good friends and families do when they assemble. Regardless of what they discuss, they bond and grow in their understanding of and appreciation for one another. They grow to like and care for one another. They deepen their trust of and reliance on one another. Such moments become the bricks and mortar for the company's culture.

Larger companies can emulate some of these "family practices," but they may not work the same way and will need to be recalibrated. The main priority is to let people know you recognize them as people, not just employee ID numbers, and appreciate their vital and unique contribution to your organization. The most important thing to convey is simply that you care about them and want them to care about each other.

SPIRITUAL VITAMIN

A company's culture must be willing and able to address tensions, stresses, and dilemmas as they arise. Especially when a leader makes a mistake or does something to violate trust, then there's only one solution to pursue in order to maintain the health of the company: forgiveness. If leaders are not willing to practice forgiveness, then the culture around them will suffer and become toxic. Such practice means that leaders ask for forgiveness when they offend or wrong others, and it also means they choose to forgive those who wrong them. Forgiveness is the essential, spiritual vitamin that keeps a company's culture healthy and strong.

Shortly after launching WWT, the importance of forgiveness met me head-on. After investing every cent of my family's savings in this new company, we struggled to make ends meet. Even after we had acquired new accounts and had shown signs of growth, we still couldn't seem to get on our firm footing financially. Then I learned that one of our company's key people, someone trusted and respected, had "creatively reallocated" several hundred thousand dollars from the company. It was not simply that it was morally and ethically wrong and a violation of God's commands; relative to our company's health, stealing this money was like removing a vital organ from a body!

When we had undeniable evidence of this individual's guilt, we confronted the person. There was no denying what was done, so this person did not refute the evidence but instead confessed and showed remorse. Unfortunately, however, the company money was spent and could not be returned.

My wife and I prayed and asked God what we should do. Thelma then opened her Bible and read to me, "For if you forgive other people when they sin against you, your heavenly Father will also forgive you. But if you do not forgive others their sins, your Father will not forgive your sins" (Matt. 6:14–15). She also reminded me of another passage with a clear indication of what God wanted in this situation: "Do not seek revenge or bear a grudge against anyone among your people, but love your neighbor as yourself" (Lev. 19:18). Although this embezzlement was a major setback to the company, we forgave him.

As angry, hurt, and disappointed as I felt, I knew it was not only what I needed to do personally but what also needed to be done for the well-being of WWT. We forgave because that person is one of God's children, so it is not for us to judge or discipline them. It is for God to discipline others who sin against us. The Lord told us to love them and pray for them.

When you don't forgive, you only hurt yourself—and your organization! The old adage is true. Refusing to forgive others is like taking a poison pill and waiting for them to die while you're the only one who is dying. But it's also like spreading a virus throughout the body of the company.

A CULTURE OF CONSEQUENCES

The Bible instructs us not to take vengeance against others. Despite the devastating impact of the embezzlement, I was free to focus on more productive things and could let God deal with vengeance. But please don't misunderstand why I shared this example. Sins must be confronted, and forgiveness extended, and often this involves consequences and making changes in order to maintain the health of the organization.

While I chose not to pursue legal action, I realize that other leaders in a similar situation may be forced to do so because of the nature of their business. For example, an investment firm, bank, or insurance company may forgive a guilty party but also be required to file for illegal deeds in order to maintain their credentials or legal standing. God commands us to forgive others, but He never tells us to ignore the consequences of their offense.

In everyday business, most common wrongdoings involve matters of poor judgment or unintentional mistakes, such as tardiness, poor service, failure to communicate, using company time doing personal activities online, and so on. With matters like these, a good leader must communicate that such behavior is unacceptable, thereby sending a message to all employees as to the values of the organization. Regarding cases of inadequate performance—such as poor follow-up in serving a customer, giving too high a bid to a vendor, quoting too low a price to a customer—a leader, while forgiving the poor performance, should use these as specific teaching opportunities for coaching and improving the individual employee's performance.

Certainly, gray areas can develop where people may not know what is acceptable behavior and what is not. A good leader lets it be known where he stands on matters of significance and avoids problems down the road. He or she also lets habitual offenders know that they will be held accountable and face consequences. And while a good leader is kind and understanding, people know that his or her forgiving nature should never be viewed as weakness. Yes, good leaders forgive people, but when appropriate, they will also demote or discharge offenders who are repeatedly unwilling to change.

Jesus Christ is the only perfect person who has ever lived, and a good leader recognizes that people make mistakes. We're reminded, "For all have sinned and fall short of the glory of God" (Rom. 3:23). A good leader knows his people are not perfect, so when someone errs, he should be understanding and forgiving. When people are treated with respect and kindness, they learn from their mistakes, and their performance generally improves. When they're given the opportunity to grow, and when others witness how they're treated, then the culture remains a healthy environment.

If you're willing to create a corporate culture based on Biblical principles and Christ-centered values, then you can always trust the people you lead!

YOUR LEADERSHIP FLYWHEEL:
Learn, Live, Lead, Legacy

1. What three words best describe the company culture where you presently lead and serve? What's unique about your company's culture compared to its peers and competitors?

2. What needs to change or could be improved in your company's culture? How can you be a catalyst for positive change toward a healthier, more vibrant, more productive environment within your workplace?

3. When have you chosen to forgive someone in the office whose offense, large or small, caused you both personal and professional disappointment? What was the hardest part about forgiving them? Why? How did your choice to forgive affect others in your company?

Dear God, You are the giver of good gifts and the source of everlasting joy and peace. I praise You for all the people with whom I'm privileged to interact each day. Bless each man and woman whom You allow me to lead and to serve. Knit us together as a united team, a loving family committed to treating each other like we want to be treated as we work hard together to do our best for You. In Jesus' name, amen.

SECTION 7

Share

CHAPTER 19

SHARE YOUR WISDOM

As iron sharpens iron, so one person sharpens another.

Proverbs 27:17

We've all had some help along the way. We get sharper by interacting with others on a regular basis. Many successful people have told me about the ups and downs they've had throughout their careers, and they emphasize the mentors they've had along the way.

One of the best examples of mentoring in the Bible is how the apostle Paul mentored Timothy, a young pastor. Earlier in his life, Paul was a mentee of the learned Jewish scholar Gamaliel, who was a member of the Sanhedrin, the highest ruling council of the Jewish people during the time of Jesus. Paul explained to Timothy, "And the things you have heard me say in the presence of many witnesses entrust to reliable people who will also be qualified to teach others" (2 Tim. 2:2). Here Paul is telling Timothy to invest in his mentees who in turn will be able to teach others. This is a call to pay it forward—to pass along what Timothy has learned from Paul. This is the essence of what it means to mentor someone.

Paul emphasized the importance of mentoring relationships when he wrote to the church in Philippi, "Whatever you have learned or received or heard from me, or seen in me—put it into practice. And the God of peace will be with you" (Phil. 4:9).

Paul was emulating Jesus, who was constantly mentoring the people who were with Him; therefore, they could model His behavior and pass it on to each subsequent generation.

Thelma and I have always believed in the vital importance of mentoring, both for our children and beyond. Many years ago, our pastor, Dr. Lynn Mims, asked us to lead a Sunday school class for businesspeople. Having visited WWT on many occasions, Dr. Mims said, "I want you to take the principles you practice at your company and teach them to others. When you do, others who follow your lead can also prosper by doing good."

Our kids were still young then, but we committed to serving in this capacity. Our class attracted about forty to fifty people each Sunday and reflected a diverse cross section of individuals, ranging from owners of new start-up companies to successful executives in huge corporations. During the course of leading that class for several years, we received visits from two different governors of Missouri as well as US senators, members of Congress, city and county councilors, and even clergy from other denominations. As a result, we enjoyed many lively discussions as we explored God's Word for wisdom about how to live out our faith in our respective places of business.

That Sunday school class extended my ability to serve others and teach them what I've learned about applying Biblical principles in business practices. Having been mentored by so many people throughout my life, I appreciate the value others have for equipping and empowering us in our faith. Teaching that class became the impetus for writing *Doing Business by the Good Book*, which in turn has opened other opportunities to mentor others, including *this* book!

PLANTING SHADE TREES

While mentoring remains a buzzword in today's business world, the concept has been around for a very long time. A Greek proverb wisely points out, "A society grows great when old men plant trees in whose shade they will never sit." Of course, we see the vital importance of mentoring throughout the pages of God's Word.

In Psalms, King David wrote, "One generation commends your works to another; they tell of your mighty acts" (145:4). To provide a little context for this observation, consider that David wanted to remind the Israelites of all that God had done for them, not just in individual lives or families but for them generation after generation. David echoes this truth again in his prayer, "Even when I am old and gray, do not forsake me, my God, till I declare your power to the next generation, your mighty acts to all who are to come" (Ps. 71:18). What a profound reminder to pass on our lessons to those whom we lead and serve! We must continually ask ourselves, "How am I sharing what God has done in my life with others? Who can I bless by sharing the wisdom the Lord has imparted to me?"

As I mentioned earlier, the way Brandon and I met reflects this mind-set—on both our parts. At the time he was participating in a mentoring program at his church that connected small minority-owned businesses with members of the church who had experiences and skills to share. One of Brandon's mentees was an entrepreneur in his early thirties whom I was also blessed to be mentoring at the time—a good reminder to have more than one mentor just as you may have several mentees. Sensing we would have a productive conversation, our mutual mentee suggested that the three of us should do a conference call.

From that initial call, Brandon and I hit it off and realized how much we had in common, including our firm belief in the power of mentoring to impact lives. That call was the beginning of an endearing friendship! After our first meeting, Brandon said, "David, I'd like you to be my mentor! Would you be willing to consider that?" I laughed and said, "I thought I already was!" From the beginning, even though he is about twenty years younger than me, I viewed Brandon as a peer, a friend, and brother in Christ. So, we began meeting for lunch or coffee, reading the Bible and discussing its truth together, and of course praying together.

WELCOME TO THE REAL WORLD

Brandon is quick to credit his mentors for both his personal growth and professional success. In his junior year at the University of Missouri, Brandon was hired by Dr. David West, a highly regarded professor who had served multiple terms as the chairman of the department of finance and also ran the real estate investment degree program. Dr. West was in his sixties and had contracted polio as a child, which resulted in him being confined to a mechanized wheelchair, but neither his age nor physical limitations slowed him down or prevented him from earning a national reputation in finance research. Dr. West invited Brandon to serve as his teaching and research assistant, while completing an MBA program there. Dr. West also hired Brandon to work at his commercial real estate investment fund off campus.

Dr. West was a wonderful mentor and set up Brandon for success in numerous ways, including introductions to other leaders in business. One of Brandon's most significant connections resulted from meeting Mark Burkhart, the former CEO of Turley Martin (later named Cassidy Turley before merging into Cushman & Wakefield), a world-class real estate firm based in St. Louis. When Burkhart accepted Dr. West's invitation to speak, Brandon escorted their guest around campus.

Following his speech, Burkhart promptly headed to the parking garage, only to glance up and see Brandon chasing after him. "Did I forget something?" Burkhart asked, to which Brandon replied, "No, I just wanted to thank you for your time today and for doing such a great job."

From that time on, Brandon considered Burkhart to be his

mentor. Burkhart offered Brandon a position after he completed his graduate program. But as graduation neared, other offers poured in, including one from a competitor of Turley Martin. Enamored by the promises of one of that firm's senior executives, Brandon turned down Burkhart's offer.

Naturally, Brandon found it awkward telling his mentor that he was joining another firm, and Burkhart's disappointment was obvious. Nonetheless, he wished his young protégé much success and concluded, "Either you will be very successful there, and I'll be calling you to join us, or it's not going to go the way they told you it would, and in that case, I'm guessing you'll be calling me. Either way, we'll stay in touch."

Sure enough, after six months working for the other firm, Brandon discovered everything that could have possibly gone wrong did indeed go wrong. His new boss and would-be mentor had many other competing priorities, and as a result, their relationship did not develop. Although Brandon had been told his MBA education and previous investment management experience would be put to good use, it was not. Brandon describes it as one of those "welcome-to-the-real-world moments."

Eventually, Brandon left the company but was hesitant to reconnect with Burkhart. Candidly he says, "Mark was right, but my ego couldn't handle it. So, instead of calling Mark right away, I began to interview elsewhere." One of Brandon's other mentors served on a board with Burkhart, and he told Burkhart about Brandon's transition. Burkhart was surprised that Brandon had not reached out to him. Eventually Brandon called Burkhart, and they agreed to meet a few days later for coffee. "Those six months took all the wind out of my sails. I had lost all my self-esteem," Brandon remembers. "Mark was gracious enough to listen as I explained the challenges that I had been going through since my graduate school days. So, I told him I had made a mistake and asked for another chance to earn his trust and confidence again. I would have been willing to sweep floors if necessary!"

Mark Burkhart, like any great mentor, understood the power of forgiveness and the importance of second chances. After a thoughtful pause, Burkhart told Brandon, "You will start with us next week. I know you'll do just fine." Instead of making the most of an "I told you so" moment, Burkhart knew he had the rare opportunity to teach Brandon a lesson in life that was just as important as, if not more than, anything the younger man learned in business school. Good mentors not only teach you about God's grace and forgiveness—they practice it!

GO FISH

Like Brandon, I've been blessed to deepen my faith as well as sharpen my business acumen through my interactions with mentors. Mentors have shown me that the highest form of charity is to help sustain a person before he becomes impoverished. And this form of giving would include helping a person find employment as they pursue discovering their purpose and living out of it as God calls them. When you do this, you make it unnecessary for that individual to become dependent on others.

If you think about it in a business context, this is exactly what mentoring does! It helps a person to succeed, and then he or she is able to be financially self-sustaining and not be dependent on anyone. It's the essence of the saying "Give someone a fish and feed them for a day—teach someone to fish and feed them for a lifetime." In addition, this kind of mentoring helps a person grow and have high self-esteem. Pouring yourself and what you've learned into another person is a wonderful gift—and an investment in them and those they will later mentor. The choices you make now determine the eternal rate of return for generations to come. The Bible tells us, "Instruct the wise and they will be wiser" (Prov. 9:9), which reminds us to selectively choose those whom we want to mentor.

As I grow older and consider the impact I want to have during my time on this earth, I see mentoring at the heart of my spiritual legacy. With each passing year, I appreciate the priceless value of time. Undoubtedly, time is our most precious asset, and the most important question we must ask ourselves each day is how we want to invest it. If you want to make an eternal difference as a servant-leader, then share your wisdom!

YOUR LEADERSHIP FLYWHEEL:
Learn, Live, Lead, Legacy

1. Who are the mentors who have had the greatest positive impact on your life? What did you learn from each of them, about faith as well as business? How have these lessons shaped the kind of servant-leader you have become?

2. Who are you presently pouring your wisdom into on a regular basis? What could you do to bless and encourage these individuals even more? Is there anyone else the Lord might be calling you to mentor right now? Ask the Holy Spirit to guide you as you spend some time in prayer with this question.

3. What spiritual legacy do you want to leave as you invest your time in the lives of others? How can you be more deliberate about how you spend your time together in order to focus on what matters most?

> *Dear Lord, I'm so grateful for the men and women who have taught me, encouraged me, coached me, and inspired me to grow in wisdom in my pursuit of serving You. Bless each one of them as You continue to use them and their investment in me, and others, to make an eternal difference for Your kingdom. Help me to be the best steward of the wisdom entrusted to me as I now mentor others. In Jesus' name, amen.*

CHAPTER 20

SHARE YOUR TREASURE

Every good and perfect gift is from above, coming down from the Father of the heavenly lights, who does not change like shifting shadows.

James 1:17

S haring your treasure means more than just giving money. It means sharing what's most important to you—your time, your skills and expertise, your heart. If you want to keep your focus on serving others, then it's important to share *all* the good gifts God has entrusted to you. What's the point of making a profit or receiving an abundance of blessings if you can't share with those around you? Daily, we should ask ourselves the sobering question Jesus put to his followers: "What good is it for someone to gain the whole world, yet forfeit their soul?" (Mark 8:36).

We are all human, and our mortal bodies will perish. Every dollar, diamond, or designer outfit ultimately doesn't matter, because no one can take anything with them when they depart this life. What matters most is your investments, often invisible to the naked eye, of eternal value. Jesus clearly cautioned us to think twice about the kind of treasure we pursue in this lifetime:

Do not store up for yourselves treasures on earth, where moths and vermin destroy, and where thieves break in and steal. But store up for yourselves treasures in heaven, where moths and vermin do not destroy, and where thieves do not break in and steal. For where your treasure is, there your heart will be also. (Matthew 6:19–21)

SHARE AND SHARE ALIKE

Sharing your treasure with those you serve seems obvious if you're a follower of Christ. When I first entered the workforce, however, I witnessed several bosses, professing believers, who were determined to keep their teams working as many hours a week as possible. It didn't matter that they came to work early and didn't leave the office until after dark. These supervisors exploited their teams with promises for advancement depending on how many unpaid overtime hours they put in. But ultimately, it was a classic case of dangling a carrot out there that can never be caught.

If those you serve share in the rewards reaped from their efforts in producing and harvesting your company's fruit, then they are much more likely to feel valued and validated. They realize it's not just the CEO and executive team benefiting from their hard work and sweat investment. A good leader who cares and loves those he serves will get better results compared to a harsh taskmaster who motivates his people by fear, intimidation, or negative reinforcement. As my mother used to say, "You attract more bees with honey than with vinegar!"

Sharing your treasure is not just about how you motivate others—it's about how you appreciate their value, not just as workers but also as human beings. At WWT, we make sure to remind our employees how important they are to the company and how much their work is appreciated. We share praise and affirm their efforts on a regular basis.

When our people put in overtime on a big project or go way above and beyond what's required and expected, we also show our appreciation by rewarding them with a special treat that takes their minds off work. These might include tickets for a concert or show at the Sheldon Concert Hall or tickets to the Harold and Dorothy Steward Center for Jazz, the use of our sky-box for a professional hockey or baseball game, or guest passes for a special event. Or, it might be as simple as a complimentary dinner out to a fine restaurant with their spouse or significant other.

In fact, we are always looking for new ways to bless others and show them how much they're appreciated. When I notice that someone has a certain hobby or interest, I try to find a gift or experience that they will especially enjoy. Thelma and I will sometimes offer our lake house or use of our vacation time-share, which has locations around the globe. Whether it's a night out on the town or a getaway vacation, we offer these gifts in or-der to share the blessings we've received. These tokens are just a way to thank people and let them know we recognize their work and care about them.

YOUR MOST IMPORTANT MEETING

Another way we try to share our treasure at WWT is by en-couraging team members to invest more in their families than in their careers. We always emphasize the importance of focusing on top priorities—faith and family—ahead of work. Some orga-nizations say this, but then they actually contradict themselves and steal this treasure by interrupting family time. However, our employees are encouraged to put their families first, and this is not just lip service—we really mean it!

The workers at other companies may receive a lot of "keep up the good work" pats on the back and high fives from these demanding bosses, but these leaders never show real concern for their workers' families, nor do they ever mention how the families should be the workers' top priority. Consequently, the attitudes of these bosses caused their workers' attitude to fester into a source of resentment and frustration. They say one thing but do another. The people they lead begin to notice their bosses' hypocrisy, whether anyone calls it that or not. Simply put, this kind of leadership does not honor God.

From the beginning at Biblical Business Training and Kingdom Capital, Brandon has emphasized the importance of family in many ways. He is careful to not interrupt family vacations with emails or calls that are not critical in nature. Also, he acknowledges that each and every weekend is important for families to reconnect after several busy days of work and school-related activities. He has even coined a phrase, that I have adopted as well, to highlight the importance of our families: "The most important meeting of the day is when you see your family!" After one's relationship with God, the people you're blessed to love and serve in your home must come first.

Because at the end of the day, if you're living for work, then you will miss out on some of this life's greatest treasures—time with your loved ones. No promotion, sales award, or performance bonus can take the place of a loving family. Creating special memories together is what it's all about. If you don't have a home where your body can rest and your soul can find refreshment, then you will not last for long, no matter how talented you are or how great your workplace is.

There's no place like going home to find peace and rest. A long time ago, when WWT was just taking off, Thelma and I talked about the kind of home we wanted. "The only way I can keep going and serving the best way I know how," I told her, "is knowing that when I'm home with you and the kids, I have sanctuary." There is no other place where I can go and get what I need.

Thelma's love and encouragement keep me going, and our kids always remind me, even now that they're adults, of the kind of legacy I want to leave. The Bible says, "He who finds a wife finds what is good and receives favor from the LORD" (Prov. 18:22).

God's Word also declares, "Children are a heritage from the LORD, offspring a reward from him" (Ps. 127:3). When I consider all the many ways God has blessed me, there's no gift of greater value than my family and no meeting of more importance than my time with them.

REST FOR THE WEARY

Sharing the treasure of our time goes beyond our families. It's also important to set aside time during the workday to give back to the community. No matter how busy someone may be, they still choose how they *invest* their time. Notice I use the word *invest* to emphasize that time is the most precious gift that God gives us. As leaders, we must be very good stewards of this invaluable resource.

Perhaps the best way to invest your time in the lives of others outside your workplace is simply to schedule it regularly, ensuring it as a priority. When you commit something to your calendar, you can usually find a way to keep that appointment. These appointments might include meeting with community leaders, volunteering at civic and charitable organizations, and mentoring rising leaders outside of your workplace. Such encounters always energize me, and we encourage everyone at WWT to find time for community service, both individually and corporately. Because our company culture centers around giving, we want to be good neighbors in every way.

Again, we try to do more than just donating money, which is still very important, so we go out of our way to show others we care. There's something life-giving about ministering to people in ways they might not expect. It keeps us from focusing only on ourselves and our own problems. Serving others provides a healthy sense of being part of a world so much bigger than yourself and your little corner of it. Ministry offers ways of looking after others and serving them in meaningful ways, both large and small. When you lead by serving like Jesus did, then you also discover how energizing it can be.

Jesus said, "Come to me, all you who are weary and burdened, and I will give you rest. Take my yoke upon you and learn from me, for I am gentle and humble in heart, and you will find rest for your souls. For my yoke is easy and my burden is light" (Matt. 11:28–30). Following Him and serving those entrusted to our care should not be exhausting but exhilarating! But in order to remain actively engaged and give our best as leaders, we must also make rest a priority.

We may not often think about rest being a requisite of sharing our treasure with others, but God certainly knew our bodies, minds, and spirits would need time for renewal when He told us to set aside the Sabbath as a day of rest. In fact, God Himself took the seventh day to rest after completing all His acts of creation. Being God, He did not need rest as we're accustomed to it, but He knew the best way to teach is by example.

Jesus would often invite His disciples to come with Him when they were tired and overworked—to take a break from their usual responsibilities. And these times were not reserved for the Sabbath, the seventh day of the week in the Jewish tradition. Christ encouraged His followers to commune with the Father anytime, in any place, and in any way. Jesus also made sure that His followers did not get burned out.

For example, when He saw all that His disciples had been doing, Christ gathered His disciples and made rest a priority: "'Come with me by yourselves to a quiet place and get some rest.' So, they went away by themselves in a boat to a solitary place" (Mark 6:31–32). Likewise, there are times when He would retreat in solitude to a quiet place to pray. Following His example, I try to read or I try to listen to the Word of God every morning. This practice energizes me so I can get ready to begin my day.

During hectic workdays, I often put aside time to pray for, or with, others. By lifting people up, I receive energy. I also meditate on the Word of God throughout the week, which rejuvenates me as well. When I'm concentrating on God's Word in my heart, then I know it affects my thoughts, my words, my attitudes, and my actions. It's internal recharging for external results! As I am lifted up, so are others. This is why I set aside multiple times to be spiritually at rest during the day.

SIMPLY SACRED

While we must recognize the value of rest, we must also use it as a resource for serving. Trying to find a balance is important, but some seasons require more from us than others. In the early years of my career, I often worked day and night to make ends meet. When I was selling FedEx services, I was often required to attend Monday-morning meetings on the West Coast, necessitating a flight on Sunday. As much as I hated leaving Thelma and our two small children to catch a Sunday-afternoon flight, my job required it. But I always did my best to make up the time with them later during the week—for their sake as well as my own.

Whenever I missed church services and spending Sunday with my family, I took comfort and found rest for my soul through praying and reading God's Word. I'd repeat those inspirational words from Psalm 91: "Whoever dwells in the shelter of the Most High will rest in the shadow of the Almighty" (v. 1). This verse reminded me to seek rest in the Lord, not only on the Sabbath, but anytime. Through prayer, I can dwell in the house of the Almighty anywhere, all the time, and it doesn't have to be in a church. I can also find rest in God by reading His Word anywhere and anytime.

We can all share in the privilege of His presence anywhere at any time. God sent Jesus to bring us into *relationship* with Himself, not to establish a religion. During His lifetime, Jesus' followers had been toiling under the burden of religious oppression with pressures that were put on those who believed in the Lord. Then, too, religious edicts were inflexible. Jesus' teachings encouraged people to have a relationship with God. He didn't propose a litany of rules and regulations that would complicate this relationship. The Lord wanted us to have a day of rest to get away from work and relax. He didn't want keeping the Sabbath to be a burden—that defeats the point for it in the first place! Jesus said, "The Sabbath was made for man, not man for the Sabbath" (Mark 2:27).

Nonetheless, I try to keep Sundays set aside as a special day of rest, renewal, and reconnection with God and with my family. Some of my happiest memories growing up emerge from Sundays with my parents and siblings. We would all go to church and usually enjoy a big Sunday lunch or dinner afterward. I can still taste my mother's fried chicken with mashed potatoes and gravy! We would eat and talk, maybe sing or just enjoy one another's company, maybe play a game or lounge outside if the weather was nice. My father worked long hours every day but always took Sunday off to be with us. Those times were simply sacred.

Thelma and I have tried to create the same kind of cherished memories for our own children. We would all go to Sunday school and then enjoy the worship service, followed by a big home-cooked meal, a picnic, or a special visit to one of our favorite restaurants. Often, we ended up discussing that day's sermon together. Thelma and I always enjoyed David II's and Kimberly's take on the minister's message. We encouraged our kids to think about their faith and what we were learning from the Bible. We would even watch sermons on TV together some Sunday afternoons!

Every day is a holy day. But setting aside one day to rest, and to do it with loved ones, makes Sundays very special. Rest allows us to share the treasure entrusted to us in an obvious but nonetheless often neglected way. With our hectic workweeks, the days can become so busy that we are distracted, and we don't take time to rest, to recharge, to praise the Lord and count our blessings. Sundays—or whatever day is set aside as a day of rest—remind us to pay attention to what really matters. We take time out to recognize how God has blessed us and to give thanks for His goodness. These times then inspire us and motivate us to share our abundance of treasure—whether money, minutes, or man power—with others.

YOUR LEADERSHIP FLYWHEEL:
Learn, Live, Lead, Legacy

1. When you think of the many ways God has blessed you, what gifts immediately come to mind? Spend a few moments thanking the Lord for these blessings and asking Him to show you how you can share them with others.

2. In this current season of your life, is it easier for you to share your time, your money, or your expertise? How have you been allocating your gifts in each of those categories? What are some other ways you can share them with the people around you?

3. How often do you take time to rest? How would you describe a typical Sunday or whatever day you set aside? What brings you the most joy during this day of spiritual rest and renewal?

> *Dear God, You have blessed me with so many good gifts. I'm so grateful for each one of them and give You thanks and praise for them all. May Your generosity grow inside me so that I will continue to share more and more of the treasures entrusted to me. Let me bless others the same way You consistently bless me. Help me to set aside time for rest and to reconnect with You and my family so that I may continue to lead by serving like Jesus. In His name, amen.*

CHAPTER 21

SHARE YOUR FAITH
IN ACTION

If anyone, then, knows the good they ought to do and doesn't do it, it is sin for them.

James 4:17

Your testimony has more power when your deeds reinforce your convictions. As you lead and serve in accordance with the Good Book, others will see your faith in action on a regular basis. Often, it's the cumulative impact of everyday, routine decisions and interactions that others notice more than anything else. Simple things like praying at the start of a meeting or checking in with someone who was out sick. Keeping your word and following through on promises made. Maintaining your convictions and obeying God's Word—especially when it might be easier or more profitable to compromise or cut corners.

The way a leader handles mistakes, disappointments, and delays communicates so much about what he or she really believes. It's one thing to say you want to do the right thing but another when you're in the moment and forced to choose. In our industry, we're constantly faced with situations that test our beliefs. For example, when we underbid a project, we're forced to choose between honoring our word and taking a loss.

The high-tech industry remains very competitive. We often bid for multi-million-dollar contracts, and some may run into eight and nine figures. Occasionally, we're awarded a contract only to realize later that we underestimated our costs. As a result, we're required to put in a lot of hard work, knowing in advance it will be a money-losing proposition. No one likes being in this kind of situation, but it helps if you know beforehand how you will handle it.

At WWT, we always honor an agreement, and if we underbid, then we try to learn from our mistakes. Our number one priority is making sure the customer's needs are served. We stick to our core values, always determined to do what we say we are going to do. Looking for ways to cut corners to "make the numbers work" is never an option. We might be forced to take a haircut at the time, but in the long run, we know doing the right thing always pays off.

SIMPLY THE BEST

In addition to serving many of the world's largest organizations, WWT also does business with many small companies, including some that are family owned and operated on a shoestring. We know what the pressures involved are firsthand, and we always try to work with these new companies and start-ups to accommodate their situations. We recently worked with a vendor, and their team needed more time to complete the work than the contract allowed. Legally, we could have pressured them to stick to the contractual deadline; instead, we waived some terms in the agreement to give them some leeway.

We didn't have to go this route, but in my mind, the spirit of the relationship was very important to us, and we wanted to protect it. This is not only the right thing to do, but over time, it's good business. We know that our clients, customers, and vendors talk to other potential partners. They may ask, "How is it when you work with WWT? What's it like to do business with David Steward and his team?" We want to make sure we know the answer every time! And we're committed to ensuring the response is more than just "OK" or "fine." We want to be the *best* at working with others in a way that reflects who we are and what we believe!

It all goes back to our core values of trust, honesty, and integrity. Although a deal might be structured one way, when I see that the other side is starting to lose money, I recognize that in a true partnership, it has to be good for both sides, a true win-win. In those situations, an honest talk with each other is in order. As a result of our conversation, we can look for a solution and terms that work for everyone. We can make it clear that we want our relationship to remain healthy more than we want to exploit an opportunity.

This way of doing business doesn't mean we're pushovers or lack strong boundaries. Just the opposite! We always do our due diligence and whatever legal and accounting principles require us to do. But at the end of the day, we focus on doing business with people whose character aligns with ours. No matter how good a deal is, or how much due diligence is done, ultimately our decision will be influenced by knowing we share the same values.

FAITH UNDER FIRE

Throughout the pages of Scripture, we find numerous examples of faithful individuals unwilling to compromise their principles. One of my favorites has to be the story of Shadrach, Meshach, and Abednego. They were friends of the prophet Daniel while being held captive, along with all the Israelites, by the conquering Babylonians. Throughout their captivity, Daniel and his friends faced numerous challenges to their faith in God. After all, the Babylonians were known for their anything-goes indulgences and their numerous pagan gods. The conflict of beliefs between the two cultures finally came to a life-or-death showdown when the king of Babylon's herald proclaimed, "As soon as you hear the sound of the horn, flute, zither, lyre, harp, pipe and all kinds of music, you must fall down and worship the image of gold that King Nebuchadnezzar has set up. Whoever does not fall down and worship will immediately be thrown into a blazing furnace" (Dan. 3:5–6).

Despite the king's threat, the three followers of Yahweh remained unwavering in their commitment to serve the Lord their God and only Him:

> King Nebuchadnezzar, we do not need to defend ourselves before you in this matter. If we are thrown into the blazing furnace, the God we serve is able to deliver us from it, and he will deliver us from Your Majesty's hand. But even if he does not, we want you to know, Your Majesty, that we will not serve your gods or worship the image of gold you have set up. (Daniel 3:16–18)

Furious, Nebuchadnezzar ordered the oven heated up *seven* times hotter than usual. Then two of his strongest soldiers were ordered to bind the three captives and throw them into the furnace, but the blistering heat was so intense it killed the two soldiers! The king and other royal onlookers then peered inside the furnace and noticed not three but four men walking around in the fiery furnace, unbound and unharmed, with the fourth appearing like "a son of the gods" (Dan. 3:25).

When the faithful trio then came out of the fire, unscathed, King Nebuchadnezzar was so impressed that he promoted the three men to high positions in his court!

Shadrach, Meshach, and Abednego refused to bend, and God demonstrated His faithfulness and protection over them. Similarly, we may go through the fires of life and face severe challenges, but if we stand by our principles, then God will honor us.

GRIP OF GRACE

Unlike Shadrach, Meshach, and Abednego, who went un-harmed in the furnace, Jesus suffered terribly. After being set up and falsely arrested, Christ was beaten, whipped, and forced to carry a heavy, rough-hewn crossbeam on his back for approximately half a mile up to Calvary. Some scholars speculate that the brutal beatings He endured would normally have killed a person under such physical punishment. Even more amazing is that while Jesus suffered unimaginable pain, He chose to forgive those responsible for His death: "When they came to the place called the Skull, they crucified him there, along with the criminals—one on his right, the other on his left. Jesus said, 'Father, forgive them, for they do not know what they are doing'" (Luke 23:33–34). Jesus' faith in His Father's goodness enabled Him to forgive those who wronged Him.

Perhaps even more remarkable is the way Jesus ministered even in His final moments before death:

> One of the criminals who hung there hurled insults at him: "Aren't you the Messiah? Save yourself and us!"
>
> But the other criminal rebuked him. "Don't you fear God," he said, "since you are under the same sentence? We are punished justly, for we are getting what our deeds deserve. But this man has done nothing wrong."
>
> Then he said, "Jesus, remember me when you come into your kingdom."
>
> Jesus answered him, "Truly I tell you, today you will be with me in paradise." (Luke 23:39–43)

Even with His final words, Jesus continued serving others by offering hope and assurance of peace, words of comfort. In His final moments, Christ extended forgiveness to someone who, by his own admission, deserved his punishment as a consequence of his crimes. Now, that's grace beyond measure! As servant-leaders, we are called to exercise the same willingness to forgive those who hurt us as well as extend grace to those who may deserve their consequences. Why? Because God has gripped each of us with His amazing grace even while we were yet sinners, just like the thief beside Jesus!

From followers of God such as Shadrach, Meshach, and Abednego to personal heroes of the faith in our lives today, we see the painful realities of refusing to compromise. Their examples, however, continue to inspire us as we seek to stand strong and share our faith in action. Ultimately, of course, the example of our Savior, Jesus Christ, fuels our ability to trust God and hold fast to our beliefs in Him. Following in His footsteps, we can set an example that inspires others to do what's right by obeying God and living by His Word.

YOUR LEADERSHIP FLYWHEEL:
Learn, Live, Lead, Legacy

1. When have you most recently faced a situation that stretched your faith or tested your convictions? How did you handle it? What consequences did you face? What did you learn from this situation about putting your faith in action?

2. Who has inspired you by the way they live out their faith and refuse to compromise their commitment to God? Why? How has their example given you strength and encouragement to always do the right thing?

3. What verse or passage in the Bible serves as your "go-to" source for strength and courage when you're facing unexpected challenges? How has God used this truth to empower you in the face of adversity?

> *Dear God, thank You for Your presence in the midst of life's challenges and daily struggles. It's not always easy to do the right thing, but I'm grateful for Your strength and power in the face of trials and temptations. May I reflect Your truth and goodness as well as the sacrificial example of Your Son, Jesus, in everything I do. In His name, amen.*

SECTION 8
Follow

CHAPTER 22

FOLLOW THE EXAMPLE OF JESUS

If anyone would come after me, let him deny himself and take up his cross and follow me. For whoever would save his life will lose it, but whoever loses his life for my sake will find it.
Matthew 16:24–25 ESV

The greatest impact a leader can have is by serving those who follow him. This is the example we see in the life of Jesus. His ministry and interactions with others consistently reflect God's love for them. When we follow Christ's example, we commit to being open, honest, respectful, and transparent with those entrusted to our care. The way we serve and lead becomes a living testimony to our commitment to follow Jesus in all areas of our lives.

His example reminds us to balance grace and truth, to add both flavor and illumination everywhere we serve. He said, "You are the salt of the earth. But if the salt loses its saltiness, how can it be made salty again? It is no longer good for anything, except to be thrown out and trampled underfoot. You are the light of the world. A town built on a hill cannot be hidden" (Matt. 5:13–14). Christ also emphasized the importance of our testimony by elaborating on this metaphor of light: "No one lights a lamp and hides it in a clay jar or puts it under a bed. Instead, they put it on a stand, so that those who come in can see the light. For there is nothing hidden that will not be disclosed, and nothing concealed that will not be known or brought out into the open" (Luke 8:16–17).

These are powerful words because Jesus basically commands us to be transparent. Openness is essential in business, and at WWT, we go beyond what the law requires. As a privately held company, it's not mandatory for us to disclose financial information that a publicly traded company is required to release. Still, we share financial information about WWT so our employees know about our profitability and our successes. They are also kept informed when we have less successful periods and lower profits.

We do this because they have a vested interest in the company. WWT's performance directly affects their lives and their futures. We want them to know the problems we face because they're often the ones who can furnish us with solutions. We provide a lot of visibility that includes the good, the bad, and the ugly!

We believe it is important for our people to have their family's support, and for this reason, they're encouraged to take home information companies do not typically share. We do it because we don't want to keep our employees' spouses in the dark. We don't want them to have unnecessary anxiety.

In volatile times when there are big swings in the market, I think that our voluntary transparency boosts morale. Our team members know we're not legally required to share certain financial information with them, but we still choose to do it. We want them informed and aware of the truth so they don't feel anxious or let their imaginations run away with a worst-case scenario. It's just another way of letting them know we care about them. We think of ourselves as a big family—and aren't family members privy to inside information? Sharing knowledge gives them a sense of ownership, and we want them invested in order to keep growing into the future. It's hard to drive to a destination if you don't have any visibility of where you are going. We want them to know we are all in this together.

SHARE YOUR FEARS

Transparency is often exhibited by how a leader will let others know some things about his or her past history. Such revelations help others appreciate your humanity as well as your understanding of the challenges they may be facing. Sharing how you've overcome obstacles or what you've learned from certain mistakes encourages them to push through and keep the faith.

While we're often taught that we shouldn't talk about ourselves, on the other hand, a leader shouldn't be so private that his people don't know who he is. There are some things you should let them know, and sometimes it's good to share the big failures you had. This lets them know that failure is acceptable and that you're human and have had your share of disappointments.

For this reason, I like telling others about the challenges we faced a few years after launching WWT. It's why I enjoy sharing the story of my car being repossessed and towed away while I was in a meeting just a few yards away. Transparency of this nature builds trust and loyalty. They probably get tired of hearing some of my stories, but I know they appreciate my willingness to be real. And why not? God is the reason for WWT's success; HE is the source—not David Steward.

RISK BY FAITH

Another reason we must practice transparency is so others can see the way we live by faith in taking risks. While writing from prison to his protégé Timothy, Paul reminds the younger believer, "For the Spirit God gave us does not make us timid, but gives us power, love and self-discipline" (2 Tim. 1:7). Not only is he imprisoned for preaching the gospel, but by the time he has written this, Paul has already endured several close brushes with death. He is encouraging Timothy to keep going and continue his ministry to build the church, realizing he will face perilous times and many obstacles.

Paul understands the persecutions the younger pastor will encounter, and yet as a servant-leader following the example of Jesus, he encourages Timothy to press forward, assuring him that his reward will be great in heaven. His courageous words remind me of another verse in the New Testament: "Without faith it is impossible to please God, because anyone who comes to him must believe that he exists and that he rewards those who earnestly seek him" (Heb. 11:6).

According to this verse, stepping out in faith and taking risks please God. This can be difficult in the face of what appears to be certain failure or defeat. But to succeed in following the example of Christ, servant-leaders must be willing to look beyond his or her circumstances. They must not succumb to discouragement in the face of failure.

When I make high-risk decisions, I often read these verses, and I am comforted to know God is with me. What others call risk taking is really just walking in faith. What truly excites me is when I am able to inspire others to take that walk in faith and seize opportunities that God has brought before them. When you can inspire someone this way, you give him or her a wonderful gift.

That's why I love rereading Scripture about how great Biblical men and women took risks against insurmountable odds. Noah building the ark. Jacob wrestling the angel. Moses parting the Red Sea. Rahab helping the Hebrew spies. And so many more! Hebrews 11 has been dubbed the "Hall of Faith" because it lists many of those who walked in faith in mighty ways. Read it every chance you get, and be inspired to walk in faith, setting an example of your own for those who follow.

YOUR LEADERSHIP FLYWHEEL:
Learn, Live, Lead, Legacy

1. What's the most difficult aspect of following Christ's example in the way you serve and lead? Why? How have you seen God strengthen and empower you in this area?

2. On a scale from one to ten, with one being "completely opaque" and ten being "completely transparent," how do you think most of the people you serve would rank you and your style of servant leadership? What score would you give yourself? Why?

3. How would you describe your style of transparency? How frequently do you share past struggles and failures? When do others see you taking risks? What kinds of sacrifices have you made for the good of your team and the people in your organization?

Dear Jesus, thank You for showing me what it means to lead others by serving them. I want to follow Your example and be salt and light to those around me. Help me to balance truth and grace so that they might glimpse Your character by the way I lead. Give me the courage to be transparent and to lay down my life for those I serve. In Your name I pray, amen.

CHAPTER 23

FOLLOW THROUGH ON YOUR WORD

But whoever keeps his word, in him truly the love of God is perfected. By this we may know that we are in him.

1 John 2:5 ESV

Good leadership requires consistency.

If you want to be a leader who serves like Jesus, then you must follow through on your word. You have to walk what you talk and live according to the same principles that you expect everyone else to follow. You cannot have standards and rules that fluctuate according to your moods, favorite people, or circumstances. Leadership by the Good Book is about aligning your beliefs, your words, and your actions with God's truth and the example of Christ. While the Bible makes this clear in numerous ways, one passage refers specifically to doing business:

> Do not have two differing weights in your bag—one heavy, one light. Do not have two differing measures in your house—one large, one small. You must have accurate and honest weights and measures, so that you may live long in the land the LORD your God is giving you. For the LORD your God detests anyone who does these things, anyone who deals dishonestly. (Deuteronomy 25:13–16)

FOLLOW THROUGH

Following through on your word not only honors God as you obey His commands, but it also demonstrates your character and the kind of business practices you follow. One memorable situation reflecting this truth occurred years ago when I was in New York City attending a conference. Numerous friends and colleagues throughout our industry attended, and I had arranged to meet with Nick De Tura, the VP over Alcatel-Lucent's supply chain and logistics, in the hotel lounge.

One of our WWT subsidiaries, Telcobuy, had been working with Nick's company for a while and now faced a tight bidding contest for the next contract. While we had served them well, I knew it could go either way because of the way business works. Nick and I were friends, and I hoped to impress upon him the value of sticking with our company. We weren't just offering another contract—we were promising to follow through on that contract and *keep* his business!

After we exchanged pleasantries, Nick said, "David, as you know, we also do business with one of your competitors. We've had a good relationship, and you know how no one wants to change."

When Nick said this, my heart sank. I figured he was looking for a nice way to inform me that we didn't win the new contract because he knew how disappointed I'd be. Nonetheless, I nodded and kept listening, waiting for the other shoe to fall.

"You know how difficult it is to pull out an incumbent," Nick continued. "When we select a vendor, before we make our decision, we do extensive research. With this one, you were up against some strong competition. Basically, the race has been a dead heat."

Nick paused as if to choose his next words carefully. The momentarily silence held the tension of what he was about to reveal. "It hasn't been announced yet, David, but the business is yours! While it was a tough call among so many excellent candidates, the tiebreaker came down to *how* you conduct business. You and your people truly share the same philosophy as mine: The customer is always right. I believe you and your team will always go that extra mile to make sure we succeed."

I smiled, letting his good news sink in.

"There's something else I want you to know," Nick added. "Some of our people wanted to try another vendor, and I had to nudge them to go with Telcobuy. I'm sticking my neck out for you because if your company doesn't do its job in handling the movement of product to our customers, my job will be on the line. I'm counting on you, David. Don't let me down."

Overwhelmed by what Nick said, I promised to use every resource at our disposal to make sure we exceeded his expectations. We shook on it, and gratitude immediately bubbled up inside me to become a prayer of thanksgiving and a praise of rejoicing. And here's the thing: The promise we made that day is the commitment we make to all our partners every day. It's *how* we always do business!

A few years later, we were given an opportunity to demonstrate our commitment to Nick and his company above and beyond our regular terms. Nick called and informed me there was a power outage in New Jersey, and they needed to get a shipment out to a customer with no power whose entire warehouse was down. I told Nick to let me see how I could help come up with a solution.

After thinking through options, I called one of my old friends, Tom Voss, then CEO of Ameren, a power company in the Midwest. Tom made some calls back East and got additional disaster support crews to help Con Edison make repairs and restore power there. With everything up and running again, we got Nick's shipment delivered to his customer on time.

"Well, David," Nick began when he called to thank me, "you said you'd do whatever was necessary when we needed help, and you came through! We were stuck and needed someone to step in and provide assistance in solving this problem. You are a man of your word, and I look forward to many more years of doing business with you and your people. I know I can always count on you to do what you promise to do."

CONSISTENCY CREATES CULTURE

Nick's words humbled me. Ultimately, though, what he said honored God because I was simply doing what I had promised to do. God is always faithful and honors His promises, and I work hard to follow through and always honor mine. It's how I want to be treated; so, it's how I treat others.

Leaders who promise one thing and do another aren't good leaders. You can't be inconsistent and lukewarm when it comes to your dedication to serving others. In the Bible, we're warned about being tepid in our faith: "I know your deeds, that you are neither cold nor hot. I wish you were either one or the other! So, because you are lukewarm—neither hot nor cold—I am about to spit you out of my mouth" (Rev. 3:15–16). This assessment was addressed to the Laodiceans, and it not only described their wishy-washy faith but did so in a way they understood all too well.

At the time this charge was made, their city drinking water traveled via an aqueduct from a spring about six miles away. By the time their water flowed that distance, it was lukewarm. Unlike the water from the hot springs that the Laodiceans used for bathing, this liquid was not cool enough for enjoyable drinking. Even today, we tend to like our beverages hot or cold! We want a hot cup of coffee and a cold glass of iced tea. Consequently, something lukewarm disappoints on both accounts—just as the inconsistent faith of the Laodiceans disappointed God.

Good leaders cannot be lukewarm. We either have to serve wholeheartedly and do the right thing every time, or else we shouldn't claim that we're following Jesus. Our behavior, the way we do business, should reflect integrity, honesty, and consistency of character. We must be compelled in our minds and hearts to represent Christ and the Word of God in a way that all people will know what to expect from us. They know who we are and what we believe because we always act in accordance with His teachings.

When others interact with us, they can anticipate what we will do because it will be what we know God wants us to do. They can expect that we will reflect scriptural principles in ways that remain consistent over time. It's easy to come in strong and make a good first impression when you're trying to attract a new customer or land a new contract. But you should never promise anything that you can't deliver. As the old saying goes, "Under-promise and overdeliver."

Following through on our promises is reflected not only in our actions but also in our words and attitudes. We should continually offer words of encouragement and hope. As Jesus' followers, we will be known by our love. We should treat people the way we would want to be treated. This applies to how we treat everyone: the sales rep, the tech support, the janitor, the receptionist, the warehouse crew—everyone. No matter what a person's job or station in life might be, we treat them with kindness and respect. We serve them by our consideration, our loyalty, and our dedication. We do everything within our power to bless them and make their lives better as a result of interacting with us.

As servant-leaders following Jesus, that's who we are. It's what makes our lives worthwhile and our service more than just good business. Consistency creates a culture, an environment, a style of relating that others cannot dismiss or ignore. People want to do business with people who are always straightforward and honorable. It's easy to play games and say what's expedient in order to tell someone what they want to hear. It's much more challenging to speak the truth and to follow through every time. But it's what Jesus did during His time on Earth and what God still calls us to do today.

SEEING IS BELIEVING

A few years ago, I visited Seoul, South Korea, to meet with Samsung SDS CEO, Yoosung Chung. We spent a couple of days together, and before each meal, I said a prayer. While Samsung's located on the other side of the world with revenues that exceed $200 billion, I prayed before meals like I always do. Nothing formal, but just the kind of prayer I'd say in a casual neighborhood restaurant with a small group of WWT associates.

This practice has been with me all my life. Whether I'm with a client, a partner, a WWT associate, or a dignitary, I am going to pray before we eat. I do this because it is important to me—in addition, it also sets the tone for others to know the kind of authentic relationship I want to have with them. It invokes God's blessing on our time together and establishes a warm basis for our conversation.

My new friends in South Korea didn't seem to mind my praying, and in fact, Chung, along with the other Samsung executives present, seemed very thankful. They saw me the way I hope everybody sees me: just being myself. To try to act like someone I'm not would be disingenuous and deceptive—simply put, it would be flat-out wrong. Whether I'm in St. Louis or Seoul, Pittsburgh or Paris, a cubicle or a café, the way I treat people should not vary. Anyone who spends time with me knows what to expect right away. I may not get it right every time, because God is still working on me, but what they see is what they get!

Everyone has a responsibility in ministry to be themselves with those they seek to serve, regardless of whether you sweep the floors or head the world's biggest corporation. We're all servants and must practice stewardship in natural, authentic ways. Interestingly enough, while it was a business trip, Chung and I talked about so much more than business. For example, we discussed our community involvement, the common traits that our companies share, and our views on the future. When others see the way we live out our beliefs in business, they glimpse God's faithfulness in our lives.

Seeing is believing!

SETTING THE STANDARD

Leading by the Good Book means being who God made us to be in all aspects of our lives. Authenticity and humility are hallmarks of this type of leadership. When you think about it, executives are no different than anyone else. The sun comes up and we get out of bed. The sun goes down and we go to sleep. We all need three meals a day. Sure, we can act like we're different, but whether you own an NFL team or drive a bus, you're still human. People are much more alike than they are different.

I can't stress enough the importance of consistency and follow-through in leadership. A great example for you to consider is the difference between a thermometer and a thermostat. One registers the temperature and the other regulates it. Good leaders are intentional and set the example. They don't lead by reacting and doing what others want or what circumstances dictate. Good leaders set the standard and maintain it.

Without a doubt, this truth undergirds the foundation of any business, of any life, of any person. This is why every time I make a decision, I challenge myself by asking if it is in line with the Word of God and what it teaches. His truth is eternal. As His Word testifies, "The grass withers and the flowers fall, but the word of our God endures forever" (Isa. 40:8). When we base our servant leadership on Biblical principles, we enjoy the freedom to lead with authenticity and consistency. We follow through on our word because we follow His Word!

YOUR LEADERSHIP FLYWHEEL:
Learn, Live, Lead, Legacy

1. What does it mean for you to follow through on your word? When was the last time you kept a promise you made to a team member, supervisor, customer, or client? How do others respond when you follow through and do what you said you would do?

2. Would the people you serve in your present role of leadership describe your style as consistent? Why or why not? What are ways you can demonstrate more consistency as you follow the example of Jesus by walking what you talk?

3. How does relying on God's Word as the basis for your leadership principles make it easier for you to serve? Have you experienced situations where it also makes it more challenging for you to serve? How so?

Dear God, You are timeless and eternal, the same "I AM" in past, present, and future. May Your consistency and faithfulness always remind me to serve honorably as Your steward. Help me to follow through on my word, Lord, and not to make promises I cannot keep. Through the power of Your Spirit in me, I want others to know that I'm Your servant and that I lead according to Your truth. In Jesus' name, amen.

CHAPTER 24

FOLLOW THOSE
YOU LEAD

So the last will be first, and the first will be last.

Matthew 20:16

Good leaders know that often it takes more than just a willingness to delegate to others—they must be willing to *follow* those they empower. This might include following their direction, their advice, their recommendation, or their leadership in a certain area of expertise. Once again, we see how trust is so vitally important. But as long as we're committed to serving one another, then the results will always honor God. We're told, "Each of you should use whatever gift you have received to serve others, as faithful stewards of God's grace in its various forms" (1 Pet. 4:10).

Serving one another within community is at the heart of team leadership.

I learned a lot about this kind of teamwork while playing basketball on an athletic scholarship at Central Missouri State. It wasn't the team that had the five best athletes on the floor that won championships—it was five dedicated athletes playing as one team. So many schools had great players with amazing abilities, but they didn't gel as a team. It takes a certain kind of humility, trust, dedication, and fellowship to be part of a team that's bigger than your ego.

EXPERT OPINION

The best leaders know how to create a team that's always greater than the sum of its individuals. In team sports, players must work in unison to win. Football, like basketball, requires everyone to execute his assignment in coordination with his teammates. If, say, a lineman doesn't block an opposing defensive lineman, the quarterback is vulnerable. It's also a busted play if a receiver doesn't run his assigned route. Every player must perform his assignment in synchronization with his teammates. Likewise, good corporate leaders manage this way and, like on any successful team, rely on specialists: accountants, attorneys, engineers, and others in production, marketing, warehousing, and in varied areas throughout the company.

As a business owner, I must rely on people in their field of expertise. It's my job to coordinate these people in leadership positions so everything comes together and runs smoothly. Personally, I don't have a particular area of expertise in any area of our business. I'm an entrepreneur and a generalist. I'm a guy who takes risks—with a high tolerance for making bold decisions. By surrounding myself with an excellent team of experts, I'm continually trying to make the odds work in our favor. Good leaders excel at uniting experts into an exceptional team.

Examples of teamwork appear throughout the Bible. Moses relied on the twelve tribes of Israel, each with different attributes while sharing the Jewish faith. The heads of these tribes reported to Moses, and his job was to have them work in unison. Similarly, Jesus had His twelve disciples that had different skills and responsibilities. Some seemed to be better at handling details and preparations. Others may have been better speakers or interacted more easily with the many crowds following Jesus.

UNITED WE STAND

Members of the same team assess things from different perspectives, which can cause conflict within an organization. Working with many specialists, each of them with a different point of view, can result in a tense group dynamic full of underlying dissention. Getting everyone in a large organization to work together as a team is quite challenging.

For example, take a department store CEO who must get his management team to agree on an annual budget. His marketing executive wants an increase in money for advertising, the merchandising manager wants more money to carry a larger inventory, the warehouse manager wants to update the distribution system, the human resources manager wants to hire more people, and the chief financial officer wants to reduce expenditures across the board. One team member's goal may appear to contradict or interfere with another's!

The leader's job is to get all members on the team to work in harmony regardless of anyone's special interests or distinct agendas. Often a generalist, such as myself, must gather all the facts and opinions of the top executives and, based on information that's not privy to everyone, make a decision that may not be well received by all members of the management team. This burden is part of the weight that a strong leader must endure— running a business is not a popularity contest! It's always about serving the best interests of the team and not any one individual or department.

DIVIDED WE FALL

When individuals work at cross-purposes, they defeat the entire team. We see an example of this kind of impasse in the early church. While imprisoned, the apostle Paul wrote to two women who were having a squabble: "I plead with Euodia and I plead with Syntyche to be of the same mind in the Lord. Yes, and I ask you, my true companion, help these women since they have contended at my side in the cause of the gospel, along with Clement and the rest of my co-workers" (Phil. 4:2–3). Here we see a reference to an earlier conflict, which only emphasizes the way good leaders face conflicts head-on.

While it may be tempting to let team members work it out among themselves or to ignore relational issues if they don't slow down production, strong leaders know that how we relate to one another matters. And sooner or later, the problem will eventually spill over into the effectiveness of the team. Paul urges us to "be of the same mind in the Lord" in order to reflect God's character and to restore unity within the church. Good leaders know this willingness to address conflicts within the team is essential for the same reasons. Because the old saying rings true: "United we stand; divided we fall."

While petty personal differences can poison the power of a team, a cooperative spirit of unity can maximize its strength. You've likely heard the expression "I've got your back"—in the military, at the big game, and across the boardroom. The adage has been around for a long time and emphasizes the way we need others to help us maximize our potential. Whether providing protection against unseen dangers or simply another pair of eyes to cover people's blind spots, good leaders always have others' backs.

The phrase also reminds us that we're stronger together than individually. People need each other to do their best. In the Bible, Solomon, considered the world's wisest man, concludes,

> *Two are better than one,*
> *because they have a good return for their labor:*
> *If either of them falls down,*
> *one can help the other up.*
> *But pity anyone who falls*
> *and has no one to help them up.*

Also, if two lie down together, they will keep warm.
But how can one keep warm alone?
Though one may be overpowered,
two can defend themselves.
A cord of three strands is not quickly broken.
(Ecclesiastes 4:9–12)

The concept of teamwork always promotes the premise that two are better than one. No matter what your accountant might say, when it comes to teamwork from the kingdom-of-God perspective, one plus one equals three! More can be accomplished when we work together as a collective force than when each team member works independently. In his reference to a third cord, Solomon also advises us that while we will have failures along the way, as a team, we can work together to overcome obstacles. As we know, a chain is only as strong as its weakest link. In the world of business, a good leader maximizes the strengths of his entire team.

Military missions are successful because they unite specialists on teams with specific goals. They often include a designated communications specialist, a navigator, a mechanic, a medic, and so on. Each excels in his or her area but has been cross-trained in leadership and knows what to do in the event that another member is harmed or incapacitated. If there's a secret to team building in business, this is it: Good leaders build teams with specialists that are well versed in areas outside their field of expertise.

BRING YOUR BEST

Circumstances are constantly changing, and well-managed teams are cross-trained so when the unexpected happens, one team player can perform another's assignment. Whether in military operations or factory production, team members learn to do a variety of jobs and roles so they can fill in for one another as needed. This way, the functional success of the team doesn't rely on any one individual. It's vital that everyone know his or her specific role on the team, but they must also be able to cover multiple roles as needed.

We certainly see this kind of global, history-changing impact in the leadership of Jesus. His selection of the particular individuals who became His disciples is especially striking when you consider that none of them had leadership training of any kind. None of them had a rabbinic background or experience leading in the temple. Not one launched his own business—unless you count the fact that seven were fishermen. They were commoners, normal everyday people leading typical lives of their time. But Jesus knew the impact they could have working together as a team and empowered by the Holy Spirit.

The same is true for us today: God knows that we're better when we're part of something bigger than ourselves. As Brandon says, "We want the best *for* you, and the best *from* you!"

YOUR LEADERSHIP FLYWHEEL:
Learn, Live, Lead, Legacy

1. What have you learned from participating in various teams over the course of your life? How has being part of a team made you a stronger, better servant-leader?

2. What criteria do you use, other than expertise in their particular areas, when selecting individuals to be part of a team you're leading? How do you handle personality differences or conflicts within your teams? When have you most recently been forced to address or resolve a conflict within a team?

3. From your experience, what qualities or traits are essential for a team to succeed? Why? How does following Christ's example help you serve your team more effectively?

Dear Lord, thank You for choosing me to serve on the only team that matters—Your team. I'm humbled to see how You continue to work through me to build teams that glorify You and advance Your kingdom. Give me wisdom, strength, and sensitivity to Your Spirit as I seek to unite those entrusted to my care in order to further heavenly causes. In Jesus' name, amen.

SECTION 9
Grow

CHAPTER 25

GROW THROUGH INTERNAL STRUGGLES

Peace I leave with you; my peace I give you. I do not give to you as the world gives. Do not let your hearts be troubled and do not be afraid.

John 14:27

As a young boy, I developed a lisp and was put in a special elocution class to help me address this setback. It took years before my speech impediment was no longer noticeable. Even into my early adulthood, I doubted that I would ever be able to speak from a podium without a lisp and becoming too self-conscious to deliver a speech or message. Any time I had to deliver a report in front of the class and later to give a speech, I relied on prepared notes, basically a script, to get me through the ordeal.

Gradually, over time, I realized that my faith in God provided me with the strength and courage I needed to win this battle. To-day, I actually enjoy speaking to people and usually don't rely on notes unless I need to quote someone or cite extensive data. My favorite thing is usually the question-and-answer sessions after I speak, which would have terrified me once upon a time. Many times, I now invite Brandon to accompany me and serve as moderator.

I remember one of the first times we shared the stage. I had been invited to speak at the governor of Missouri's prayer breakfast several years ago. I insisted that Brandon be the moderator because he and I share the same sensitivity to the Holy Spirit's prompting on stage. When Brandon began to prepare for the event, he developed several questions that would help facilitate our conversation on stage, as led by the Holy Spirit. He asked if I wanted to review the questions in advance, which, I might add, is a reasonable question. However, I told him that I wanted my answers to be spontaneous, not prepared in advance, so people can know that what I say comes from my heart. As the Good Book says, "For out of the abundance of the heart his mouth speaks" (Luke 6:45 NKJV).

TURN HURT INTO HARVEST

While overcoming my lisp and the accompanying feelings it produced, I often thought of something my mother frequently said. Anytime one of my siblings or I faced adversity, my mother would remind us that the Bible says we should "turn our hurt into harvest," her abbreviated version of Psalm 126:6. This is probably the way her parents and grandparents who toiled the soil said it. I never forgot those words, and they have helped get me through many difficult times. They provide a reminder that faith in God combined with hard work can overcome what appears to be sure defeat. We can choose self-pity and passivity, or we can choose to act in faith and trust God with the results.

Unfortunately, many people submit too easily to adversity, or they avoid it altogether. Once knocked down, they stay down. When their path gets blocked or their plans derail, they give up instead of growing up. They assume the world is against them and that they are powerless to change their circumstances or influence their future. Because they cannot see a way to move forward and fulfill their dreams, they quit and look for an escape from the pain of their lives, pain compounded by their own self-defeating behavior.

Today, I see many young adults struggling with the pressure to be an overnight, viral sensation. They have watched their peers seemingly turn an online song, comedy monologue, or acting or musical performance into "instant" success, so they assume they should expect the same. They've seen college dropouts launch profitable online businesses, create video games, and invent new service apps and appear to become instant millionaires. Then when they can't get funding for their new start-up, they lose enthusiasm for their idea and lose confidence in themselves.

But that's simply not the way success works for most people, even in our age of social media and instant online connections. No matter how talented someone might appear to be on social media or otherwise, or how much financial support they have from investors, success still requires hard work, dedication, and perseverance. You will have times when you're exhausted, frustrated, overwhelmed, doubtful, and disappointed. Which is why in order to lead and succeed, to serve and not swerve, you must have faith!

The Good Book tells us that faith is "confidence in what we hope for and assurance about what we do not see" (Heb. 11:1). Faith, like a muscle in our body, requires exercise to grow. When we choose to give our best and trust God for the rest, as Brandon and his family say, then we begin to surrender our will to His more and more easily. We see Him do things that we know we could never have done on our own. Every time I pull into our parking lot at WWT or walk through my office door, I can't help but smile and say a silent prayer of humble thanks. Despite how hard I've worked, I know the only reason WWT has succeeded and continues to grow is by God's power and through His goodness.

FAIL WITHOUT FAILING

Instead of giving in when circumstances don't seem to go as planned, leaders who serve like Jesus know they must rely on God to guide them, empower them, and sustain them. These are the people who refuse to give in, no matter how overwhelming the odds against them. While grit does not assure positive results, it goes a long way in determining success. You will always face internal struggles that come and go depending on your circumstances, your moods, and the reactions of those around you. Wise leaders, however, learn, that faithful persistence pays off.

Successful people in all fields refuse to allow fear of failure to defeat them. They accept failure as an inevitable part of the process of growth, regroup and refocus, and figure out other ways to move toward their goals. It's been said, "The secret of success is to go from failure to failure without failing."

Like all great leaders and innovators throughout history, we will each face adversity in pursuit of the destination to which God calls us. In order to persevere and succeed, we must learn to change the way we view our failures and the resulting internal struggles we may experience. The Bible reveals the secret to this transformative endeavor: "Consider it pure joy, my brothers and sisters, whenever you face trials of many kinds, because you know that the testing of your faith produces perseverance. Let perseverance finish its work so that you may be mature and complete, not lacking anything" (James 1:2–4). This passage has given me strength, comfort, and incentive to keep going on countless occasions.

BLESSED ASSURANCE

One of the best examples of someone learning to rely on God to overcome their internal struggles has to be Moses. For more than forty years, he led the people of Israel on their exodus out of bondage in Egypt and into the freedom of the Promised Land. However, as a consequence of his disobedience, Moses knew that he would never enter the Promised Land. Nonetheless, he reassured the Israelites that under Joshua's leadership and with God's blessings, they would live and thrive in the land that the Lord had promised to their fathers. "Be strong and courageous, for you must go with this people into the land that the LORD swore to their ancestors to give them, and you must divide it among them as their inheritance. The LORD himself goes before you and will be with you; he will never leave you nor forsake you. Do not be afraid; do not be discouraged" (Deut. 31:7–8).

When he offered this blessing of reassurance, Moses was 120 years old. Instead of focusing on his personal disappointment or sense of loss, he chose to see the bigger picture of God's hand at work and to encourage the people he had been leading and serving for four decades. Moses himself knew the power that words of encouragement carry when faced with internal struggles of fear and doubt.

Right after God called Moses to lead and serve, he initially resisted because of what would be required of him, including a showdown with Pharaoh. "Who am I that I should go to Pharaoh and bring the Israelites out of Egypt?" he asked (Exod. 3:11). Even after God reassured Moses of His presence, the man who would soon part the Red Sea continued thinking of excuses and worst-case scenarios: "Suppose I go to the Israelites and say to them, 'The God of your fathers has sent me to you,' and they ask me, 'What is his name?' Then what shall I tell them?" To which God replied, "I AM WHO I AM. This is what you are to say to the Israelites: 'I AM has sent me to you'" (vv. 13–14).

Similarly, when Moses died and his mantle of leadership went to Joshua, the Lord provided the same kind of blessed assurance to the new leader: "No one will be able to stand against you all the days of your life. As I was with Moses, so I will be with you; I will never leave you nor forsake you. Be strong and courageous, because you will lead these people to inherit the land I swore to their ancestors to give them" (Josh. 1:5–6). God goes on to tell Joshua two more times to "be strong and courageous" (vv. 7–9). When the Lord tells you something three times in a row, you would be wise to listen!

Moses and Joshua are not the only examples, of course. Throughout the pages of Scripture, we see God consistently encouraging His people when they're battling internal emotions of fear, doubt, and insecurity. Really, it's not surprising when you think about it, because after all, the Bible is the most inspirational book ever written! The essence of God's Word is good news offering hope and encouragement.

When looking for a personal dose of divine medicine, consider the Lord's promise to us: "So do not fear, for I am with you; do not be dismayed, for I am your God. I will strengthen you and help you; I will uphold you with my righteous right hand" (Isa. 41:10). When you keep your faith in God and glimpse the extent of His power, you can expect to see the unexpected!

REINFORCE YOUR DREAMS

Another way to overcome internal struggles is to reinforce your dreams. Back in the days when I was sharing Thelma's car because mine had been repossessed, the four of us would pile in to take a Sunday drive. I would drive us to the most affluent residential neighborhoods in St. Louis and cruise by the biggest mansions in town. We would all take turns pointing out our favorites as we oohed and aahed over these homes that looked more like museums than private residences. During those hard times, I promised Thelma that someday we would live in one of the most beautiful homes in all of Missouri. She would smile and tell me the same thing every Sunday: "As long as the four of us are together, I'm willing to live in a house made of cardboard boxes if necessary. I love you, David, and I believe in you."

My wife is not the only one who has reinforced my dreams by their encouragement. From a young age, I was blessed with a mother who was always giving me words of encouragement and constantly lifting me up. She told me that I was special and that there was no limit to what I could accomplish. She was quite convincing! There were also Boy Scout leaders, teachers, and coaches who were there for me during times when I struggled or doubted myself. I was blessed to be in a community of believers—people of faith—who saw more in me than I could see in myself at times. Their faith not only inspired me but also prepared me for what I would do with my life.

Just as others have inspired me to grow through my internal struggles, I have tried to pass on what I learn in order to encourage and support the people who are entrusted to my care. This isn't just my natural tendency but obedience to God. We're told, "Therefore encourage one another and build each other up, just as in fact you are doing" (1 Thess. 5:11). Encouraging people and lifting their spirits is an important part of my daily routine and should be for all leaders.

Every single day, I praise people for their good work and thank them for their contributions. Whenever there is an opportunity to pat someone on the back for doing a good job, I do it. It's an essential responsibility of leadership. A "well done!" from a business owner, CEO, or supervisor can make someone's day. Helping someone feel good about their contribution doesn't take much effort, not to mention it makes me feel good to see the other person's positive reaction. It's like throwing a boomerang. You throw something out and it comes back, often with more force than you threw it out with. Once again, it comes back to reaping and sowing. Sometimes the best way to overcome our internal struggles is to help someone else overcome theirs!

Clinging to my faith and encouraging others has always enabled me to keep the right attitude every day, which wasn't always easy in the early days when I had to be excited about the future of this business even when it didn't look promising to others. I recall a conversation with Luke Fouke, who was my first landlord as well as a good friend and mentor. At a time when the company was on the verge of going under, Luke said, "David, what do you see here that I don't see? What is it about this company that makes you so excited?"

My answer was simple: I was excited because my company was my ministry, and I had a commitment to my people that we would succeed. God had assured me that my dream was possible. With His help, I was determined not to disappoint my family, my partners, bankers, or our WWT team. I was completely blinded to negative thoughts and what must have seemed obvious—imminent failure and probable bankruptcy—to others. As I look back, those initial obstacles were so enormous that we could never have possibly succeeded without God. Seeing Him at work back then confirmed my faith and confidence in God and assured me that all things are possible through Him.

Our internal struggles are no match for the power of God!

YOUR LEADERSHIP FLYWHEEL:
Learn, Live, Lead, Legacy

1. What are the greatest personal struggles you have overcome in your life? What did you learn from this experience? What role did your faith in God play in your victory?

2. What internal struggles continue to challenge you? How do they manifest themselves in the way you lead and serve? What promises from God's Word offer you strength and courage as you win the battle over these personal struggles?

3. Who has reinforced your dreams by believing in you and encouraging you in the midst of particularly trying times? How are you now passing on this kind of encouragement to others?

> *Dear Lord, I'm so grateful for the many ways You have empowered me to overcome the various challenges of my life. When I feel afraid, uncertain, desperate, or insecure, I know that You are with me and will not abandon me. Help me to rest in Your holy presence and to trust You with all that I need to lead and serve in my present role. May I continue to encourage others as so many people have encouraged me during times of stress and struggle. In Jesus' name, amen.*

CHAPTER 26

GROW THROUGH EXTERNAL CHALLENGES

The righteous person may have many troubles, but the LORD delivers him from them all.

Psalm 34:19

In addition to the growth opportunities presented by our internal struggles, leaders are also stretched by external challenges. The two—internal struggles and external challenges—are intertwined, and one often leads to the other. Regardless of the form it takes, however, adversity also forces us to be resourceful, resilient, and reliant on God in ways we might never have discovered otherwise.

One of my favorite examples to illustrate this point emerges from Enterprise, Alabama, early in the twentieth century. When the boll weevil devastated the farming community's cotton fields from 1915 to 1918, most farmers lost their entire cotton crops. At the time, King Cotton continued to be the primary cash crop in the South, but instead of accepting their circumstances and giving into defeat, these "Enterprising" farmers decided to grow another crop—peanuts.

Not only did the switch return vital nutrients to the soil depleted by decades of cotton cultivation, but peanuts also became an even more lucrative crop. The change from cotton to peanuts made Coffee County, Alabama, where Enterprise is the county seat, one of the richest areas in the country. Eventually, residents erected a monument honoring the boll weevil! The monument serves as a reminder that when faced with adversity, perseverance combined with innovation and hard work can turn what appears to be defeat into victory.

BIGGER, NOT BITTER

I learned this lesson throughout my childhood and adolescence. Like most African Americans growing up in rural Missouri in the 1950s and 1960s, I faced racial discrimination on a daily basis. Some incidents remain more vivid than others. As I mentioned in an earlier chapter, when I was around ten years old, I went door-to-door selling Christmas cards to earn money to pay for Scout camp the next summer. After school, I'd walk through the various mostly white neighborhoods nearby hoping to find people who could afford to buy the cards.

At that time Clinton, Missouri, was a segregated town, and many of those residents I called on had never had a black person knock on their door to sell them something. Some folks were kind and politely said, "No, thank you," while a handful actually ordered a box or two. Others, however, slammed their door in my face while making derogatory remarks. Their racial slurs were particularly hurtful. On several occasions, I came home with tears stinging my cheeks.

While comforting me, my mother never let my hurt feelings fester into bitterness or hatred. She would always manage to find a verse or story in her big King James Version of the Bible, its cover cracking and pages dog-eared from use. I can still hear her soft voice: "Avenge not yourselves, but rather give place unto wrath: for it is written, Vengeance is mine; I will repay, saith the Lord" (Rom. 12:19). She would look up and tell me, "There are mean-spirited people in this world. Don't let their words hurt you. And never become bitter because that will hurt you, not them—they don't care how you feel."

Her words soothed me and gave me the courage to go out the next day to sell more Christmas cards. Looking back, I know how much it must have hurt her to see people vent their racial prejudices on one of her children. Her maturity of faith, however, strengthened her commitment to teach us how to love others—even our enemies. My mother was determined that I would not quit, and I was able to save up enough money to go to camp that following summer.

IN THIS CORNER...

While I faced many instances of racism growing up, I also enjoyed the respect and kindness of other people. One person in particular showed me how friendship transcends race and endures beyond childhood. My friendship with Bob Cox, now an attorney in Clinton and still my good friend, goes back to when we were boys attending grade school together. In fact, back then Bob may have been my only friend at school!

As the only African American boy in my class, I could hardly escape the attention of my classmates, especially a handful of bullies. My nickname back then was Spider because I was so tall and gangly, all arms and legs, and while I wasn't the biggest or toughest kid, I always had grit. Bob Cox, who was the biggest kid in our class, easily outweighed me by a hundred pounds, but when I asked if he wanted to wrestle with me, he agreed. While we had fun together, I also figured that if the bullies saw that I was willing to wrestle the biggest kid day after day, then they would leave me alone. It worked—with a little help from Bob.

You see, every day at recess, while Bob and I wrestled, I would always try to grab his arm and throw him over my shoulder, the way I had seen wrestlers do it on TV. With Bob so much bigger and heavier than I was, though, there was really no way I could successfully flip him to the ground. Nonetheless, I kept trying. Then one day a group of kids gathered around to watch us, and one of the bullies made a racist comment. I knew better than to respond to it, but I could tell that the bully's remark also upset Bob. He didn't say anything, but that day when I tried to flip him, he fell to the ground! Our little audience gasped in surprise, and from then on, none of the bullies ever bothered me again. We never talked about it, but I've never forgotten the gift my buddy Bob gave me on the playground that day!

Another childhood incident I'll also never forget revealed where Bob picked up his kind nature and respect for all people. As I recall, he had invited me to play with him at his home after school one day. His family lived on a farm, and his mother operated a beauty shop out of their home. While Bob and I were running around playing that afternoon, I saw one of his mom's customers glaring at me. "What's *he* doing here?" I overheard her say. "You have to get him out of here right now!"

You could've heard a pin drop in that moment. Bob was visibly upset, and the lady's words definitely hurt me. But then Bob's mother stopped what she was doing and went over to the lady and calmly said, "Please leave my house right now—you are *not* welcome here. Take your business elsewhere." Bob and I looked at each other and enjoyed the bond of our friendship, communicating once again without saying a word.

RAILROAD TIES

Friends like Bob Cox and his family definitely helped me persevere in the face of racism. Nonetheless, by the time I graduated from Central Missouri State University (now University of Central Missouri) with a BS degree in business administration with an emphasis on industrial organization, I had vowed never to go into sales. As an African American with only an average GPA, I figured it would simply be too hard to overcome most people's prejudiced perceptions. Unable to find a business-related job, I accepted a part-time position as a substitute teacher in a St. Louis public school.

Working part-time on a teacher's salary wasn't enough to get by, and after months of searching, I was finally hired by the Boy Scouts of America, an improvement from subbing, but not a position in business. So, I continued sending out resumes to companies and finally landed at Wagner Electric as a supervisor in manufacturing. Unfortunately, less than a year later, I was laid off. So I had to start all over again by sending out more resumes.

For the first couple of years after college graduation, it was two steps forward and one step back. I probably sent out about four hundred resumes and averaged a couple of job interviews per week. If I didn't know what rejection looked like before, I sure did by then! Eventually, I got my first break when a series of interviews at Missouri Pacific Railroad Company led to a marketing and sales position.

It was my dream job. The company was committed to hiring African Americans, and I was one of the first on its payroll. Following an extensive yearlong training program, I became the first person of color to sell rail services in the railroad industry. I will always be grateful that Missouri Pacific invested so much in my training and gave me the opportunity to sell its services.

After my training, the company sent me to New Orleans. Just imagine a six-foot-five black man with a mustache, wearing an Afro that made me six foot eight, calling on people that had never had a business discussion with anyone of color in their entire lives! I was clearly an outsider, and the message was clear about how they viewed me. Not only did they dislike my coming to call on them, but their attitude reflected outrage. "How *dare* the railroad send this person of color! They want our business, and *this* is who they send?"

Some customers would make derogatory remarks about me to management, calling and writing to complain, and insist that I never return. Having grown up in a segregated town, I was disappointed but not surprised. To the railroad company's credit, management was solidly behind me. Customers were told in no uncertain terms that I was the company's representative in their area, and nothing was going to change that fact. If they wanted to have their goods shipped by the railroad, I was the person they would have to consult. They had a choice to either do business with David Steward or take their business somewhere else.

So, I kept calling on them, always courteous and eager to serve them. Eventually, knowing that I was their only option if they wanted to ship on the Missouri Pacific, a high percentage of them stayed with the company. Over time, most of them realized that I was fully capable of servicing their account, and some even said I was the best person in my position with whom they had ever worked. A few not only raved about my service and professionalism, but they also became lifetime friends.

I have to say that these friendships were not easy for me at first. They took some forgiving and walking in God's love. But then I realized that these people had never worked with a person of color who had my competency. All of their lives they had only known persons of color to work as domestic help. In my customers' eyes, I was an anomaly, but I knew if I did outstanding work, then the doorway would be opened for others in the future.

WORKING OUT

Building on what I learned in my previous jobs, by 1984 I had left my sales job at Federal Express to launch Transportation Business Specialists (TBS), a company that audited and reviewed freight bills and overcharges for the railroad industry. Seeing the way the industry worked, it wasn't long before I also formed a sister company, Transport Administrative Services (TAS), which uncovered invoice errors of shippers underpaying the railroad and then collected those payments owed.

As I mentioned previously, the Union Pacific Railroad hired TAS to audit $15 billion of rate information in 1987. To do this, TAS built a local area network to handle the data, and by using new technology, it had the capacity to audit forty times faster than the method used by Union Pacific. We made a lot of money for them, and they were thrilled with the service we provided. As we neared the end of our two-year contract, I was looking forward to renewing it for a longer term. Then, out of the blue, I got a call from one of their vice presidents.

"David, we're totally satisfied with the wonderful service you provided," he said. "You've saved us millions."

Momentarily relieved, I said, "It's our pleasure," hoping our conversation would shift to the new contract.

"We have no complaints, and in fact, your work was so efficient that we're now in a position to do the work internally. We will not be renewing our contract."

Our company had worked itself out of our biggest job! Their business accounted for 70 percent of our total revenues. To say I was devastated would be an understatement! How would we pay our bills? Meet payroll? Survive until we found a replacement client? Even as fear tried to take a foothold in my heart, I knew that the Lord was on my side and would not let me down. I remembered Philippians 4:13—"I can do all things through Christ who strengthens me" (NKJV)—and I did a lot of praying that night.

By the next morning, I was ready to go back to work and figure out what we could do to keep our company intact. This adversity opened my eyes to seeing a bigger opportunity: If we could solve problems for the railroad industry, why not use our technology expertise to solve problems for companies in other industries? This obstacle caused me to think beyond our company's present focus, which eventually led to launching WWT.

ACCEPTING ADVERSITY

We've certainly encountered our share of setbacks and external challenges at WWT over the years. For instance, in 1992, our sales had shot up from $3 million to $8 million, and we were thinking about how we could be a $10 million–plus company in 1993. Then a major personal computer deal with the U.S. Army Tank-automotive & Armaments Command, then comprising nearly 80 percent of our revenues, was not renewed. The reason? We were *twelve minutes* late in submitting the bid. I kid you not! We should have known better—that's the way it works when you're late in submitting a government bid. When you're late, you're late—end of story!

We paid a price for our mistake. We had to reduce our workforce from twenty employees to ten, and that really hurt. It not only grieved me to let good people go, but it also crippled our young company's ability to go after new business. As you've seen by now, I always dream big and swing for the fences! The upside is when you land a big account, there's a lot of money on the table. The downside, however, is that it hurts that much more when you lose a big account!

Working overtime with a reduced team, we nonetheless kept swinging for the fences in hopes of a grand slam—or at least a single. Through sheer tenacity and the grace of God, by 1994 our sales were $17 million. That year, we put in six months of hard work and invested $150,000 in out-of-pocket expenses preparing a bid to win a large contract with the army—so large, in fact, that it would triple our revenues!

In the first round of bidding, we outbid four companies. It was then down to one other company and WWT. We had then invested so much time and money that we felt confident we'd win the bid. We knew we had done everything right and deserved to get the job. Apparently, the other company had also worked smart and hard, and it won the job. Again, another huge disappointment!

But these ups and downs are par for the course in business, particularly the tech industry. Over the years, I've had my share of adversity, and if there's one thing I know for sure, it's that I'll face more external challenges as WWT continues to grow. Our company is living proof of what my father always said: "What doesn't kill you makes you stronger." His message echoes a similar truth, although expressed differently, in the Bible: "Not only so, but we also glory in our sufferings, because we know that suffering produces perseverance; perseverance, character; and character, hope. And hope does not put us to shame, because God's love has been poured out into our hearts through the Holy Spirit, who has been given to us" (Rom. 5:3–5).

Ultimately, my outlook on adversity is similar to what M. Scott Peck wrote in his classic book, *The Road Less Traveled*: "Life is difficult. This is a great truth, one of the greatest truths. It is a great truth because once we truly see this truth, we transcend it. Once we truly know that life is difficult—once we truly understand and accept it—then life is no longer difficult. Because once it is accepted, the fact that life is difficult no longer matters." Leadership is also difficult. But as a leader, facing adversity is part of the job and can help you grow. Once you accept that fact, you can trust God and focus on serving others!

YOUR LEADERSHIP FLYWHEEL:
Learn, Live, Lead, Legacy

1. What external obstacles or limiting circumstances did you encounter while growing up that shaped your present style of leadership? What did they teach you about problem solving? About trusting other people? About trusting God?

2. What current conflict, problem, or roadblock is frustrating you the most? Why? How is it preventing you and your organization from growing? What do you need to do in order to surrender this obstacle to God?

3. How have you seen God work through the external challenges you've encountered in your career? How can you accept adversity as part of the process of your growth as a leader committed to serving others?

Dear God, when setbacks and obstacles come up, I often get frustrated, impatient, and afraid. I sometimes try to take control and fix everything on my own, acting as if I no longer trust You to lead, guide, and direct my every step. Forgive me, Lord, for those times when I try to conquer life's problems by myself. Thank You for Your loving presence and for the power and wisdom You provide. I trust You to help me grow as a leader so that I may serve others like Your Son, Jesus, did. In His name I pray, amen.

CHAPTER 27

GROW THROUGH SHARED VICTORIES

For lack of guidance a nation falls, but victory is won through many advisers.

Proverbs 11:14

If we want to be a servant-leader to others, then we must realize that our organization's growth requires teamwork, open communication, and collaboration in order to achieve the shared victories that signal true success. The Bible reminds us to be open to advice because others may have differing views that may be better than our own.

Every day, I'm surrounded by smart people, so when they bring ideas to the table that differ from mine, I listen carefully to what they say. I make it known that I am always open to their viewpoints. There's no possessive, competitive, or defensive posturing, because we're all committed to our shared values and business objectives. We create safe spaces for brainstorming ideas and finding imaginative solutions for our customers' needs.

In a business such as ours, we all need feedback from specialists who know more than we do as individuals. WWT requires having accountants, lawyers, engineers, technicians, and many other professionals under our roof. They work at WWT because they are very good at what they do. Going back to the beginning of WWT, my background was sales and marketing. There

I was in the IT industry, knowing that there were many people out there who knew so much more about technology than I did. I had no choice but to rely on their advice and fresh ideas, and when they were not like mine, you can be sure I listened very carefully to what they had to say.

How well I understood, then as now, that while I may have been the founder and owner of the company, our future success relied on their knowledge, expertise, and the collective wisdom of our teams trusting each other and working together. If a leader doesn't communicate to her people that they should challenge authority, the likelihood and opportunity for change is unlikely. That's when you end up doing the same old thing the same old way, and you have no competitive advantage. Good leaders are not threatened by the ideas of others, because they understand that fresh viewpoints from distinct areas of expertise are required. No matter how successful you are, you must continue to change in order to stay ahead of your competition.

Once again, we come back to the Biblical wisdom of how we're all parts of the same body, distinct and yet unified by a greater purpose. "But in fact God has placed the parts in the body, every one of them, just as he wanted them to be. If they were all one part, where would the body be? As it is, there are many parts, but one body" (1 Cor. 12:18–20). Similarly, a successful organization has people with different skill sets coordinating and collaborating to function as one. Successful businesses rely on all of their parts working in harmony, each having a different function. In order to reach their shared goals, every department, team, and individual must align and synchronize.

CULTURE OF COLLABORATION

To maximize our success at WWT, we have always recognized the importance of gathering a diversity of people from various backgrounds and having a multiplicity of experiences. This collaborative approach enables us to have the benefit of looking at opportunities and new ventures with many unique perspectives. This directive also holds true within each individual company unit. For instance, not all accountants or lawyers or engineers share the same thoughts. To consider only one point of view in any area would not only be foolhardy, but it would be dangerous. If you do not listen to people with different views, then you're essentially tying the organization's hands behind its back. Having diversity but not utilizing it accomplishes nothing but frustration. A strong team is able to select from the best of all ideas that are presented as well as discover new possibilities from the combined interaction of their wisdom.

This is one of many reasons we treasure a diverse workforce. Over the years, WWT has developed a reputation for welcoming people from dissimilar backgrounds who think differently. Everyone knows from his or her first day here that we consider diversity a valuable asset. We value it as one of our strengths. Everyone is encouraged to speak openly and to never hold back his or her opposing ideas. We want to hear them, even the ones that may seem very far outside the box.

Synergy is a key factor that has enabled us to leapfrog over competitors who were bigger, better financed, and established long before we had the audacity to call ourselves World Wide Technology. We relish ideas and opinions that seem so far out that others sometimes may view them as laughable. And the best ideas come from collaborative, creative conversations.

NO ONE IS GREATER THAN EVERYONE

Oliver Wendell Holmes Sr. said, "Many ideas grow better when transplanted into another mind than in the one where they sprang up." This wise observation reminds us that when a leader is surrounded by people willing to consider more than one option in their exchange of ideas, then any one idea suddenly has the potential to evolve into a better idea. A good leader lets people brainstorm, and the synergy from their collective thinking forms a better solution than any single person in the group might have had on his or her own.

This happens often at our Advanced Technology Centers (ATCs). There, we've worked hard to create an environment where people come together seeking solutions, working with coworkers, partnering with different companies, and even working with competitors to cooperatively solve mutual problems. In order for a collaboration to occur at an ATC, people must be open to different points of view that will make his or her company better or perhaps add value to their particular industry. For this approach to work, respect for others, including one's competition, is crucial. Every day, our team members at our ATCs illustrate the old saying "No one of us is better than every one of us."

In order for team members and stakeholders to work in harmony and to take advantage of synergy, they know they must check their egos at the door. The way we work is not centered on any one individual, department, or core group. There's no room for showboats and prima donnas! Ego-driven leadership fosters an unhealthy individualism that results in a lack of trust. As I mentioned earlier, I believe that *ego* stands for "edging God out."

In a "me first" situation, there's no room for "we first" solutions. Everyone worries about getting credit, blaming others, or covering his or her own back. No one can relax, because the emphasis is on asserting oneself and one's ideas to the detriment of others' ideas and shared goals. Communication ends up being filtered, censored, and edited in order to always anticipate what others will think and to make oneself look good. Ego-driven leaders exhaust themselves by promoting themselves instead of serving others and the mission of their organization.

Instead of being driven by one's ego, shared victories are

always fueled by humility. A willingness to put others first goes a long way in effective leadership. Scripture urges us, "Do nothing out of selfish ambition or vain conceit. Rather, in humility value others above yourselves, not looking to your own interests but each of you to the interests of the others" (Phil. 2:3–4). Humility of strength enables a leader to say, "I don't have all the answers; however, together we can figure this out." No one person should be the go-to problem solver, rainmaker, or creative genius. Everyone should fulfill those roles and more!

People feel important when their voices are heard. They want to feel empowered. They want to know they are making a difference. A good leader gives them credit and thanks them for their contributions. She lets them know it is not just them—it's the entire team that makes things happen.

BALANCED AND ALIGNED

While it's important to listen to opposing views, when a leader does not agree with what his people say, he should thank them for speaking out and explain why he disagrees. He should not discourage them from offering other contrasting views in the future, even when previous ideas or input might have missed the target. When opposing views conflict with a company's values and beliefs, however, a leader must speak directly and honestly about why they are unacceptable.

Occasionally, you may be the only leader at the table who resists an idea that the majority of your team endorses. Depending on your reasons and what's at stake, you must reject the temptation to give in if you feel strongly about this particular decision or course of action. You must not appease the majority but instead make it crystal clear why you're unwilling to compromise. Again, principles must never be compromised. Shared victories sometimes require the leader who is ultimately accountable to exercise the judgment, authority, and wisdom he or she wields.

With this in mind, I try to listen to all viewpoints before supporting a particular course of action. And I ask myself, Does this solution align with those core values I believe in? The ones that we share and have committed to fulfill in all that we do as a company? Does this direction align with the Word of God that I know to be true and timeless?

A good leader will always have alignment between the cornerstone and the foundation, based upon God's Word. If those are anchored by His truth, then the structure will be sound. Otherwise, like the house built on sand, it will not survive the storms of life. When there is complete alignment between core convictions and strategic action, then the outcome is a shared victory for both heaven and earth.

YOUR LEADERSHIP FLYWHEEL:
Learn, Live, Lead, Legacy

1. When was the last time you asked someone to speak up in a meeting or to share more about their point of view in a group discussion? From your experience, why is it essential to invite all participants to give input?

2. How often do you struggle with letting others share ideas that are different than your own? What do you do when you feel your ego getting the best of you? How do you continue to serve others in the midst of such moments?

3. What are some ways in which you encourage communication, collaboration, and cooperation among your team members? How does your leadership style liberate others to be part of something bigger than their individual ideas and department goals?

Dear God, thank You for inviting me, along with all Your children, to be part of advancing Your kingdom and sharing the gospel of Christ. I'm grateful for the freedom we have to use our gifts collaboratively so that we might accomplish mighty deeds as we rely on Your power and guidance. Keep my mind open, Lord, to new ideas and perspectives different than my own. Thank You for the many unique and diverse people I'm blessed to serve and lead. In Jesus' name, amen.

SECTION 10

Celebrate

CHAPTER 28

CELEBRATE THE DAILY
GIFT OF HEALTH

Each of you should use whatever gift you have received to serve others, as faithful stewards of God's grace in its various forms.

1 Peter 4:10

Celebration is about stewardship.

Not only are we to receive and use God's gifts and provisions, but we're also called to be good stewards who share our blessings with others. Healthy living—physically, emotionally, spiritually—is the most basic form of stewardship. Paul reminded the early Christians in Corinth, "Do you not know that your bodies are temples of the Holy Spirit, who is in you, whom you have received from God?" (1 Cor. 6:19). In appreciation to our Creator, you must take good care of your physical body and your mind as well. You do it by eating properly, getting sufficient sleep, and following a regular exercise program.

GOOD STEWARDS BECOME GREAT LEADERS

Keeping physically fit encompasses maintenance of body, mind, and soul. As we see in Daniel's example, discipline is required. We have to say no to certain options that might taste good, feel good, or seem good in the moment in order to take the long view about what is best for our health, what will allow us to be the best stewards of the physical body God has given us for this life. We also have to commit to habits and practices that will facilitate our health and keep us strong.

For example, twenty years ago I set a daily goal to do 100 consecutive push-ups. Now, please realize that this was quite a goal for a man who's six foot five and who was in his forties. It took a while, but eventually I worked myself up to 100 and then kept training over time until I increased my personal high to 140 push-ups. When I turned sixty, I cut back to protect my back, but I still exercise. It doesn't matter if I have an early appointment or am on a trip, exercise is part of my daily routine. Just as I pray in the morning, I exercise.

My daily workout lasts thirty-five minutes, enough to build up some strength and get my heart rate up. When I'm traveling, I'll do my exercises in my hotel room, basically the same workout I do at home. While I'll never be in good enough shape to play in the NBA, my daily routine keeps me energized. It keeps me mentally fresh and alert. Staying healthy physically motivates me to be a good steward in all the other areas of my life as well. My family tells me that it's part of my personality to push beyond the limits. Completing my daily exercise regimen is a vital part of being the good steward (and—forgive my pun—the good Steward!) God calls me to be.

The benefits of being good stewards of our bodies transcend the obvious personal health benefits. One of the greatest beneficiaries of a leader's fitness is his team—we set an example for giving our best self. I've gone through periods where I haven't maintained my fitness level like I should, and my ability to lead effectively has suffered. When I'm taking care of my body, I have more endurance to help my team solve problems and generate new ideas. As a leader, your ability to absorb adversity, while thinking clearly, is paramount to helping your team thrive. They rely on your energy, vision, and stamina to motivate the group and keep everyone focused.

A good workout can sometimes make you feel like a brand-new person. And, in a way, that feeling may be literally true. Over the past three decades of research in neuroscience, researchers have identified a robust link between aerobic exercise and subsequent cognitive clarity. For many in this field, the most exciting recent findings involve neurogenesis, the process by which our brains repair themselves and create new neurons.

Recent studies in animal models have shown that new neurons are produced in the brain throughout its life span. So far, vigorous aerobic exercise is the only known activity to trigger the birth of these new neurons. Research has revealed that these new cells pop up in the hippocampus, a region of the brain associated with learning and memory, which explains why other studies have identified a link between aerobic exercise and improvement in memory. So physical fitness contributes significantly to neuro-fitness. If you want to be a great leader, then be a good steward of your body—and your mind!

REJECT A ROYAL DIET

Both Brandon and I travel extensively, and we often discuss the inherent challenges of being on the road constantly. Whether dining at an airport café or a five-star restaurant, we both know we have to be very careful about what we eat. It's so easy to go with the flow and just do whatever you feel like doing to get by, but here's the problem: The flow never stops! There's always going to be comfort food, junk food, and delicious food available, not to mention a variety of beverage choices.

With our busy schedules combined with the abundance of delicious foods, the devil offers many allurements to tempt us from caring for our bodies. Our enemy plays on our weaknesses and knows that it's easier for us to make choices requiring less effort and discipline. As human beings, we naturally seek pleasure and comfort—often to our detriment in the long run. This is why celebrating the daily path of stewardship is so important. We must maintain our eternal perspective on a daily basis, focused on God's big picture while we cultivate habits of good stewardship.

It reminds me of Daniel's predicament after the Israelites were taken captive by the Babylonians after they had conquered Jerusalem. Daniel, along with many of the young men taken prisoner, was trained to serve in the royal court of King Nebuchadnezzar there in Babylon. The prisoners were expected to abide by Babylonian customs and accept the hedonistic culture of their captors. Consequently, Daniel and his fellow trainees received a daily portion of the king's rich food and wine, per the royal dietary habits. While this might not sound like harsh treatment, such a menu violated the Hebrew religious dietary laws God had given them.

Rather than go on a hunger strike or compromise his beliefs and accept the king's meals, Daniel convinced the guard in charge of their care to allow him and his friends to only eat vegetables and water for ten days. If they then appeared as healthy as their Babylonian peers on the royal diet, then they would be allowed to maintain their simple, all-natural, and God-pleasing menu. Not surprisingly, "at the end of the ten days they looked healthier and better nourished than any of the young men who ate the royal food. So the guard took away their choice food and the wine they were to drink and gave them vegetables instead" (Dan. 1:15–16).

Daniel demonstrates several important lessons for us today as we practice good stewardship. In addition to eating healthy and drinking water, we must not allow our environment to dictate our choices for taking care of our health. All of us are too busy to exercise based on the number of demands and responsibilities we carry. But if we're committed to serving those we lead to the best of our ability, then we will make stewarding our health a priority—for our sake as well as theirs.

AN ATTITUDE OF WELLNESS

WWT has a wellness program because we care about our people's health and welfare. Employees are encouraged to join fitness centers and make other healthy choices. There are also several paths and walking trails near our locations, and we even have workstations with treadmills for people to exercise while working on their computers. In addition, we provide on-site family health centers that serve all employees and their dependents at no charge.

Our wellness program goes beyond physical fitness. Our employee assistance program is a free benefit for all employees, including all the members of one's household, and provides confidential, professional assistance for a wide range of personal concerns. Coaching with professional trained consultants allows team members to address a variety of issues related to physical and mental health, including diet and nutrition, substance abuse, tobacco cessation, elder care, and child care. Additional benefits also cover matters such as identity theft, will preparation, education planning, and much more.

This program goes much further than simply encouraging our people to take good care of themselves physically and mentally. We want to help them find practical, affordable, healthy solutions to the stressors that we all face in various seasons of life. This goal emerged when we first provided health insurance coverage and wanted to facilitate healthy lifestyles. As WWT grew, one thing led to another, and when we could afford to do more for our employees, we did. We are always looking for ways to improve their lives.

While small companies and start-ups may not be able to afford the same kind of care, they can still establish an attitude of wellness. It took us a while before WWT could offer the spectrum of services we now provide for our employees, but we practice many little things that virtually any company can afford. For example, to improve cardio health, we encourage our people to walk during the workday by having "mobile meetings" and outdoor gatherings. Not only is it healthy to get some fresh air and exercise, but there are no interruptions such as texts, calls, and emails.

While it varies, walking meetings are typically held with two or three people over a set route and time period—often thirty minutes. They can take place on campus, at a nearby park, or even in our office hallways. Studies have shown that the more participants engage in moderate physical activity at work, the less likely they are to miss work for health reasons. On the other hand, doctors are now linking being sedentary for long stretches to obesity, type 2 diabetes, and a range of other harmful conditions.

Although standing desks have received attention in recent years, studies have also shown that standing doesn't burn many more calories than sitting. Experts emphasize the other benefits of mobile meetings, especially the way they can remove barriers between team members and increase unity and cohesion. Studies also show that creative output increases when people are walking or exercising.

We have also been very deliberate about providing free healthy snacks, including fruits and vegetables, granola, energy bars, bottled water, and juices. Many employees enjoy flexible hours that permit them to make the most of seasonal activities and recreational opportunities. This flexibility allows them to make the most of summer so they can enjoy time hiking, swimming, biking, or gardening. We're serious about offering real perks that help our people in tangible ways. We want to reduce stress not only at work but also in all areas of their lives.

REST, RELAX, RECHARGE

Many of the other leaders whom I know also make healthy living a priority. Brandon enjoys biking and has competed in several Olympic-distance triathlons.

He and I agree that it goes back to what God has called us to do as leaders—to be our best in every situation He puts us in. We're called to be good stewards, which means practicing habits that make the most of the many gifts and opportunities He has given us. In order to glorify God in all we do, we must maximize our talents. We want to set good examples and model the behaviors and lifestyle habits that we want to share with our team members. In many ways, it's a celebration of all He's bestowed upon us—our health, our families, our careers.

Many of my friends who have extraordinary leadership skills keep physically fit by working out with a trainer and going to the gym regularly. They are taking good care of the temple God has given them. Many young leaders do not respect the vital importance of sleep. They pride themselves on the fact that they can get by on only a few hours each night. As you age, however, you will acquire some wisdom and realize that when you get a good night's sleep, your thinking is clearer, and you have more energy. When you are rested and thinking clearly, you are more attuned spiritually—plus, you will find more time for prayer and Bible study.

Rest is vital for you to lead by the Good Book. When a person is tired, it colors his or her lens on life and often produces a more critical attitude. Fatigue can become cumulative and lead to various ailments and injuries, as well as to depression and anxiety. When you're exhausted, it's impossible to give your best efforts or freshest thoughts. God rested on the seventh day after completing His creation, not because He needed rest, but because He knew we would need to rest; so, He modeled it for us. Therefore, He commanded us to honor the Sabbath as a day of rest. We need downtime to relax, recharge, and rejuvenate if we're going to maintain our ability to serve and lead.

As leaders committed to serving as Jesus served, we must focus on being the best stewards we can be. This mind-set and the practices we cultivate create dividends on a daily basis as well as on an ongoing—even eternal—basis. We share the blessings of life by making the most of them for God's glory and for His kingdom purposes. And that's always a reason to celebrate!

YOUR LEADERSHIP FLYWHEEL:
Learn, Live, Lead, Legacy

1. How do you presently celebrate the many gifts God has given you on a daily basis? What does it look like for you to be a good steward of His gifts? How are you sharing these gifts with those you serve?

2. On a scale from one to ten, with one being "rarely" and ten being "always," how often do you make your health the priority it needs to be in order for you to lead and serve most effectively? What area of your health needs the greatest attention? Diet? Exercise? Stress management? Sleep? Downtime? Something else?

3. How do you promote wellness and healthy living in your organization? What programs, facilities, and resources are available to your team members? What incentives do you provide for them to exercise and practice healthy habits? How does your attitude and example influence them to participate?

Dear Lord, thank You for the many blessings You continue to pour into my life! I have been entrusted with so many gifts, and I know You want me to use these to bless others so that they may know You and enter Your kingdom. Give me the strength, stamina, and discipline to make my physical and mental health a priority so that I can be the best leader for those I serve. May I promote an attitude and example of wholeness and wellness in all that I do. In Jesus' name I pray, amen.

CHAPTER 29

CELEBRATE MILESTONES
ON THE JOURNEY

I will remember the deeds of the LORD; yes, I will remember your wonders of old.

Psalm 77:11 ESV

From our early days at WWT, we have always measured the milestones of progress together. Whether celebrating our winning bid on a contract or acknowledging the contribution of someone retiring from the company, we share in the satisfaction that comes from working hard together and harvesting fruit as a team. While we do our best to recognize individual milestones, such as birthdays and graduations, sharing company trials and triumphs uniquely bonds us together in our WWT family. These celebrations take many forms, from family picnics and seasonal events to department meals and team activities.

In addition to sharing food and fellowship, one of the primary ways we try to celebrate our milestones is by remembering how far we have come. Sharing stories about the early days of our company makes celebrating our present successes even sweeter. We can look back and give thanks to God for all He's done to bring us so far. Celebrating our milestones becomes an opportunity to praise and worship because we know that He is the reason we've not just survived but thrived all these years.

NEVER FORGET

Based on what we see in the Bible, celebrating God's goodness on a regular basis helps us grow stronger in our faith. One of the recurrent themes throughout the Old Testament is remembering and honoring past events. God wanted the people of Israel to remember all that He had done for them in order to grow in their faith and trust Him during challenging times.

They were told, "Then take care lest you forget the LORD, who brought you out of the land of Egypt, out of the house of slavery" (Deut. 6:12 ESV). This included creating the feast day of Passover to commemorate not only their exodus from bondage but also escaping the angel of death's visit during the plagues on the Egyptians. God told Moses to instruct the people to place blood from a sacrificial lamb on their doorposts so the angel of death would not linger but would pass over them (see Exod. 12:23).

Clearly, for the people of Israel, remembering their milestones also included the hard times and the challenges they endured. Prior to entering the Promised Land, the Israelites were urged to "remember the whole way that the LORD your God has led you these forty years in the wilderness, that he might humble you, testing you to know what was in your heart, whether you would keep his commandments or not" (Deut. 8:2 ESV). As difficult as it was, they persevered—even when they strayed from and disobeyed God—and celebrated the goals they achieved and the miracles God performed along the way.

Similarly, we can follow the Israelites' example and celebrate how God sustained us during those times when we saw no way forward. We can let others see what He has done for us as we steward His gifts in order to bless others. Sharing those memories together and thanking God keeps us grounded and reminds us that it is His power fueling our accomplishments. Recalling all that the Lord has done for us inspires us to keep taking risks and to forge ahead toward the next summit on our journey.

No wonder, then, that Jesus instituted a unique celebration to help His followers remember all that He sacrificed for them by dying on the cross. Gathered with His disciples to celebrate the Passover meal, Christ knew He would be arrested later that night and then crucified. This would be the last time He would be with them all before His death, and He wanted to create a memorable celebration:

> While they were eating, Jesus took bread, and when he had given thanks, he broke it and gave it to his disciples, saying, "Take and eat; this is my body."
>
> Then he took a cup, and when he had given thanks, he gave it to them, saying, "Drink from it, all of you. This is my blood of the covenant, which is poured out for many for the forgiveness of sins. I tell you, I will not drink from this fruit of the vine from now on until that day when I drink it new with you in my Father's kingdom."
>
> When they had sung a hymn, they went out to the Mount of Olives. (Matthew 26:26–30)

Jesus took items from the meal on their table and used them to mark the occasion in the most powerful, symbolic way possible. "Do this in remembrance of me," He told them (Luke 22:19). As His followers, we continue to celebrate what is usually called the Lord's Supper as a special observance that resonates historically as well as personally, physically as well as spiritually. When we share these elements together, we celebrate the greatest gift of all time: our salvation through the sacrifice of Jesus Christ.

TELL ME ABOUT IT

One of the best ways we can celebrate together is by telling the stories related to our milestones. Just as Passover recalls the Israelites' exodus from Egypt and the Lord's Supper recalls Christ's death and resurrection, we repeat the story to honor what God has done in the past and to reflect on the ways these events shape our lives now. Christmas would not be complete without the story of Jesus' birth at the center of it. Similarly, Easter is not just about rebirth in the springtime but about the resurrection of our Savior in His victory over sin and death.

The very fact that these stories from the Bible, and so many more, continue to inspire us encourages us to share our own tales of trials and triumphs. Through storytelling, we commemorate the milestones that led us to our present destination. We can acknowledge the path and recognize the pattern of God's hand guiding us through what often felt like a wilderness at the time. This seems important on so many levels to both honor Him as well as give Him the glory for what we're doing as individuals and as a company.

When people hear a well-told story about someone, they can relate to it. Words paint a picture of the experience and make it possible for them to feel the pain and suffering more than they would by simply reading about the large numbers of people that suffered. Conversely, an uplifting story fills them with joy and may bring just as many tears as a story of lament. Likewise, a good speaker will talk about a personal experience, and this, too, has an emotional impact on his audience. The best stories are rooted in the personal but transcend circumstances to point out the timeless truths of God's Word.

Storytelling also informs an audience that the speaker has earned his stripes because he's been in the trenches, faced challenges, and overcame them. For example, when talking to a group of young people that come from modest backgrounds, I let them know that I grew up poor. While often joking about it, I also make sure they grasp the reality of what my family experienced. Young adults today sometimes find it hard to believe that we didn't have an indoor bathroom or that I was eighteen years old when I ate my first meal in a restaurant. But in order to appreciate what God has done with WWT, they need to see the miracles He's done in my life.

As I've shared in previous chapters, I also love telling the story about how my car was repossessed shortly after WWT launched. I tell this story to let people know that like them—and everybody—I've had my share of tough times. Being able to see how far God has brought us is vitally important in order for us to practice gratitude and to look ahead. For the most part, the stories I tell about myself are about my hardships and failures. I tell them in order to inspire others' dreams and to give them hope about what God can do in their lives. They need to hear about my journey in order to realize that God is on their side. With hope and faith in Him, they will succeed.

LEGACY OF DREAMS

Hearing stories of victories achieved and sacrifices made and about the role of faith in the way we live our lives has always inspired me. Growing up in the African American community, my siblings and I heard many stories about our ancestors, an important part of our history because most of these stories were not recorded in writing. The African slaves that were brought to America had no formal schooling, and as a result, their word-of-mouth stories about their lives in Africa were passed on to future generations. They were good storytellers, and they repeated stories that dated back many generations from their elders.

We also heard stories more directly related to our own immediate family. My mother shared personal stories about her experiences when she was young as well as those passed down from her parents and grandparents. For instance, she told us about moving to Chicago with her family when she was growing up because she could not attend the segregated public high school in Clinton, Missouri, where her family lived. They stayed in Chicago until she and her siblings finished school and then returned to Clinton for its small-town values and low crime rate. Her parents believed in the importance of quality education so much that they were willing to uproot their entire family to secure their children's future.

Other stories I heard affected me more directly and were ongoing. When I entered first grade in 1957, *Brown v. Board of Education* had ended segregation three years earlier. Nonetheless, the Ku Klux Klan in our area actively attempted to stop school integration in Clinton. During that time, my father and some of his friends patrolled the town many nights to protect the black community from being harmed by KKK members. As I was growing up, I often heard about my father and those other brave men who protected us. Consequently, I have also told that story to my children and look forward to sharing it with my grandchildren once they're older. Through the years, shared stories become the legacy of our ancestors' dreams.

These stories at home helped me appreciate and celebrate my heritage in ways that I didn't experience at school. From my parents and others in our community, I heard many stories about remarkable people of color, and of course, my mother told us stories from the Bible about God's people having courage, faith, and confidence. These stories reminded me that God loves all people regardless of color or any of the other characteristics that differentiate us from one another. After all, He created all His children in His own image!

When we'd talk about people of color in the classroom, however, it was always about slavery. There were rarely stories about nonwhite heroes. And whenever the historical issue of slavery arose, everyone in class usually turned to stare at me since I was the only person of color in the room. While I tried to ignore my classmates' stares, my internal reaction was, *Why are you looking at me? I wasn't there!* Some kids would usually make unkind remarks after class or during recess after those particular lessons.

Even though I developed a kind of defensive posture from

those uncomfortable moments, they also taught me about persevering, and through these challenges, I learned about self-control. In spite of being treated this way, I was taught that you can't stop trusting people and become consumed with animosities. If that happens, you lose. It was from my Bible lessons and attending church services that I learned to love people in spite of their shortcomings. Looking back, I thank God for those experiences and celebrate them because they proved to be life lessons that can never be taken away from me.

THAT'S OUR STORY

In His role as a teacher, Jesus was the greatest storyteller who ever lived. He often told stories to His followers—a majority of whom were likely illiterate—drawn from their culture and familiar surroundings. These stories, often called parables, could easily be understood while also revealing new insight into God's character and our relationship with Him. In order to reach as many listeners as possible, Jesus often described the kingdom of heaven differently to fit His audience.

For example, Jesus chose a fishing metaphor to explain how God assesses people: "Once again, the kingdom of heaven is like a net that was let down into the lake and caught all kinds of fish. When it was full, the fishermen pulled it up on the shore. Then they sat down and collected the good fish in baskets, but threw the bad away" (Matt. 13:47–48). His audience merely had to look toward the water or sniff the air to experience the comparison. No one, then or now, wants to be a smelly fish that's gone bad!

Well aware of His listeners' familiarity with the challenge of producing life from the dry, sandy soil in their arid climate, Jesus also said, "The kingdom of heaven is like a mustard seed, which a man took and planted in his field" (Matt. 13:31). He also appealed to listeners with experience as merchants, shopkeepers, and vendors: "The kingdom of heaven is like a merchant looking for fine pearls. When he found one of great value, he went away and sold everything he had and bought it" (vv. 45–46).

As the Scriptures reveal, Jesus told vivid parables that were tailored for the people He addressed. Today, skillful speakers adapt their message to their listeners, emulating how Jesus did it in ancient times. Likewise, a good speaker chooses the right story to tell his audience. Had Jesus talked about fishing when He addressed farmers, for example, they might not have been receptive to His message.

The Scriptures we have today are based on stories told by Jesus and by those who were with Him. For example, Matthew and John were disciples, and Luke was a companion of Paul. When the time came to give a testimony or witness, the Holy Spirit would give them the necessary words. After Jesus' death and resurrection, these stories were repeated. Likewise, having been taught by Jesus, these men were adept at telling about His death and how He ascended into heaven. Through the power of the Holy Spirit, these stories were shared over and over and eventually recorded in written form. The number of Jesus' followers grew and multiplied, and today the Bible remains the best-selling book of all time.

Everyone loves a good story and the joy of seeing something familiar in new ways. Celebrating, remembering, and storytelling allow us to connect, which in turn feeds our ability to collaborate and create community. As the Good Book says, "Rejoice in the Lord always. I will say it again: Rejoice!" (Phil. 4:4). When we celebrate milestones together, we honor the past and anticipate the future. We give God the glory for all He's done, all He's doing, and all He will do!

YOUR LEADERSHIP FLYWHEEL:
Learn, Live, Lead, Legacy

1. What are the biggest milestones you've celebrated personally in the past year? In your company or organization? How did you recognize all the hard work and sacrifice that went into these achievements? What are some ways you can continue to celebrate them moving forward?

2. How often do you share stories, both casually and formally, in your communications with those you serve? What are your favorite stories to share about how God has brought you to where you are now? Why are those your favorite?

3. What's the next major milestone you anticipate celebrating corporately in the coming months? How can you make this celebration a unique event that glorifies what God is doing?

Dear God, when I look back over my life and see Your hand at work time and time again, I am in awe. Thank You, Lord! I give You thanks and praise for the many milestones You've allowed me to celebrate. It's through Your power alone, along with the contributions of so many people in my life, that they have been reached. Help me always to remember what You've done for me as I look ahead at where You will lead me next. In the name of Jesus, amen.

CHAPTER 30

CELEBRATE THE DESTINATION AHEAD

May the God of hope fill you with all joy and peace as you trust in him, so that you may overflow with hope by the power of the Holy Spirit.

Romans 15:13

In June 2016, we celebrated the development of our new WWT global headquarters building by placing the final I beam on the 208,000-square-foot, seven-floor structure. That beam is inscribed with a favorite Bible passage that seems all too appropriate:

> Built on the foundation of the apostles and the prophets with Christ Jesus himself as the chief cornerstone. In him the whole building is joined together and rises to become a holy temple in the Lord. And in him you too are being built together to become a dwelling in which God lives by his Spirit. (Ephesians 2:20–22)

We put this Scripture on the new building to invoke the Holy Spirit to live, reign, and always be present at WWT. While the building should last for many decades, the Spirit will live forever. When we lead by serving those God has entrusted to us, we're responsible for making decisions that will improve the lives of people a thousand generations from now. My life is dedicated to passing on the Word of God, which means all my decisions today are not about the here and now as much as the there and then. They are for eternity!

When we allow God's Spirit to guide us, we look ahead and plan for the future not only in yearly increments but for eternity. Following God and obeying His Word, we celebrate the destination ahead by being the best stewards we can be today. Long-range planning is not about sacrificing short-term gains for sustainability—long-range planning is about investing in a legacy that will have the greatest impact for God's kingdom!

AHEAD OF THE CURVE

As we look ahead, we know that we have to remain relevant. In the fast-changing high-tech industry, a company cannot resist change and rest on its past successes. We all know technology changes at such a rapid pace that in order to be a successful enterprise today, you must always stay ahead of the competition. And in our world today, everyone embraces the fact that they have to incorporate technology and online availability if they want to succeed and thrive. No one will disagree that technology is crucial to his or her success in the twenty-first century.

As a leading company focused on technology and helping others utilize it effectively in their realms, WWT has a culture that continues to be entrepreneurial. This has enabled us to be innovative, creative, and flexible. Consequentially, we are always open to new ideas and concepts that utilize technology. Unlike a publicly traded company, we are not under pressure to sacrifice long-term goals with short-term profits to make our quarterly numbers look favorable to shareholders. As a privately owned corporation, we are entrepreneurs. Typically, major corporations don't have the flexibility to pivot as we do.

The company we are today is not the company we were yesterday, nor is it the company we will be tomorrow. If we don't continually change and improve, we'll be put out of business by our competition. You have to constantly find ways to improve and differentiate yourself from your competition in order to set your organization apart. This is a responsibility of everyone in the organization—everyone must have this same attitude.

An organization must always have a mind-set that demands excellence. All of its people must collectively strive for excellence, and they must not tolerate anything less from their teammates. Most of all, they must hold each other accountable for excellence.

The bar should be so high that when somebody says a task isn't possible, a leader replies, "Let me know what you need for us to make this happen." Too often leaders accept constraints as givens and they throw in the towel without challenging the impossible to find out if it actually is possible, let alone stepping out in faith to follow where God leads. Strong, faith-driven leaders will challenge their people to work hard in order to achieve more than they think they can. These faith-driven leaders push toward a future that only God can ultimately orchestrate.

Good leaders make sure their people know they are respected and that their ideas and contributions are welcome. At WWT, our people appreciate our company's willingness to invest in the next generation of technology, which will allow them to learn and grow. They know we will be in the forefront, always working with our partners and customers. In turn, we can push the envelope when we work with our partners and customers—many of whom are considered the world's top technology-driven organizations. At WWT, our people get up every day knowing they have the best tools and training for finding solutions for our customers. Knowing that our services cannot be matched by our competition does wonders for their self-confidence!

SACRED SUCCESSION

In addition to looking ahead and trying to stay ahead of the tech curve, we must also invest in leadership for our future. Succession planning is a top priority for boards of directors and strategic planning teams at both public and private companies, like WWT. Because leadership can change quickly, virtually all companies, colleges, governments, and well-managed organizations have a succession plan in place. No leader lives forever and may need to be replaced for a variety of reasons, including retirement, disability, irresponsibility, misconduct, or a personal or family crisis.

Organizations and companies should be strong enough to endure a major change in leadership for whatever reason. Institutions and businesses should not be so tied to any one person's personality or skill set that they cannot exist without that individual. Responsible management makes plans in advance for a time when its current management team's key people become inactive. When properly executed, a seamless transition occurs, and the business of the corporation continues without missing a beat. Good leaders invest in creating a legacy of leadership that endures long after they themselves have retired or left the company.

While it may seem that succession planning is more of a modern business phenomenon, it's actually a timeless principle of strong servant leadership. In fact, many succession plans appear in the Bible. As Moses' successor, Joshua became responsible for the division of the land among the Israelites, among other duties.

Similarly, we see King David summon all of Israel's officers and important officials to his palace. There, he then declared God's decision for his successor:

> Of all my sons—and the LORD has given me many—
> he has chosen my son Solomon to sit on the throne of

the kingdom of the LORD over Israel. He said to me: "Solomon your son is the one who will build my house and my courts, for I have chosen him to be my son, and I will be his father. I will establish his kingdom forever if he is unswerving in carrying out my commands and laws, as is being done at this time."

So now I charge you in the sight of all Israel and of the assembly of the LORD, and in the hearing of our God: Be careful to follow all the commands of the LORD your God, that you may possess this good land and pass it on as an inheritance to your descendants forever.

And you, my son Solomon, acknowledge the God of your father, and serve him with wholehearted devotion and with a willing mind, for the LORD searches every heart and understands every desire and every thought. If you seek him, he will be found by you; but if you forsake him, he will reject you forever. Consider now, for the LORD has chosen you to build a house as the sanctuary. Be strong and do the work. (1 Chronicles 28:5–10)

With these words, David revealed that the Lord had chosen Solomon to succeed him as the next king of Israel. Notice the way David not only explained the transition in leadership but also charged his successor and those present to continue obeying God and completing what David had started. There's not only a specific plan but also a kind of blessing and a charge that's passed along.

SPIRITUAL LEGACY

We see these same elements in the succession plan Jesus gave His disciples. After handpicking them and teaching them how to lead by serving others, He made it clear how they would carry on the ministry after He returned to heaven: "Therefore go and make disciples of all nations, baptizing them in the name of the Father and of the Son and of the Holy Spirit, and teaching them to obey everything I have commanded you. And surely I am with you always, to the very end of the age" (Matt. 28:19–20).

As the greatest leader who ever walked the earth, Jesus knew His investment in those He served would live on. Confident that they were prepared to spread the Word, Jesus assured them He would always be with them and all humankind: "I will not leave you as orphans; I will come to you. Before long, the world will not see me anymore, but you will see me. Because I live, you also will live. On that day you will realize that I am in my Father, and you are in me, and I am in you" (John 14:18–20).

Jesus' plan of succession ignited a passion for sharing the good news of the gospel that continues burning bright to this day. And to ensure His succession plan would endure even beyond His disciples, Jesus sent the Holy Spirit, the Counselor and Comforter, to empower, guide, and direct us. The Holy Spirit sustains our direct relationship with the Lord and allows us to fulfill the charge Jesus gave His followers: "You will be my witnesses in Jerusalem, and in all Judea and Samaria, and to the ends of the earth" (Acts 1:8). From generation to generation, we invest in the spiritual legacy of those believers before us in order to pass it along to those who follow.

ETERNAL IMPACT

In servant-led companies, leaders throughout the organization develop other team members to replace them when they move up the corporate ladder. With succession plans at different levels within an organization, people are constantly advancing to positions with more responsibilities and opportunities to receive higher compensation without impeding the company's productivity. Each person realizes their value extends beyond their current role as they collaborate with those they serve as well as those they follow.

Unfortunately, not all leaders in every organization think this way. Instead, they may believe themselves to be irreplaceable. They falsely assume, "As the only one who can do my job, I have complete job security. The company needs me and will never discharge me. I'm special!" This kind of thinking has several fallacies. First and foremost, such an individual is not a team player and does not act in the best interest of the organization. Second, they often hamper the growth of those they serve, damaging team morale. Such a leader not only fails to serve those they lead but also fails to recognize the gifts that God has given others. Finally, some managers and senior executives, both covertly as well as blatantly, put their personal self-interests above others. They want to climb the career ladder and make as much money as possible without serving anyone but themselves.

Good leaders, on the other hand, always look ahead at the best interests of their people and want them to grow and excel. These leaders look to Jesus as their example and understand that following Biblical principles is always their highest priority. They invest in those they serve on a consistent, daily basis and give generously to everyone around them. They're not worried about job security or making the most money because they're trusting God. They know if they serve to the very best of their abilities, the Lord will take care of the rest.

Now at an age when many people retire, I'm blessed with a leadership team in place at WWT that continues to look ahead and seek God's guidance. Consequently, my focus now is on how I can continually support them. Throughout WWT and its departments and business units, we have men and women of integrity committed to leading by serving at every level. In many cases, I've had the privilege of working side by side with them for more than a quarter of a century, and they, like so many others, are family to me. They have made commitments to the company, and they have made sacrifices, and they will continue growing our company long after I'm gone.

As long as WWT's core values remain intact, my succession plan will allow for the smoothest transition possible. This is why WWT remains a privately held company, to avoid any conflict that could occur in a publicly held company where shareholders, often with short-term views on fast profits, don't always serve the best interests of employees and customers. We strive to preserve our culture of innovation, creativity, and risk—a culture with an entrepreneurial spirit.

If you're serving those you lead, then you are already investing in your succession plan. As you look ahead and continue striving for excellence as unto the Lord, may the principles we've explored in these pages serve you well. I'm beyond humbled to impart to you any wisdom that I've gleaned over the years from all that God has revealed to me. May He give you a fresh infusion of clarity, power, and purpose as you continue leading and serving those He has entrusted to your care.

Our new global HQ building is just a few blocks from our original office where I experienced real despair. Frequently, I drive past that small building and recall that poignant memory from 1993 that I shared with you at the beginning of this book. It seems like yesterday when I was sitting there engulfed in emotional and psychological darkness. WWT and I were truly at an all-time low. However, there in the darkness, there was a glimmer of hope, and it came from God's Word in Psalm 91. In the darkness, Scripture truly became a lamp for my feet. God's Word illuminated my path.

As we conclude our study of the timeless principles from God's Word that enable us to have the greatest eternal impact, my prayer is that this book will inspire and encourage you to rely on God's Word. And that Scripture will be a lamp for your feet and the light that God uses to guide you along your path. May you continue to love others and serve as Jesus did, with complete humility and deep compassion, with God's limitless power and infinite wisdom, and with the bold assurance that your leadership can change the world and advance God's kingdom. Godspeed on your journey as you learn from the past and look to the future, stepping out in faith toward all that God has for you!

YOUR LEADERSHIP FLYWHEEL:
Learn, Live, Lead, Legacy

1. How are you presently investing in an eternal legacy? What daily habits help you focus on investing in others and God's kingdom? What are some ways you could increase your investment in the priorities that matter most?

2. What is your long-term succession plan? Who are the team members you're presently grooming and coaching to lead and serve in your role should you leave the organization? How could you give them more responsibility toward making this transition?

3. Which chapters and principles have resonated with you the most as you've read this book? Why? How is God using your experience reading *Leadership by the Good Book* to make you a stronger leader?

Dear Lord, thank You for the wisdom You've revealed to me through these pages. May Your Spirit continue to guide me as I seek to implement these leadership principles so that I might serve You, and those entrusted to me, more fully. Help me to look ahead and focus on what matters most: investing in others, sharing the gospel, and advancing Your kingdom. You are the source of my life, my love, and my leadership! With praise and thanksgiving, I pray all this in Jesus' name, amen.

BIBLICAL
BUSINESS
TRAINING

THANK YOU for choosing our book! All proceeds from the sales of our book support Biblical Business Training (BBT), a global nonprofit ministry. BBT's mission is to help people apply Biblical principles at work. But this is more than a mission; it is a movement of men and women from a wide range of communities and churches meeting in small groups to sharpen and develop each other's leadership for the Lord.

YOU ARE INVITED to join the BBT movement and continue your leadership development on the *Leadership Flywheel.* You have been called to lead for a time such as this!

May God continue to bless you as you leave a legacy for Him!

Yours in Christ,
David and Brandon

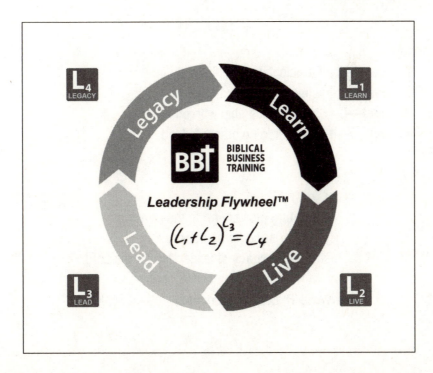

The *Leadership Flywheel* is a relational process focused on increasing an individual leader's spiritual growth in Jesus Christ with the goal of encouraging and equipping the development of other spiritual leaders. The *Leadership Flywheel* process is specifically designed to continually grow through an individualized coaching process of assessing, equipping, and encouraging leaders to develop themselves and invest in those entrusted to their care.

The purpose of the *Leadership Flywheel* is to produce Christ-centered, spiritual leaders.

Leadership Flywheel **is expressed as the following equation:**

$$(L_1 + L_2)^{L_3} = L_4$$

1. **Learn—L_1**: Participating in Bible study
2. **Live—L_2**: Inviting others to participate
3. **Lead—L_3**: Sharing leadership with others
4. **Legacy—L_4**: Encouraging others to lead

Learning plus **Living** to the power of
Christ-centered **Leadership**
results in a **Legacy** of leadership for the Lord.
Join the movement at
www.B-B-T.org/LeadershipbytheGoodBook

ACKNOWLEDGMENTS

David and Brandon's acknowledgments: While many voices contributed to these pages, we have done our best to make attributions clear and to give credit to the various amazing individuals responsible for this book and its collective wisdom. Any mistakes are ours, not theirs, and we take ultimate responsibility for the quality of how their ideas are expressed.

We would both like to thank Biblical Business Training's board of directors, led by Chairman Dennis Muilenburg, and BBT's staff, led by Executive Director and CEO Robert Millar, for their prayerful support and encouragement throughout this journey. Also, we would like to thank Bob Shook and Dudley Delffs for their gifted writing and editing. Special thanks to our agent, Jan Miller, who has been a tireless advocate for our book.

Brandon's acknowledgments: First and foremost, I praise God for allowing me to coauthor this labor of love with my dear friend and mentor David Steward. Our journey together is a testimony for Ephesians 3:20!

Likewise, the same verse applies to my family, beginning with my precious wife, Lisa. Ever since we were high school sweethearts, you have prayed with me and for me. To each of our three amazing children, Logan, Kaitlyn, and Gavin, thank you for inspiring me to love and lead well every day. My parents, Dr. James and Ruth Mann, provided a solid faith foundation for me to develop my personal relationship with Christ.

Thank you, Mom and Dad, for your unwavering, faith-filled encouragement and love!

Thank you, Michelle Hackmann, my executive assistant, for your support and partnership. You are awesome! Finally, as I reflect on my personal journey, there are two mentors, in addition to David Steward, whom I must thank for challenging and empowering me during various stages of my leadership development: University of Missouri finance professor David A. West and Cassidy Turley CEO, Mark E. Burkhart. Both are referenced in this book, but I wanted to personally thank them for "loving me through it!" May God continue to bless you all.

David's acknowledgments: All thanks be to God, who has loved, guided, and been so patient with me through the trials and tribulations of starting businesses and facing other challenges. Praise Him for the things He has done. Thelma, I love you. Thank you for faithfully supporting all the endeavors that I have been called to pursue. Your unwavering love exemplifies God's love. Thelma, my words of appreciation are less than adequate; so I will rely on God's Word in Proverbs 31:29 to sum up my feelings: "Many women do noble things, but you surpass them all."

David II, Mary, and Kimberly, and my precious grandsons, David III and Julian—I love you. Thank you for blessing me with your tremendous support throughout our lifelong journey. Thank you, Dorothy and Harold Steward, my mom and dad, and Dorothy Willis, my mother-in-love, for paving the way for all of us. I strive daily to live my life worthy of your sacrifices and your love.

Thank you, Brandon, for your unyielding faith in, and love for, Christ. You represent the next generation of Christ-centered leaders in a uniquely gifted way. Thank you for answering the call to the mission field of work and for coming alongside me to represent our Lord and Savior Jesus. I know you did not do this alone; so I must thank your precious family, Lisa, Logan, Kaitlyn, and Gavin, for their love and support.

Thank you, Mary Unnerstall, Patti DeSoto-Carr, Julie Council, and Michele Stallmann, my executive assistants, for your tireless support and help with this book. There are a few very special "greatest generation" mentors for whom I have the deepest admiration and respect: Herschel Parks, a WWII Navy veteran and a spiritual leader at Union Memorial Methodist Church for forty years. Sam and Marilyn Fox, who inspire Thelma and me as a family, community and business leaders, entrepreneurs, and dear friends. Finally, the late Des Lee, for his tremendous community leadership like few others have ever exemplified and his goal to "give it all away" in his lifetime, and accomplishing just that. All influenced me as an adult in immeasurable ways.

SPECIAL ACKNOWLEDGMENTS

No single person builds a successful organization. As it says in Scripture, "Again, truly I tell you that if two of you on earth agree about anything they ask for, it will be done for them by my Father in heaven" (Matt. 18:19). I am forever grateful to the many men and women who work at WWT; without them, this company would neither exist nor would this book have been written. While it is not possible to list the individual names of the thousands of WWT family members globally, I would be remiss if I didn't acknowledge Jim Kavanaugh, who helped launch WWT back in 1990, with the addition of Joe Koenig, Tom Strunk, and the executive management team, who joined in the ensuing years. Our shared commitment to excellence and core values has evolved into a unique brand of leadership. Working as a team for many years, we have developed a strong bond and unique spirit that has yielded a special relationship among us rarely exhibited in the workplace. May God continue to richly bless these individuals and the WWT family.

APPENDIX OF
SCRIPTURES CITED

A Note to Readers

Romans 8:28

Introduction by Brandon K. Mann

2 Corinthians 5:20

SECTION 1: SERVE
Chapter 1: Serve a Higher Purpose

Mark 10:43–45
Psalm 91
Proverbs 29:18
Hebrews 11:1
Ephesians 3:20
Proverbs 18:22

Chapter 2: Serve Those Around You

1 Peter 5:2–3
Matthew 22:36–40
Matthew 26:52–54
John 10:11
John 15:12–13
Proverbs 22:1
Mark 10:43b

Chapter 3: Serve Those in Need

Hebrews 13:16
Luke 23:43
Luke 12:48
1 Peter 4:10
Mark 12:41–44
Luke 10:30–37
Proverbs 13:22

SECTION 2: LOVE
Chapter 4: Love What You Do

1 Corinthians 10:31
Deuteronomy 7:11–12
Romans 5:2–4
Exodus 3:10
Jonah 1:1–2
Matthew 28:19
Matthew 7:12
Colossians 3:23
Romans 12:11
Philippians 3:5
Acts 9:3–6

**Chapter 5: Love Others—Family,
Friends, Employees, Customers**

John 13:35
John 3:16

Proverbs 16:18
Romans 12:3
John 13:6–9
John 13:15–17
Matthew 21
Zechariah 9:9
Leviticus 19:18
1 John 4:11, 20–21
Mark 12:3
Matthew 22:39
Luke 10:27
Galatians 5:14
John 13:34
1 Corinthians 12:4–6
1 Corinthians 12:21–27
1 John 3:18
1 John 3:16
1 Peter 3:9

Chapter 6: Love God and His Word

Deuteronomy 6:5
1 John 4:7–8
1 John 4:16
Matthew 6:33
Galatians 5:22–23
1 Corinthians 13:13
Matthew 6:5–8
Matthew 6:9–13
1 Thessalonians 5:17
1 John 4:19
Isaiah 55:11
Psalm 91:1–2
Psalm 91:15–16
Romans 10:17
Philippians 4:6–9

SECTION 3: IMAGINE
Chapter 7: Imagine Your Vision Realized

Proverbs 29:18
Isaiah 41:10
Romans 8:28

Chapter 8: Imagine Your Future Success

Matthew 17:20
Mark 11:12–14, 20–24
Hebrews 11:1
Numbers 13:18–19
Numbers 13:27–28
Numbers 13:31–33
Numbers 14:7–9
Matthew 7:6
James 2:14–17
Matthew 13:31–32

Chapter 9: Imagine Your Eternal Legacy

John 14:12
Matthew 6:33
1 Peter 2:24
Acts 1:8
2 Timothy 2:2
Ephesians 3:20–21

SECTION 4: INVEST
Chapter 10: Invest in Your Vision

Jeremiah 29:11
Ephesians 3:20
John 3:16

Proverbs 29:2
Proverbs 3:5–6
Hosea 4:6
Matthew 5:17–18
Romans 12:2

Chapter 11: Invest in Your People

Proverbs 11:25
Exodus 18:18
Exodus 18:22–23
Proverbs 16:18
John 14:12
John 15:16
Matthew 10
Luke 16:10

Chapter 12: Invest in God's Kingdom

Matthew 6:19–21
Hebrews 13:8
Luke 3:23
Luke 19:10
John 3:16
Matthew 5:16
John 13

SECTION 5: RISK
Chapter 13: Risk Your Heart

Psalm 31:24
1 Samuel 16:7
Matthew 22:36–40
Exodus 18:21
Proverbs 22:1
Matthew 5:37
Luke 4:16–22

Chapter 14: Risk Your Best Efforts

Romans 12:11
1 Samuel 17
Romans 8:17
Joshua 1:9
Psalm 90:12
Ecclesiastes 3:1
Mark 1:35
Ephesians 5:15–17

Chapter 15: Risk Your Reputation for What's Right

2 Timothy 1:7
John 7:12
Exodus 14:12
Exodus 32
John 15:2

SECTION 6: TRUST
Chapter 16: Trust God for the Impossible

Matthew 19:26

Chapter 17: Trust God's Word for Guidance

Psalm 119:105
Jeremiah 29:11
Joshua 1:9
James 1:22–25
Deuteronomy 31:8
Proverbs 3:5
Romans 10:17
Hebrews 4:12

Chapter 18: Trust the People You Lead

Ephesians 4:32
Matthew 6:14–15
Leviticus 19:18
Romans 3:23

SECTION 7: SHARE
Chapter 19: Share Your Wisdom

Proverbs 27:17
2 Timothy 2:2
Philippians 4:9
Proverbs 9:9
Psalm 145:4
Psalm 71:18
Proverbs 9:9

Chapter 20: Share Your Treasure

James 1:17
Mark 8:36
Matthew 6:19–21
Proverbs 18:22
Psalm 127:3
Matthew 11:28–30
Mark 6:31–32
Psalm 91:1
Mark 2:27

Chapter 21: Share Your Faith in Action

James 4:17
Daniel 3:5–6
Daniel 3:16–18
Daniel 3:25

Luke 23:33–34
Luke 23:39–43

SECTION 8: FOLLOW
Chapter 22: Follow the Example of Jesus

Matthew 16:24–25
Matthew 5:13–14
Luke 8:16–17
2 Timothy 1:7
Hebrews 11:6

Chapter 23: Follow Through on Your Word

1 John 2:5
Deuteronomy 25:13–16
Revelation 3:15–16
Isaiah 40:8

Chapter 24: Follow Those You Lead

Matthew 20:16
1 Peter 4:10
Philippians 4:2–3
Ecclesiastes 4:9–12

SECTION 9: GROW
Chapter 25: Grow Through Internal Struggles

John 14:27
Luke 6:45
Psalm 126:6
Hebrews 11:1
James 1:2–4
Deuteronomy 31:7–8

Exodus 3:11

Exodus 3:13–14

Joshua 1:5–6

Joshua 1:7–9

Isaiah 41:10

1 Thessalonians 5:11

Chapter 26: Grow Through External Challenges

Psalm 34:19

Romans 12:19

Philippians 4:13

Romans 5:3–5

Chapter 27: Grow Through Shared Victories

Proverbs 11:14

1 Corinthians 12:18–20

Philippians 2:3–4

SECTION 10: CELEBRATE
Chapter 28: Celebrate the Daily Gift of Health

1 Peter 4:10

1 Corinthians 6:19

Daniel 1:15–16

Chapter 29: Celebrate Milestones on the Journey

Psalm 77:11

Deuteronomy 6:12

Exodus 12:23

Deuteronomy 8:2

Matthew 26:26–30

Luke 22:19

Matthew 13:47–48

Matthew 13:31

Matthew 13:45–46

Philippians 4:4

Chapter 30: Celebrate the Destination Ahead

Romans 15:13

Ephesians 2:20–22

1 Chronicles 28:5–10

Matthew 28:19–20

John 14:18–20

Acts 1:8

Psalm 91

DAVID L. STEWARD

David is founder and chairman of World Wide Technology. After founding two successful start-up companies, Mr. Steward founded World Wide Technology in 1990. Since then, World Wide Technology has grown into a global technology solutions firm with more than 6,000 employees globally and more than $12 billion in revenue.

David is also founder and chairman of Kingdom Capital, a values-driven private investment and philanthropic firm based in St. Louis, Missouri, that seeks to transform the world through a virtuous cycle of capital. David is the author of *Doing Business by the Good Book*, published in 2004.

After graduating from Central Missouri State University in 1973, David relocated to St. Louis. He was the first person of color ever hired by Missouri Pacific Railroad Company to sell rail services. Upon leaving Missouri Pacific Railroad Company, he joined Federal Express as a senior account executive. During his tenure at FedEx, David was recognized as salesman of the year and was inducted into the company's sales hall of fame in 1981.

David is a member of the Horatio Alger Association of Distinguished Americans and serves on their board of directors. He also serves on the boards of National Academy Foundation (NAF), United Way of Greater St. Louis, Washington University, Variety the Children's Charity of St. Louis, Boy Scouts of America Great St. Louis Area Council, and is the founding vice chairman of Biblical Business Training, and other organizations.

BRANDON K. MANN

Brandon has been blessed with more than twenty-five years of diverse executive and board leadership experience. He is the cofounder, managing partner, and CEO of Kingdom Capital, a values-driven private investment and philanthropic firm that seeks to transform the world through a virtuous cycle of capital.

Brandon serves as an advisor to the board of directors of World Wide Technology, a global technology solutions firm. Brandon is the founder and executive chairman of Biblical Business Training, a global nonprofit ministry that helps people apply Biblical principles at work.

Prior to founding Biblical Business Training, Brandon served in a variety of key executive and board roles helping develop the country's largest privately held commercial real estate services firm. Brandon also has served on a wide variety of nonprofit and ministry leadership and board roles.

Brandon graduated top of his BSBA and MBA programs at the University of Missouri in 1994 and 1996 respectively. Originally from Hannibal, Missouri, Brandon is married to his high school sweetheart, Lisa, and they are blessed with three children: Logan, Kaitlyn, and Gavin.